The Use of
Documentary Evidence
in the Study of
Roman Imperial
History

Sources in Ancient History
General Editor: E. A. Judge, Macquarie University
This series is designed to provide translations of substantial bodies of
source material with accompanying discussion particularly suitable for
tutorial use by students of ancient history or of political and social
institutions.

The Athenian Half-Century
A. French

The Politics of Friendship:
Pompey and Cicero
Beryl Rawson

Religious Conflict in
Fourth-Century Rome
Brian Croke and Jill Harries

The Spectre of Philip
J. R. Ellis and R. D. Milns

The Use of Documentary Evidence
in the Study of
Roman Imperial History
B. W. Jones and R. D. Milns

The Use of Documentary Evidence in the Study of Roman Imperial History

B. W. Jones and R. D. Milns

Sydney University Press

SYDNEY UNIVERSITY PRESS
Press Building, University of Sydney

UNITED KINGDOM, EUROPE, MIDDLE EAST, AFRICA
HB Sales, Enterprise House, Ashford Road
Ashford, Middlesex TW15 1XB, England

NORTH AND SOUTH AMERICA
International Scholarly Book Services, Inc.
P.O. Box 1632, Beaverton
Oregon 97075, USA

National Library of Australia
Cataloguing-in-Publication data

Jones, B. W.
  The use of documentary evidence
  in the study of Roman imperial history.

  Bibliography.
  Includes index.
  ISBN 0 424 00105 5.

  1. Rome – History – Empire, 30 BC–284 AD –
  Sources. I. Milns, R. D., 1938–   . II. Title. (Series: Sources in
  ancient history).

937'.07

First published 1984
© B. W. Jones and R. D. Milns 1984
Printed in Australia at Griffin Press Limited
Marion Road, Netley, South Australia

Contents

List of Illustrations   vii
Abbreviations   viii
Introduction   xi

Part I   Coins   1

Part II   Inscriptions   20
A.   Official Documents   20
    i. Major Enactments   20
    ii. Minor Administrative Records   52
B.   Tributes to Particular Persons   82

Part III   Papyri   118
A.   Official Documents   119
B.   Semi-Official and Private Documents   142

Examples of Historical Reconstruction   163
A.   A Vespasianic War of Conquest in Germany   163
B.   The Revolt of Saturninus   171

Appendices   177
1   Constitutional Matters   177
2   Imperial Propaganda   178
3   Religious Aspects of the Emperor's Position   178
4   Municipal and Provincial Administration   178
5   The Army   179
6   The Frontiers   179
7   The Imperial Civil Service   179
8   Roman Egypt   180

Glossary of Military, Administrative and Official Terms   181
Select Bibliography   186
Comparative Tables   188

Indexes
1   Chronological   193
2   Names   195
3   Places   199
4   Major Topics   201

Illustrations

An *as* of Vespasian (Obverse and Reverse, Document 11).
  Reproduced by courtesy of the Trustees of the British
  Museum.   11

An *aureus* of Nerva (Obverse and Reverse, Document 14).
  Reproduced by courtesy of the Trustees of the British
  Museum.   11

The so-called law on Vespasian's imperial powers (Document 27).
  Reproduced by courtesy of Licinio Capelli.   33

The sepulchral inscription of Tiberius Plautius Silvanus
  (Document 58). Reproduced by courtesy of Licinio Capelli.   89

A section of Claudius' letter to the Alexandrians (Document 79).
  Reproduced by courtesy of Licinio Capelli.   121

A section of a letter from Adrastus to Spartacus (Document 94).
  Reproduced by courtesy of the Egypt Exploration Society of
  London.   149

Abbreviations

AE	*L'Année Epigraphique*, Paris 1888 ff.
BGU	*Ägyptische Urkunden aus den staatlichen Museen zu Berlin. Griechische Urkunden*, Berlin 1895 ff.
BMC I	*Coins of the Roman Empire in the British Museum*, Vol. I, ed. H. Mattingly, London 1923.
BMC II	*Coins of the Roman Empire in the British Museum*, Vol. II, ed. H. Mattingly, London 1930.
BMC III	*Coins of the Roman Empire in the British Museum*, Vol. III, ed. H. Mattingly, London 1936.
CIL	*Corpus Inscriptionum Latinarum*, published under the auspices of the Berlin Academy, 1863 ff.
CPL	*Corpus Papyrorum Latinarum*, ed. R. Cavenaile and others, Wiesbaden 1958.
Church and Brodribb	*The Complete Works of Tacitus*, tr. A. J. Church and W. J. Brodribb, ed. M. Hadas, New York 1942.
E&J	*Documents Illustrating the Reigns of Augustus and Tiberius*, ed. V. Ehrenberg and A. H. M. Jones, Oxford 1949, 2nd edn, with addenda, 1976.
IG	*Inscriptiones Graecae*, ed. F. Hiller von Gärtringen and others, Berlin 1873 ff.
IGRR	*Inscriptiones Graecae ad Res Romanas Pertinentes*, ed. R. Cagnat and others, Paris 1911–27.
ILS	*Inscriptiones Latinae Selectae*, ed. H. Dessau, Berlin 1892–1916.
Jones	*A History of Rome Through the Fifth Century*, ed. A. H. M. Jones, 2 vols, New York 1968 and 1970.
Lewis and Reinhold	*Roman Civilization*, ed. N. Lewis and M. Reinhold, 2 vols, New York 1951 and 1955.

M&W   *Select Documents of the Principates of the Flavian*
       Emperors including the Year of Revolution AD 68–69,
       ed. M. McCrum and A. G. Woodhead,
       Cambridge 1961, repr. 1966.

OCD²   *The Oxford Classical Dictionary*, ed. N. G. L.
       Hammond and H. H. Scullard, 2nd edn, Oxford
       1970, repr. 1973, with corrections.

OGIS   *Orientis Graeci Inscriptiones Selectae*, ed. W.
       Dittenberger, Leipzig 1903–5.

P. Berl.   *Griechische Papyri aus dem Berliner Museum*, ed. S.
       Möller, Gothenburg 1929.

P. Fayum   *Fayum Towns and Their Papyri*, ed. B. P. Grenfell,
       A. S. Hunt and D. G. Hogarth, London 1900.

P. Fouad   *Les Papyrus Fouad I*, ed. A. Bataille and others, Cairo
       1939.

P. Gen.   *Les Papyrus de Genève*, ed. J. Nicole, Geneva 1906.

P. Giessen   *Griechische Papyri im Museum des oberhessischen*
       Geschichtsvereins zu Giessen, ed. P. Eger and others,
       Leipzig-Berlin 1910–12.

P. Lond.   *Greek Papyri in the British Museum*, ed. F. G. Kenyon
       and others, London 1893 ff.

P. Michigan   *Michigan Papyri*, ed. C. C. Edgar and others, Ann
       Arbor 1931 ff.

P. Oxy.   *The Oxyrhynchus Papyri*, ed. B. P. Grenfell and
       others, London 1898 ff.

P. Ryl.   *Catalogue of the Greek Papyri in the John Rylands*
       Library, Manchester, ed. A. S. Hunt and others,
       Manchester 1911 ff.

P. Teb.   *The Tebtunis Papyri*, ed. B. P. Grenfell and others,
       London 1902 ff.

RIB   *The Inscriptions of Roman Britain*, ed. R. G.
       Collingwood and R. P. Wright, Oxford 1965.

RG   *Res Gestae Divi Augusti: The Achievements of the Divine*
       Augustus, ed. P. A. Brunt and J. M. Moore,
       Oxford 1967, repr. 1973, with corrections.

S   *Documents Illustrating the Principates of Gaius, Claudius*
       and Nero, ed. E. Mary Smallwood, Cambridge
       1967.

SEG   *Supplementum Epigraphicum Graecum*, ed. J. Hondius
       and others, Leiden 1925 ff.

SIG³   *Sylloge Inscriptionum Graecarum*, ed. W. Dittenberger,
       3rd edn, Leipzig 1915–24.

S. *N–H*   *Documents Illustrating the Principates of Nerva, Trajan and Hadrian*, ed. E. Mary Smallwood, Cambridge 1966.

SP   *Select Papyri*, ed. A. S. Hunt and others, London and Cambridge 1932–42.

TAM   *Tituli Asiae Minoris*, ed. E. Kalinka and R. Herberdey, Vienna 1901 ff.

Introduction

The history of the early Roman empire in the modern sense could not be written on the basis of the surviving literary sources alone. For these accounts, as is well known, tend to be limited in their outlook to matters of political and military history and to the actions and intrigues of the small number of people who formed the governing élite of the empire: the emperor himself, his family and the leading senators and *equites*, who governed the provinces of the empire, commanded its armies and helped the emperor in the formation of policy and law. History at that time was a subject of great dignity, which described great events and the fortunes and vicissitudes of great men and women, and was intended to have an edifying and instructive effect upon its reader. The minute details of the normal routines and procedures of administration, the accurate study of information which might throw light upon social and economic trends and policies, the consideration of the living standards, the aspirations and hopes of the millions of people who formed the population of the empire – these were not for the Greek or the Roman writer of history. Such writers would find it hard to understand their modern counterparts, who spend most of their time in archives and records-offices, poring over documents, minutes and correspondence in their attempt to piece together and to understand a picture of the whole structure, not merely certain aspects of one small part of it, important though the influence of this small part was on the whole.

Nor can it be said that there was a lack of documentary material in the early Roman empire. Every town and city in the empire, beginning with Rome itself, had its senate, town council or similar body, of whose transactions often detailed records were kept and whose major decisions were publicly set up on durable tablets of stone or bronze. The bureaucracy at Rome, which continually grew larger and more efficient as it reached into more and more areas of public and private life, maintained full and accurate files and records of official correspondence, of decisions given by officials of all levels up to the emperor himself and of receipts and disbursements of money from all sources. This was inevitable and necessary; for no large and complex institution can function if it does not have the ability to store away and retrieve when desired all the information relevant to its efficient and proper functioning. It is, of course, uncertain what access an ancient writer would have had to these official records and documents, had he sought to make use of their evidence. The Roman empire was not a relatively open democracy, like the USA, with legislation which guaranteed the publication of or access to much statistical information collected by government. It was basically an authoritarian system, bearing a closer resemblance in its practices to the Soviet Union than to the USA, and governments of this kind are not in the habit of allowing the inspection and revelation to public scrutiny of the resources and discussions that produce their policies. It is possible that certain material would have been made available to historians for their perusal and other material kept from them as being 'classified', if we may use the current terminology. We can well imagine that detailed information and reports about the empire's military establishment and its financial management would not have been made readily available, nor would the confidential 'minutes' – for such must surely have been kept – of the emperor's discussions with his private and most intimate advisers. Nevertheless, there was much information available to the ancient writer in published material and the possibility of access to at least some part of the central government's files and records. But the occasions on which resort was made to any of this information were rare indeed.

What the ancient historians of Rome chose not to do, or did not consider doing, cannot now be done by their modern counterparts. For the records-offices and files of the many governmental bureaux of Imperial Rome have been lost and destroyed for ever. But there has survived to our times a vast quantity of non-literary material, which we can refer to as 'documentary' evidence, which has enabled modern scholars and historians to present a fuller and more analytical picture of the empire and its working than that of the ancient writers. The evidence, fragmentary and disjointed as it often is, of this mass of material has enabled us to modify the accounts and judgements of our literary sources by providing us with new information or new ways of looking at the information of our writers and even by opening up to us whole areas of knowledge left untouched by them. It is instructive to read Tacitus' account of the Julio-Claudian era in his *Annals* alongside M. Rostovtzeff's *Social and Economic History of the Roman Empire* (Oxford 1957). The difference in approach, treatment and scope is immediately apparent; and the greater breadth and depth of the modern account is due essentially to the use of the evidence provided by this documentary material. The history of the Roman empire, at any period, cannot be written without the help of documentary evidence and often must largely be based upon it; and each new piece of evidence that is discovered adds to the reconstruction of this history.

What do we mean, in the context of the history of the Roman empire, by the term 'documentary evidence'? We have already defined it broadly as non-literary material, that is, material, normally verbal and written, which was not intended to be a work of literature, appealing to the aesthetic, intellectual and emotional nature of the reader, but which, whether directly or indirectly, helps to throw light on a particular historical inquiry or problem. It is a term of wide application; and we should rid our minds of the more limited and modern idea of documents as being essentially dealings and records, written on paper and carefully stored away in archives. The documents with which the Roman historian deals are written or engraved on stone, various metals and pieces of papyrus, and have in common the fact that they were not intended to form an historical narrative or part of such a narrative. They are such items as inscriptions, coins, brick tiles and lead pipes and have, for the most part, been preserved to modern times and discovered by chance and good fortune. They may be broadly divided into two main categories: official and non-official documents. By 'official' we mean documents that emanated from a source of recognized authority and as such bore the mark of government approval; any other document – whether it be a letter from a friend to a friend or a commemorative plaque set up by a soldier to honour his former commanding officer or a petition from a private individual to an imperial agent – we may call non-official, though it may well be argued that examples of the last kind would more appropriately be called 'official' correspondence. In other instances, too, we may find it hard to make a fine and precise definition. But it can be seen that a roof tile stamped with the name and number of a particular legion may be said ultimately to have been made with the approval of the emperor himself and that a decree of a town council honouring a person has the authority of a duly constituted and recognized organ of government.

It has been stated that there is an enormous mass of this documentary evidence available to the historian, and we need go no further than the various collections of Greek and Roman inscriptions and coins of the imperial period to see how true this is. But it is a mass of material that, by its very nature and the manner in which it has reached us, presents the historian with great difficulties and problems. The random and fortuitous nature of its survival must often raise the question of how representative is the documentary evidence dealing with this or that problem. The fact that many 'official' documents, especially coins, contain officially inspired messages must cause them to be handled with caution and even suspicion. Often, too, it is not immediately or obviously apparent how a piece of documentary evidence can help the historian or how, if at all, it is related to other pieces of evidence. It we think of the task of reconstructing the history of the early Roman empire as similar to that of putting together a jigsaw puzzle, we must bear in mind that we do not have a picture of the puzzle that we are trying to reconstruct – the picture will only emerge as the pieces are fitted together – and that a large proportion of the pieces of the puzzle have been irrecoverably lost. The result is that we have to accept that there will never be a complete or even fairly complete picture and that many of the pieces of the puzzle will have to be assigned a conjecturally approximate place in the picture. There is a further complication, if we continue our analogy of the jigsaw puzzle, in that many of the pieces that we do possess have survived to us in a broken and fragmentary form, so that we have to try to reconstruct the piece before we can try to fit it into the picture. This is especially true with the documentary evidence of inscriptions and papyrus writings. Thanks to the ravages of time and the destructive energies of humans, the original stone or metal plaque on which the inscriptions were engraved has often been badly broken, mutilated and defaced, while the sands of Egypt have yielded up mostly torn and tantalizing fragments of the original papyrus documents.

All these factors mean that the use of the available documentary evidence by the historian is a highly complicated and technical business, which can be quite bewildering to the student newly arrived at the study of Roman history and untrained in the handling of such material. Yet, as we have indicated earlier, it is not possible even to begin to obtain a realistic idea of the Roman empire on the basis of the literary remains alone; and, while there are many works available which can help the student to examine critically the virtues and defects of the major literary historians, there is no such work in existence that performs a similar function for the study and evaluation of the documentary evidence.

The purpose of this book, then, is not to be a selective 'source book' of documentary evidence for the early empire, but to attempt to solve a more basic problem by indicating to the student of Roman history the main types of documentary evidence that exist for the early empire and to demonstrate the sort of information that can be extracted from these documents and the ways in which it can be put to use by the historian. We believe, however, that our selection of documents is such that the book can be used by the lecturer or teacher to illustrate many aspects and important issues of the early empire, and therefore we have added a number of appendices in which we suggest some of those aspects and issues that might be handled in the classroom and which of our selection of documents might be used for each of those topics. Because the large majority of students who study Ancient History in the high schools and universities have little or no acquaintance with Latin or Greek, the languages of almost all the documents, we have translated the documents selected into an English style which, we hope, retains the spirit of the original document as much as possible. We have tried, as far as possible, to select documents that can be regarded as 'significant' and that involve a minimum of conjectural restoration. In every case we have stated whether the original language of the document is Greek or Latin, and have indicated, whenever possible, where the document was found.

The chronological period covered by the selected documents goes from the reign of Augustus to the emperor Hadrian. We have done this for a number of reasons: this is the period richest in both literary and non-literary evidence; it is the period of Roman imperial history most commonly studied in schools and universities; and it is the period when the imperial 'constitution' was growing towards its definitive form and when the empire itself was growing to its fullest form geographically and the administrative machinery that ran it was rapidly developing in order to cope properly and efficiently with the routine tasks of government.

The work is divided into three parts, of which parts II and III contain further subdivisions. In parts I, II and III we set out and give examples of each of the main classes of documentary evidence: coins, inscriptions and papyri. Part II is subdivided into three sections in order to separate what may be called 'personal' documents (e.g. honorific and funerary inscriptions of both a private and a public nature) from 'official' documents, such as laws and imperial edicts and rescripts, on the one hand, and military diplomas, milestones, roofing tiles of military buildings, on the other hand. We have also provided two examples of how documentary evidence can be used in the reconstruction of historical events; and have used, where possible, documents already cited and discussed in the earlier chapters. We have added a glossary of the military, administrative and official terminology found in the documents that we have used and in our discussions of them. It will be noticed that in some instances we have given an English version of the Latin or Greek terminology and in others have retained the original word. This is because some terms can be given a reasonably precise English translation, involving little or no cumbersome paraphrase, whereas other terms can only satisfactorily be given in the original language, with an explanation of the terms in the glossary. Thus *imperator* can readily be translated as 'emperor' and *vigiles* as 'the watch', but *quaestor* cannot be given a straightforward translation that describes both the functions and the associations of the office. Similarly, *legatus Augusti propraetore* can be translated 'legate of the emperor with the rank of propraetor', but the subtle essence of the 'rank' of propraetor cannot be conveyed in a brief, all-embracing translation. It should be noted that, with the exception of the historical reconstructions, we have not inserted marks of any kind to show conjectural restorations in the texts of our selection of documents. This is because we felt that to indicate such restorations would not only be distracting to the eye, but involve us in our comments on the documents in technical discussions which would be inappropriate to the purpose of the book.

In the list of abbreviations (pp. viii-x) we have given the major collections and selections of documents dealing with the first and second centuries AD, both in the original language and in English translation. Much use has been made of the collections of documents of Ehrenberg and Jones, Smallwood, and McCrum and Woodhead, though in every case where we have cited a document from these collections we have also made cross-reference to other major collections (e.g. Dessau, *ILS*), where the documents can be found. We have also tried to give references to similar documents in the more important English 'source books', in order that students may extend their acquaintance with the various kinds of document. The collections of Lewis and Reinhold and of A. H. M. Jones have been particularly valuable here.

Our hope, then, is that this book will help the undergraduate or high school student, who has little or no Latin and Greek, to appreciate the variety and amount of documentary evidence surviving for the early Roman empire, the sorts of information that can be obtained from these documents and the ways in which such information can help modern historians in their task of reconstructing, analysing and understanding the early Roman empire.

Part I
Coins

During the Roman empire, an enormous number of coins were minted, both in Rome and in the provinces, and many thousands have survived. They are of immense value to the historian in that they must have been one of the few means available to an emperor to advertise his achievements and intentions throughout the empire (e.g. Trajan's building programme in Rome, **17**) and also to persuade and reassure his subjects (e.g. Augustus' 'victory' over the Parthians, **2**). In short, they clearly present the official viewpoint on a variety of matters; to some extent, the 'message' they contain might be described as official propaganda. The front or 'Obverse' of an imperial coin normally consists of a representation (sometimes, but certainly not always, idealized) of the reigning emperor together with his titulature – hence they can be dated (see **13**). On the other side, the 'Reverse', a variety of information is provided; each emperor issued many coins and, in general, it was the Reverse that was most often changed. Since so many coins have survived and since they can be dated with a fair amount of precision, their value to the historian is immense. That they must be read with caution is obvious – the information is selective and biased. A good introduction to Roman coinage is provided by Michael Grant in his *Roman History from Coins* (Cambridge University Press Paperback, 1968), the subtitle of which, *Some Uses of the*

Imperial Coinage to the Historian, is an accurate summary of its contents.

1   (*BMC* I, p. 106, No. 650 = E&J 15)

'Caesar, consul for the 6th time' (Obverse): 'For the capture of Egypt' (Reverse, with a representation of a crocodile).

This coin is a *denarius*, minted in the East; its legend is in Latin. Since Augustus held his sixth consulship in 28 BC and his seventh in 27 BC, it can be assigned to the former year.

The annexation of Egypt to the Roman empire in 30 BC was commemorated on the new ruler's coins and inscriptions: e.g. 'I added Egypt to the empire of the Roman people' (*RG* 27.1); whilst the obelisk he erected on the *spina* of the Circus Maximus and now to be found in the Piazza del Popolo in Rome bears the inscription, 'The emperor Caesar, son of the deified (Julius Caesar), Augustus, pontifex maximus, saluted as victorious commander 12 times, consul 11 times, of tribunician power for the 14th time, gave (this) as a gift to the Sun for the reduction of Egypt to the power of the Roman people' (*ILS* 91 = E&J 14: to be assigned to 10/9 BC from the tribunician year).

The simplicity of Augustus' titulature is noteworthy – compare the later excesses of Trajan (**77**). The name 'Augustus' was conferred in 27 BC, but the eastern mint still retained the old style.

2   (*BMC* I, p. 73, No. 427 = E&J 27)

'The senate and the Roman people to the emperor Caesar Augustus, consul 11 times, of tribunician power for the 6th time' (Obverse): 'For the citizens and the military standards recovered from the Parthians' (Reverse, with triumphal arch).

The coin is an *aureus* of Augustus, probably minted in Spain; the legend is in Latin. It portrays Augustus on a chariot receiving the standards from two Parthians and can be assigned to the period between 27 June 18 BC and 26 June 17 BC, when Augustus was holding tribunician power for the sixth time; however, the fact that it refers to his eleventh consulship is of little assistance in dating it, as this reference appeared on coins and inscriptions from 23 to 6 BC. The coin highlights the problems Augustus faced on his eastern frontier, and indicates, not how he solved them, but rather how he wanted the Romans to believe he had solved them. The message was frequently repeated – the coin was issued in

18/17 BC, but the 'victory' had taken place in 20. Rome's prestige had suffered three severe blows in Parthia, with the defeat of Crassus at Carrhae in 53 BC, of L. Decidius Saxa in 40, and of M. Antony in 36. Yet Augustus had wisely not used the great forces at his disposal in an effort to avenge them. The futility of such a project was impressed on the Romans a century or so later after Trajan's campaigns in the area. What Augustus did was to take advantage of the Parthian king's internal and external difficulties, bring diplomatic pressure to bear on him, and thereby restore something of Rome's prestige. In 20, as a result of these man-oeuvres, the surviving prisoners and the captured standards were restored by the Parthians, and Augustus persisted in celebrating his success in his official propaganda, on a series of inscriptions and coins such as this: thus, in the *RG* (29.2) he stated: 'I compelled the Parthians to restore to me the spoils and standards of three Roman armies, and to ask as suppliants for the friendship of the Roman people'. This he achieved by non-military means; but such was the character and temperament of his people, especially of the upper classes, that he felt it essential to proclaim himself a military conqueror. Nor was Augustus the only emperor to use diplomatic pressure to ensure peace on the frontiers; it became a regular procedure, one that was far less expensive than conducting a major campaign and maintaining a permanent garrison in the conquered area. Most emperors, too, adopted the device of portraying their victories as a military rather than as a diplomatic success.

3   (*BMC* I, p. 133, No. 95 = E&J 91)

'By decree of the Senate: Drusus Caesar, son of Tiberius Augustus, grandson of the deified Augustus, priest, of tribunician power for the 2nd time' (Obverse).

The coin is an *as* of Tiberius issued by the mint of Rome; its legend is in Latin. In 22 Tiberius was aged sixty-four, and only three years previously had become the grandfather of twin boys, a fact of which he was inordinately proud; thus, on the reverse of this coin are portrayed two *cornucopiae*, from the mouth of each of which is emerging the bust of a little boy. The twins' names can be discovered from an inscription: 'To Livia (Julia, wife) of Drusus Caesar, mother of Tiberius Caesar and Germanicus Caesar' (*ILS* 170). Tacitus refers to the fact that their birth 'so delighted the emperor that he did not refrain from boasting before the senators that to no Roman of the same rank had twin offspring ever before

been born' (*Annals* 2.84: translated Church and Brodribb). Nor was
his elation diminished by the death (in 19) of his nephew and heir,
the famous Germanicus, which left his own son Drusus, the twins'
father, with no clear rival as heir apparent – apart, of course, from
Germanicus' young sons – and Drusus' position was immensely
strengthened when his twin sons, Tiberius and Germanicus, were
born. A clear indication of his status is given by Tacitus: 'Next
followed (i.e. in AD 21) Tiberius' fourth, Drusus' second consulship,
memorable from the fact that father and son were colleagues. Two
years previously the association of Germanicus and Tiberius in the
same honour had not been agreeable to the uncle, nor had it the
link of so close a natural tie' (*Annals* 3.31: translated Church and
Brodribb). On inscriptions, too, Drusus' place in the dynasty was
stressed, e.g. '. . . to Drusus Caesar, son of Tiberius Augustus,
grandson of the deified Augustus, great-grandson of the deified
Julius . . .' (*ILS* 168 = E&J 92a). But Drusus' wife, Livia Julia, who had
previously been married to Augustus' grandson Gaius Caesar, was
to poison Drusus in the following year at the instigation of her
lover, the praetorian prefect Sejanus. One of the twins, Germanicus, died in the same year, leaving the other, Tiberius (Gemellus),
to become joint heir with Germanicus' son Gaius (= Caligula). In
this coin, however, Tiberius clearly stated the position held by the
twins' father Drusus in 22, with the grant to him of tribunician
power for the second time.

4   (E&J 50a)

'Tiberius Caesar, son of the deified Augustus, Augustus'
(Obverse): 'The municipality of Augusta Bilbilis: Tiberius
Caesar for the 5th time and Lucius Aelius Sejanus, consuls'
(Reverse).

The legend, which is in Latin, is from a bronze coin of Tiberius
minted in Spain and can be assigned to the first months of AD 31
when Tiberius held his fifth consulship (E&J, p. 42). It is particularly
significant because it indicates publicly the power and prestige of
Lucius Aelius Sejanus, Tiberius' colleague as ordinary consul. Note,
however, that Sejanus' name does not appear on the official list of
consuls for 31: see **75**. Before this time, the only senators allowed
to hold such a post were those whose fathers had themselves been
consuls. But Sejanus' father (like his son) not only lacked consular
status, he had not even been a senator. A marble tablet found in
Volsinii (modern Bolsena) provides precise evidence of the father's
status: 'Lucius Seius Strabo prefect of Egypt and Terentia, daughter

of Aulus, his mother, and Cosconia Gallitta, daughter of Lentulus Maluginensis, his wife, after buying the buildings and razing them to the ground, gave the baths with all their equipment to the people of Volsinii for public use' (*ILS* 8996 = E&J 220). Sejanus' father, then, was named Seius Strabo and had married into a noble family (the Lentuli); he gained the highest post then available to a man of equestrian rank, the prefecture of Egypt; his son was probably adopted by Aelius Gallus, and hence acquired the name Aelius (from his adoptive father) Sejanus (from his natural father). The son's rise to power is well documented. By 31 he was all but supreme in the state: 'His birthday was officially celebrated, oaths were taken by his fortune, and sacrifices were offered to his statues, as they were to those of Tiberius himself. He was at last betrothed to Livia Julia: the rivalry of Agrippina was no longer a source of danger and Tiberius himself was by this time sufficiently devoted to Sejanus to defy opinion. He was publicly saluted by Tiberius as the partner of his counsels' (R. Seager, *Tiberius*, London 1972, p. 213).

The emperor publicly indicated his trust in Sejanus with the award of an ordinary consulship, an award all the more striking since Tiberius was still on Capri and absent from the seat of power. Moreover, since his accession he had held only two ordinary consulships, one with his nephew (and adopted son) Germanicus and the other with his son Drusus. Both men were regarded as Tiberius' heirs when they shared the consulship with him, and, more significantly, when Tiberius and Germanicus held the office in AD 18 the emperor's name alone appeared on a coin from Augusta Bilbilis (Spain) similar to the one under discussion.

It would appear that Sejanus celebrated his success with some sort of arranged popular election, held not in the traditional place, the Campus Martius, but in a spot with popular associations, the Aventine. Such is one interpretation of a fragmentary inscription found in Rome: '. . . the sinister assembly of the traitorous Sejanus, which was held on the Aventine when he was made consul . . .' (*ILS* 6044 = E&J 53). At all events he was now at the height of his influence in the capital, lacking only tribunician power. But his success was short lived, for Tiberius denounced him at a meeting of the senate on 18 October of the same year and he was put to death.

5 (*BMC* I, p. 151, No. 33 = S 276)

'Gaius Caesar Augustus Germanicus, pontifex maximus, of tribunician power' (Obverse): 'Address to the Troops' (Reverse, with a representation of Gaius standing on a platform, addressing five soldiers).

The coin is a *sestertius* of Gaius from the mint in Rome; its legend is in Latin. It refers to an incident early in Gaius' reign when he paid the praetorian guard (represented on the coin by five soldiers) a huge donative to ensure their loyalty, for Tiberius Gemellus was at this time (AD 37/8) still alive – see **3** for Gemellus' relationship to the late emperor Tiberius. Dio describes the incident as follows: 'In company with the senate, he inspected the praetorians at drill and distributed to them the money that had been bequeathed them, amounting to a thousand sesterces apiece; and he added as much more on his own account' (59.2.1: Loeb translation). It is important to note that the donative was not regarded by the emperor as something unofficial, that should not be publicized: on the contrary he proclaimed it on his coins for all to see.

6   (*BMC* I, p. 200, No. 1 = S 106)

'Agrippina Augusta (wife) of the deified Claudius, mother of Nero Caesar' (Obverse): 'To Nero, son of the deified Claudius, Caesar Augustus Germanicus, emperor, of tribunician power; in accordance with a decree of the senate' (Reverse, surrounded by an oak-wreath).

The coin is an *aureus* of Nero from the mint in Rome; its legend is in Latin. Usually, it is assigned to AD 54, the first year of his reign. The obverse depicts the emperor and his mother facing each other, and is quite remarkable in that this was the first occasion that a living female member of the imperial family appeared on the obverse of a coin with the emperor. Whilst her unprecedented power is attested in the literary sources, the coin's frank presentation of it is most important, since it proves that Nero's subjects were deliberately informed of her position. As in Nero's other early coins, there is a reference to his adoptive father Claudius, but before long his name, like that of Agrippina, disappeared from the official titulature. He also used the title 'Germanicus', reminding the people of his famous grandfather who had died thirty-five years previously and whose popularity was apparently still considerable. Of some significance is the reference to the senate on the reverse. In theory, the emperor was responsible for the gold and silver coinage, whilst the bronze was left to the senate; usually there was a statement to this effect on the so-called senatorial coins. The legend on this coin stated that it was issued 'in accordance with the senate's decree', but it is a gold and not a bronze coin. Apparently Nero's advisers were advocating a policy of co-operation with the senate; it was an exercise in propaganda, designed to improve the relationship between it and the throne which had deteriorated under Claudius.

A further point of interest is the fact that the words 'in accordance with a decree of the senate' are surrounded with a representation of an oak-wreath, i.e. a chaplet of oak leaves. This so-called 'civic crown' was an honour bestowed on a soldier who had saved the life of one of his colleagues. Augustus had received it as the saviour of the citizens and later emperors often made use of it as well. One of Nero's advisers, Seneca, had, at this very time, written an essay addressed to the emperor; it was intended to guide him towards the ideal of a merciful and popular ruler – hence its name, the *De Clementia* ('On Mercy'). The last surviving section of this work notes the relevance for the eighteen-year-old prince of the 'civic crown': 'True happiness consists in . . . earning the civic crown by showing mercy. No decoration is more worthy of the eminence of a prince or more beautiful than that crown bestowed for saving the lives of fellow-citizens' (*De Clementia* 1.26.5: Loeb translation). The senate is thus seen as not only authorizing the issue of this coin but also conferring the civic crown on the new emperor.

7 (*BMC* I, p. 251, No. 261 = S 57)

'Nero Caesar Augustus emperor' (Obverse): 'The quinquennial contest established at Rome, by decree of the senate' (Reverse, with a representation of an urn and a wreath on a gaming table).

The coin is a *semis* from the Rome mint; its legend is in Latin. The contest referred to on the reverse is described by Suetonius: 'Nero was the first to establish at Rome a quinquennial contest in three parts (music, gymnastics and riding) after the Greek fashion, which he called the "Neronia"' (*Nero* 12.3: Loeb translation). This occurred in 60 and was repeated at the due time, five years later; the coin was issued for the latter celebration. The wreath on the reverse was intended for the victor, whilst the urn was for the votes of the judges. Although the coin was designed to illustrate the official view of the new institution, it must not be imagined that everyone was prepared to agree with it. Tacitus reports on the hostility of one section of the senate which could see resulting 'a degeneracy bred by foreign tastes . . . (and) a licence to vice'; but he

admits that the 'entertainment . . . passed off without any notorious scandal' (*Annals* 14.20, 21: translated Church and Brodribb).
The official attitude was obviously more enthusiastic, as the coin
indicates. Apparently the practice was discontinued on Nero's
death, and revived some twenty years later by Domitian, an
emperor equally unpopular with the senate (see Suetonius, *Domitian* 4.4).

8   (*BMC* I, p. 369, No. 10 = M&W 82)

'Aulus Vitellius Germanicus, emperor, of tribunician power'
(Obverse): 'Lucius Vitellius, consul 3 times, censor' (Reverse).

The coin is an *aureus* of Vitellius from the mint of Rome; its legend
is in Latin. Note the absence from the emperor's official titulature
of the word 'Caesar': the omission is discussed in **9**. During his brief
reign, Vitellius resorted to various devices to enhance his status.
Not infrequently, his coins refer to the eminence of his famous
father, Lucius. According to Suetonius, Lucius Vitellius 'became
consul, and then governor of Syria where, with masterly diplo-
macy, he induced Artabanus, king of the Parthians not only to
attend a parley but also to do obeisance to the standards of the
legion. Afterwards, Lucius shared two ordinary consulships and
the censorship with the emperor Claudius, and took full charge of
the empire while Claudius was away on the British expedition'
(*Vitellius* 2.4: Loeb translation, adapted). His posts, noted on the
coin's reverse, were particularly significant in that at this period it
was quite rare for a senator who was not a member of the imperial
family to hold more than one consulship. Not all the literary
sources were as flattering in their account of the elder Vitellius.
According to Tacitus, 'Through fear of Gaius Caesar and intimacy
with Claudius, Lucius degenerated into a servility so base that he
is regarded by an after-generation as the type of the most
degrading adulation. The beginning of his career was forgotten in
its end, and an old age of infamy effaced the virtues of youth'
(Tacitus, *Annals* 6.32: translated Church and Brodribb). Vitellius
himself naturally preferred a somewhat different version. The
significance of the title 'Germanicus' is discussed in **16**.

9   (M&W 79)

'A. Vitellius Caesar Augustus Germanicus emperor' (Obverse).

The coin is a *billon* of Vitellius minted in Alexandria; its legend is
in Greek. Its interest lies in the emperor's titulature, for the title

'Caesar' has been assigned to him. The literary evidence is inconsistent on this point. According to Suetonius, Vitellius 'eagerly accepted the surname "Germanicus", which everyone offered him, hesitated to accept the title "Augustus", and forever rejected the surname "Caesar" ' (Suetonius, *Vitellius* 8.2: Loeb translation). Plutarch supports his statement: 'He accepted the title of "Germanicus" which (the soldiers) conferred on him, though he rejected that of "Caesar" ' (Plutarch, *Galba* 22: Loeb translation). Tacitus, on the other hand, whilst noting that 'Vitellius forwarded to Rome a decree postponing his acceptance of the title "Augustus" and refusing that of "Caesar" ', also states that, a little later, 'he consented to be addressed as "Caesar", a title which he had previously refused' (*Hist.* 2.62 and 3.58: translated Church and Brodribb, adapted). Usually, Tacitus is more reliable than Suetonius in matters of fact, and the coin could perhaps be considered as supporting Tacitus' view. On the other hand, it should further be noted that Vitellius' coins do not usually include the title 'Caesar', and that this rare example is from Alexandria: because of the brief duration of this emperor's reign and the time required for the various areas of the empire to be informed of any official changes in the imperial titulature, one is inclined to suspect that 'Caesar' was included automatically, on the analogy of previous reigns, rather than as a result of an official modification of the earlier Vitellian titulature. On one other document from Egypt, a tax receipt from the city of Thebes, 'Caesar' is also assigned to him, and presumably for the same reason: 'In the 1st (year) of Aulus Vitellius Caesar Augustus Germanicus, emperor, June 16th . . .' (M&W 35).

10   (*BMC* II, p. 180, No. 748b = M&W 83)

'The emperor Caesar Vespasian Augustus' (Obverse): 'Caesar, son of Augustus, consul: Caesar, son of Augustus, praetor: by decree of the senate' (Reverse).

The coin is an *as* of Vespasian; its legend is in Latin. On the reverse are busts of the emperor's sons, Titus and Domitian, and since Titus is recorded as consul (for the first time), it can be assigned to AD 70. Once he seized power Vespasian was determined to consolidate it, and he made every effort to enhance his own status, together with that of his family. The vital problem, one that had plagued Augustus, was the succession, but here Vespasian was more fortunate as he had two adult sons, and he proclaimed the fact regularly on both coins and inscriptions. It was an advantage already stressed by his close associate Mucianus, governor of Syria, when he urged him to march on Vitellius: 'I count myself better than Vitellius; I count you better than myself. Your family can boast . . . the presence of two young men, one of whom is already competent to hold the position of supreme commander, and in the first years of his military career won distinction in the eyes of the very armies of Germany' (Tacitus, *Hist.* 2.77: translated Church and Brodribb). Once Vitellius was defeated, Vespasian held the ordin-ary consulship of 70, with Titus as his colleague (both of them *in absentia*), whilst Domitian was appointed 'praetor with consular authority' and remained in the capital as the family's official representative. Tacitus describes the senate's actions as follows: 'There was no want of deference on the part of the senate. On the emperor and his son Titus the consulship was bestowed by decree; on Domitian the office of praetor with consular authority' (*Hist.* 4.3). The coin faithfully reflected the senate's awards and ensured that the Flavians' position escaped no one's notice.

11   (*BMC* II, p. 131, No. 604 = M&W 44)

'The emperor Caesar Vespasian Augustus, consul 3 times' (Obverse): 'Judaea captured: by decree of the senate' (Reverse).

The coin is an *as* of Vespasian from the mint in Rome; its legend is in Latin. It was issued in 71, when he was consul for the third time. On the reverse is a representation of a 'Jewess seated . . . at (the) foot of a palmtree, in (an) attitude of dejection' (M&W, p. 39). The Jewish rebellion, which broke out in 66, was virtually crushed with the destruction of Jerusalem in 70; the latter task was accomplished by Titus, and not by his father who, although appointed by Nero to superintend the campaign, was at that time more concerned with consolidating his position in Rome. For the first three years of the reign, resistance in Judaea remained strong in some scattered pockets until the fall of Masada. By that time the Flavian propaganda had long been proclaiming the emperor's success, and indeed, ten years later, the victory was still being commemorated (see **30**).

12   (*BMC* II, p. 311, No. 62 = M&W 114)

'Domitia Augusta, (wife) of the emperor Domitian' (Obverse): 'Deified Caesar, son of the emperor Domitian' (Reverse).

The coin is an *aureus* of Domitian minted in Rome; its legend is in

Document 11   An *as* of Vespasian (Obverse and Reverse).
Reproduced by courtesy of the Trustees of the British Museum.

Document 14   An *aureus* of Nerva (Obverse and Reverse).
Reproduced by courtesy of the Trustees of the British Museum.

Latin. The absence of Domitian's frequently used title 'Germanicus' makes it almost certain that it was issued during the period 81
to 84. The reverse of the coin is described as follows in M&W, p. 50:
'Naked infant boy (Divus Caesar as baby Jupiter) seated on a globe,
stretching out hands. Around, seven stars'. The child is Domitian's
son who had died during the early years of Vespasian's reign
(Suetonius, *Domitian* 3).

On his accession, Domitian made determined efforts to enhance
his family's status – and with it, his own. Consequently, his wife
Domitia was almost immediately awarded the title 'Augusta', his
brother Titus was deified as was his own young son.

13   (*BMC* II, pp. 323–6, Nos 111, 115, 129)

(A) 'The emperor Caesar Domitian Augustus Germanicus, pontifex maximus, of tribunician power for the 7th time' (Obverse): 'saluted as victorious commander 14 times, consul 13 times, perpetual censor, father of his country' (Reverse).
(B) 'Saluted as victorious commander 14 times, consul 14 times, perpetual censor, father of his country' (Reverse).
(C) 'Saluted as victorious commander 15 times, consul 14 times, perpetual censor, father of his country' (Reverse).

The coins are *denarii* of Domitian from the mint in Rome; the legends are in Latin; each coin has the same legend on the obverse as does (A). At times it is possible to assign a fairly precise date to Roman coins. These *denarii* were all minted between 14 September 87 and 13 September 88, since the obverses refer to Domitian's seventh tenure of tribunician power. Further precision in dating is possible from an examination of his consulships. He held this office every year during the period 82–9, being consul for the thirteenth time in 87 and for the fourteenth in 88. Therefore, coin (A) must be assigned to 87, but not earlier than 14 September. The consular year of coins (B) and (C) indicate that they both were issued in 88, but before 13 September (from the tribunician year) with (B) preceding (C) – from the salutations.

14   (*BMC* III, p. 1, No. 4 = S. *N–H* 91a)

'The emperor Nerva Caesar Augustus, pontifex maximus, of tribunician power, twice consul, father of his country' (Obverse): 'Concord of the armies' (Reverse).

The coin is an *aureus* of Nerva, minted in Rome; its legend is in Latin. Nerva was consul for the second time in 90, during Domitian's reign, and for the third time in 97; it must have been minted, then, in 96, after Domitian's death on 18 September. References to 'concord' in the army are rare on Roman coins, except during a period of civil war (e.g. 68–9), and perhaps such a legend often represented an ideal rather than reflected the true state of affairs. In the first months of Nerva's brief reign there was mutiny amongst the praetorians and unrest in the army in general: Syria was unsettled, whilst it is not unlikely that Nerva was subjected to considerable pressure when he adopted Trajan, the legate of Upper Germany. The coin, then, presumably expresses little more than a pious hope on the new emperor's part, and is intended to disguise the true state of affairs.

15   (S. *N–H* 208)

'The emperor Nerva Trajan Caesar Augustus Germanicus' (Obverse): 'In the proconsulship of (Gaius) Julius Bassus' (Reverse).

This is a bronze coin of Trajan from Bithynia. Its legend is in Greek, and since there is no reference to the emperor's victory in Dacia (commemorated after 102 by the addition of 'Dacicus' to his titulature), we may assign the coin, and Bassus' proconsulship, to the period 98–102. This is a valuable item of information for the reconstruction of the senator's career. According to Pliny (*Ep*. 4.9), he had been indicted in Vespasian's reign but acquitted after a lengthy trial; subsequently he was banished by Domitian only to be recalled by Nerva. Despite his unpromising record, he was sent by Trajan to govern Bithynia, and on his return faced trial for extortion. Pliny appeared for the defence, claiming that 'in all innocence Bassus had thoughtlessly accepted certain gifts from the provincials' (*Ep*. 4.9.6), and the jury, composed entirely of senators, not unexpectedly accepted this naive explanation, and acquitted Bassus. The coin is most valuable in that it enables an approximate date to be assigned both to the delinquent's proconsulship and also to his trial.

16   (*BMC* III, p. 108, No. 531 = S. *N–H* 108)

'Marciana Augusta, sister of the emperor Trajan' (Obverse): 'Caesar Augustus Germanicus Dacicus, consul 6 times, father of his country. Matidia Augusta' (Reverse, with a representation of Matidia seated with two children).

The coin is a *denarius* of Trajan, minted in Rome; its legend is in Latin. Trajan held his sixth consulship in 112, and on 29 August in that year his sister Marciana died and was almost immediately deified. Evidence is provided by that part of the consular list for 112 that survives: '. . . 29 August. Marciana Augusta died and was deified . . . 3 September: Marciana Augusta was buried with a state funeral . . .' (S. *N–H* 22). This coin, then, can be assigned to the first eight months of 112, since Marciana lacks the cognomen *diva* (i.e. 'deified'). Her daughter, Matidia, now appeared on the coins for the first time, together with her two children (Vibia Sabina the wife of Hadrian, and Matidia the Younger). Trajan deliberately tried to enhance his family's status, just as the Flavians had done, and so his female relatives appear fairly regularly on his coins and inscriptions, with their appropriate titles – thus his wife Plotina as well as his sister Marciana and her daughter Matidia received the title 'Augusta': the latter two appear as such on this coin whilst Plotina is recorded as 'Augusta' somewhat earlier , in AD 104/5 (S. *N–H* 106). In this context, one might compare a recently discov-ered inscription with a dedication in Greek to Matidia the Younger: 'Matidia daughter of Augusta, sister of Augusta, granddaughter of Augusta' (*AE* 1950, 32) – where reference is made to her mother Matidia, her sister Vibia Sabina and her grandmother Marciana. Of interest, too, is the title 'Dacicus' or 'conqueror of Dacia'. During the first century of the empire, various emperors had styled themselves or their sons 'Germanicus' or 'Britannicus'; Domitian used the former title frequently, always in the sense of 'conqueror of Germany', whereas, for the Julio-Claudian emperors it indicated relationship with Germanicus (see **6**). With Vitellius, on the other hand, it was intended to show that he had been 'appointed by the legions of Germany'.

17 (*BMC* III, p. 94, No. 454 = S. *N–H* 378b)

'To the emperor Trajan Augustus Germanicus Dacicus, ponti-fex maximus, of tribunician power, consul 6 times, father of his country' (Obverse): 'The senate and Roman people to the Best of Rulers' (Reverse, with a representation of Trajan's Column).

The coin is a *denarius* of Trajan minted in Rome; its legend is in Latin. Since the title 'Optimus' (i.e. 'the Best') appears only on the reverse, it must have been still unofficial, and hence the coin was minted before 114. On the other hand, he held his sixth consulship in 112, and therefore we can assign it to the period 112–13.

Trajan's Column, one of the most impressive surviving monu-ments of ancient Rome, is some 128 feet high and is composed of seventeen superimposed marble drums. 'Its outer surface takes the form of a ribbon, about three feet wide and 670 feet long, twisted round it in twenty-three spirals. The spirals cover 400 slabs and are carved with reliefs containing more than 2500 figures' (L. Rossi, *Trajan's Column and the Dacian Wars*, London 1971, p. 13). They represent the entire history of the Dacian wars and provide an important source of information about the progress of the war and the Roman army of Trajan's reign, whilst the Column's unusual proportions were intended to symbolize the effort he had made to overcome natural problems for the adornment of Rome. This was made clear in the inscription on its base: 'The senate and people of Rome (erected this) for the emperor Caesar, son of the deified Nerva, Nerva Trajan Augustus Germanicus Dacicus, pontifex maximus, of tribunician power for the 17th time, saluted as victorious commander 6 times, consul 6 times, father of his country, in order to show how high was the hill and the place that was excavated for these great works' (S. *N–H* 378a: December 112/December 113). The consular list for 113 (the *Fasti Ostienses*) provides the precise date of the Column's dedication: '. . . 12 May. The emperor Trajan dedicated the temple of Venus in Caesar's Forum and the Column in his own Forum' (S. *N–H* 22).

18 (*BMC* III, p. 100, No. 498 = S. *N–H* 133)

'The emperor Trajan Augustus Germanicus Dacicus, pontifex maximus, of tribunician power, consul 6 times, father of his country' (Obverse): 'The deified Nerva and the deified Trajan senior' (Reverse).

The coin is an *aureus* of Trajan from the Rome mint; its legend is in Latin. On the reverse is a representation of Nerva and Trajan senior facing each other. Probably it was minted between 112 and 114, for there is a reference to the emperor's sixth (and last) consulship, which he held in 112, but no indication of the title 'the Best' ('Optimus') which he received in 114 and subsequently used quite regularly on his coins and inscriptions. There is some dispute about the interpretation of the legend on the reverse. It used to be thought that the reference to the elder Trajan's deification indicated that he had just died. But he had been a senior consular late in Vespasian's reign, so had certainly been well over forty on that emperor's death some thirty-three years previously; on the other hand, senators aged over ninety are not unheard of (e.g. Verginius Rufus). A sentence in Pliny's *Panegyricus*, however, which was delivered in 100, seems to indicate that he was then already dead: 'You also, Trajan senior (Pliny had just mentioned the deified Nerva) – for you too, though not raised to the stars, must surely occupy the nearest place – must experience great pleasure to see your son, who was tribune and soldier under you, now risen to be supreme commander and emperor' (*Pan.* 89.2: Loeb translation). The inference is that the elder Trajan was dead but not deified ('not raised to the stars') in 100 – a defect that his son remedied twelve years later. Moreover, in 112 the emperor was engaged in his grandiose eastern expedition, acquiring the title 'Conqueror of Parthia' three years later, and was anxious to attach to himself his father's military renown gained in that same region.

19   (*BMC* III, p. 237, No. 5 = S. *N–H* 110b)

'To the emperor Caesar Trajan Hadrian, the Best, Augustus, Germanicus Dacicus' (Obverse): 'Parthicus, son of the deified Trajan Augustus, pontifex maximus, of tribunician power, consul, father of his country. Adoption' (Reverse, with a representation of Trajan and Hadrian clasping hands).

The coin is an *aureus* of Hadrian, minted in Rome; its legend is in Latin. Hadrian held his first consulship in 108 and his second in 118, and since he came to the throne in August 117, the coin must be assigned to the last five months of that year. At this period, and indeed until July of the following year (see **20**), Hadrian remained in the East until affairs could be settled in the capital. In this coin, Trajan's honorific titles ('the Best', 'Germanicus', 'Dacicus' and 'Parthicus') have been carried directly over to his successor, but they were not retained subsequently by him. One element included in Hadrian's titles is particularly interesting. According to the *Life of Hadrian* 6.4, the new emperor 'refused for the present the title "father of his country", offered to him at the time of his succession and again later on, giving as his reason the fact that Augustus had not won it until later in life' (Loeb translation). It did not become an offical part of Hadrian's titulature until 128 yet does appear on this coin and also on an early inscription: 'To the emperor Caesar, son of the deified Trajan Parthicus, grandson of the deified Nerva, Trajan Hadrian Augustus, pontifex maximus, of tribunician power for the 2nd time, consul, father of his country. The colony Ulpia Traiana Augusta Dacica Sarmizegetusa' (*CIL* III 1445 = S. *N–H* 111). The colony referred to, Dacica, was founded immediately after Trajan's conquest of Dacia by Decimus Terentius Scaurianus (see **37**), the first governor of the province, cf. *CIL* III 1443 = S. *N–H* 479: 'On the authority of the emperor Caesar, son of the deified Nerva, Trajan Augustus, when the colony of Dacica was founded by the legion 5 Macedonica. Scaurianus, his legate with the rank of propraetor gave this as a gift.' The appearance of the title 'father of his country' on these early documents is no doubt due to analogy with the titulature of previous emperors, almost all of whom included it immediately after their accession, as the last item in their titles.

   Of considerable importance is the reference to Hadrian's adoption by Trajan. Throughout his reign, Hadrian stressed his 'relationship' to his two predecessors (see, for instance, S. *N–H* 111, translated above, from the early years of his reign, and also S. *N–H* 478 from the fourteenth year, both of which refer to him as the deified Nerva's grandson), and although the relationship may well appear rather tenuous, it was none the less vital if Hadrian was to establish the legitimacy of his new position. It must, of course, be remembered that the adoption by a 64-year-old man of someone aged 42 would not, in itself, have been regarded as unusual by the Romans.

Trajan's wife Plotina and the praetorian prefect Acilius Attianus (Hadrian's former guardian) claimed that before dying Trajan had adopted his second cousin Publius Aelius Hadrianus, and on 11 August the army of Syria hailed Hadrian as emperor. Not everyone accepted the official version: Dio, for instance, writing a century later, flatly contradicts it: 'Hadrian had not been adopted by Trajan . . . My father, Apronianus, who was governor of Cilicia, said that the death of Trajan was concealed for several days in order that Hadrian's adoption might be announced first. This was shown by Trajan's letters to the senate, for they were signed, not by him, but by Plotina, although she had not done this in any previous instance' (Dio 69.1.1–4: Loeb translation). Hadrian, however, throughout his reign, stressed the legitimacy of his position in his offical propaganda. Compare the legend on an *aureus* issued by the Rome mint in 117: 'The emperor Caesar Nerva Trajan, the Best, Augustus Germanicus Dacicus' (Obverse, with a representation of Trajan): 'To Hadrian Trajan Caesar' (Reverse, with a representation of Hadrian: S. *N–H* 110a) – it was not the regular practice for an emperor to relegate his image to the reverse of his own coins. On the other hand, as late as the period 134–8 the Rome mint issued another *aureus* with the legend: 'Hadrian Augustus, consul 3 times, father of his country' (Obverse): 'To his deified parents' (Reverse, with a representation of Trajan and Plotina, and a star above each: S. *N–H* 141b).

20   (*BMC* III, p. 401, No. 1120 = S. *N–H* 62)

'The emperor Caesar Trajan Hadrian Augustus' (Obverse): 'Pontifex maximus, of tribunician power, consul twice; by decree of the senate; the arrival of Augustus' (Reverse, with a representation of Roma in military dress, seated, clasping hands with Hadrian).

The coin is a *sestertius* of Hadrian, minted in Rome; its legend is in Latin. As Hadrian was consul for the second time in 118 and for the third time in the following year, we may assign this coin to the former year. It commemorates the emperor's arrival in the capital, almost twelve months after Trajan's death in August 117. At that time Hadrian was governor of Syria, and he remained there whilst his supporters removed any opposition in Rome. Four senior ex-consuls, all close friends of Trajan, were condemned to death and executed, for reasons that are not known. Hadrian later protested that the executions had taken place without his knowledge or consent. Possibly they had opposed the adoption of Hadrian during Trajan's lifetime (Hadrian's so-called adoption is discussed under **19**) or again, they may have expressed their concern at the new emperor's proposed frontier policy, one that was openly defensive, a return to Flavian frontiers. We happen to know the precise date of Hadrian's entry into the capital from an entry in the minutes of a meeting of the Arval Brothers (see **33**): 'In the consulship of Lucius Pomponius Bassus and Titus Sabinius Barbarus (i.e. AD 118), on 10 July, the Arval Brothers met on the Capitol because of the arrival of the emperor Caesar Trajan Hadrian Augustus . . .' (S. *N–H* 6, p. 21).

21   (*BMC* III, p. 544, No. 1919 = S. *N–H* 119b)

'Lucius Aelius Caesar' (Obverse): 'Of tribunician power, twice consul. Pannonia. By decree of the senate' (Reverse).

The coin is a *sestertius* of Hadrian minted in Rome; its legend is in Latin. It must have been issued in 137 — Aelius was awarded his second consulship in that year but died on 1 January 138.

When Hadrian became ill towards the middle of 136, he began to consider the problem of the succession. The obvious choice was his only living blood relation, his grand-nephew Gnaeus Pedanius Fuscus Salinator, who was the grandson of Hadrian's ninety-year-old brother-in-law, Lucius Julius Ursus Servianus (probably the adopted son of the Lucius Julius Ursus of **85**). Apparently there was a good deal of intrigue on their behalf and the emperor had them both executed in 136; then he surprised the senate by adopting one of their number, Lucius Ceionius Commodus Verus who was henceforth known as Aelius Verus. He had been praetor in 130 and was already consul for 136. Hadrian then gave him tribunician power in December of that year, a sure sign that he was regarded as heir apparent. During 136 and 137 he governed both Upper and Lower Pannonia, being also awarded a second consulship. Unfortunately, Verus was subject to tuberculosis and died on 1 January 138.

The coin is interesting in that the evidence it provides helps to correct the version of these events in the *Life of Hadrian*. The latter claims that 'on the occasion of the adoption (i.e. of Ceionius Commodus), Hadrian gave games in the circus and bestowed

largess upon the populace and the soldiers. He dignified Commodus with the office of praetor and immediately placed him in
command of the Pannonian provinces, and also conferred on him
the consulship together with enough money to meet the expenses
of office. He also appointed Commodus to a second consulship.
And when he heard that the man was diseased, he often used to
say: 'We have leaned against a tottering wall and have wasted the
four million sesterces which we gave the populace and the soldiers
on the adoption of Commodus' (*Life of Hadr.* 23.13–15: Loeb
translation). The legend on the coin contradicts the statement that
he was placed in command of Pannonia before his second
consulship and it notes his receipt of tribunician power which the
Life omits; on the other hand, the last sentence is a frank admission
of the role (and expense) of the imperial propaganda machine.

Part II
Inscriptions

A.   Official Documents

i.   Major Enactments

The following eleven inscriptions are all examples of documents
which either emanated from the emperor, in the form of letters
of reply to petitions (rescripts), decrees or dedications of public
works, or were set up in honour of or reference to the emperor by
bodies such as the senate or the Arval Brethren or gave the text
of legislation concerning the emperor. The type of information
that can be gained from such documents is very varied, reflecting
as they do general imperial policies, particular solutions to
particular problems and even the personality of the emperor
himself. We have tried in our comments to emphasize what we
regard as the most significant features of each document and the
most important information it contains. One obvious feature is the
use by the emperor or the initiators of the document of the
imperial titles; and we have tried to show how a formal and
regular imperial titulature developed from the time of Augustus,
the first emperor, and what the significance is of each part of this
titulature.

22 (*ILS* 113 = E&J 82)

The emperor Caesar, son of the deified, Augustus, pontifex maximus, consul 13 times, saluted as victorious commander 20 times, of tribunician power 37 times, father of his country and Tiberius Caesar, son of the deified Augustus, pontifex maximus, consul for the 4th time, saluted as victorious commander 8 times, of tribunician power for the 22nd time, gave (this bridge).

The inscription, which is in Latin, is from the bridge at Ariminum, on the Adriatic coast of Italy. The bridge apparently was begun by Augustus and completed by Tiberius; hence its dedication in the names of both emperors. The inscription can be dated to the year AD 21 from Tiberius' tribunician power, which also coincides with the year in which he held his fourth consulship. Tiberius' tribunician dating is somewhat confusing unless it be remembered that he had two periods of tribunician power under Augustus' reign, both of which he counted in his tribunician numbering when he became sole emperor. His first tenure of the power was from 6 BC to 2 BC, when he was of tribunician power for the fifth time; his second tenure began in AD 4, when he became of tribunician power for the sixth time. The numbers then increased by one each year, so that at Augustus' death in AD 14 he is of tribunician power for the sixteenth time and in AD 15, his first full year as sole emperor, for the seventeenth time. The inscription is of interest as showing the full list of Augustus' official titles, as they stood at his death in AD 14, and those of his successor, Tiberius.

(i) The first point to notice is that Augustus has the *praenomen imperatoris*, i.e. the 'first name of emperor', which is not used by Tiberius. Augustus places this word *imperator*, which grew to indicate 'emperor' and which we so translate, as almost a personal name and one showing his successful prosecution of Rome's wars. The normal word used in Augustan Rome to denote the emperor was *princeps*, which is often translated as 'prince', but really means something like 'the first citizen'. So closely was the 'imperial first name' bound up with Augustus that none of his Julio-Claudian successors (except Nero in his last years) used it as a title in official documents, though it gradually became more and more prevalent as the everyday word for 'emperor'. Vespasian, on his accession to power, resumed the Augustan practice of 'the imperial first name' and henceforth it was used in the same way that we use 'emperor', as an official title. But note, once again, that in AD 21 the ruling emperor Tiberius does not use it. It will also be noted that Tiberius does not have the title 'father of his country', which appears at the end of Augustus' titles. Suetonius, *Tiberius* 26, says of him that he 'refused to put the title "emperor" before his name, or "father of his country" after'. He maintained that this title, which had been conferred on Augustus in 2 BC, was, like 'the imperial first name', the exclusive property of Augustus. However, inscriptions from the provinces give Tiberius the title of both 'emperor' and 'father of his country'. Gaius Caligula refused the title of 'father of his country'; but both Claudius and Nero accepted it after an initial delay and henceforth it formed a part of the imperial titulature.

(ii) 'Caesar': placed second in sequence. Augustus had a right to this name through his adoption by Julius Caesar, and Tiberius after his adoption by Augustus. When Claudius, who had no blood relationship with the Julian family, took the name Caesar, it effectively became a title and no longer a name. Eventually, from the time of the Flavian emperors, 'Caesar', when used without 'Augustus', came to designate the sons and heirs-presumptive of the emperors.

(iii) 'Son of the deified': Augustus, through his adoption by Julius Caesar, became this after Julius' official deification in 42 BC. He always used it, since its religious significance added to his prestige and influence. Tiberius, after Augustus' deification, had two deities as his immediate forebears. The next emperor to be 'son of the deified' was Nero, after the deification of Claudius.

(iv) 'Augustus': this name was conferred on Augustus on 16 January 27 BC by the senate, in recognition of his great services to the state. Tiberius, with his usual deference and sense of modesty, is said by Suetonius to have declined to use 'Augustus', even though it was his by right of inheritance, except when writing to foreign monarchs. But inscriptions and coins show that he did use it. Tiberius' successors accepted 'Augustus' automatically and it ceased to be a name, but became a title limited absolutely to the reigning emperor. This can be seen very clearly in the case of Vespasian and Titus: though they were virtually co-emperors, Vespasian, the nominee of the senate and people, was always entitled 'Augustus', Titus never until Vespasian's death.

(v) 'Pontifex maximus': Augustus became pontifex maximus in 12 BC; Tiberius immediately after his accession; and after him every succeeding emperor was head of the Roman state religion.

(vi) 'Saluted as victorious commander': every Roman general fighting as an independent commander ('under his own auspices', to use the Roman phrase) was entitled to be saluted as *imperator* by his troops after a victory. But it rapidly became the rule that only the reigning emperor, not his legate (i.e. deputed commander), should receive these salutations; and thus, as with 'Augustus', it became a title appropriate to and designating the emperor (though Titus was allowed by Vespasian to receive these 'imperial saluta-tions' along with himself). We have given this translation of 'imperator', when it indicates salutations for victories, to distin-guish it from the same word used as a *praenomen* (see discussion under (i) above).

(vii) 'Of tribunician power': the tribunician power, which Augus-tus received in 23 BC and Tiberius, for the first time, in 6 BC, was always used by the ruling emperor to date the years of his reign. Thus Augustus was in his thirty-seventh year of tribunician power at his death in AD 14. Tiberius, at his death in AD 37, was in his thirty-eighth year of tribunician power (see above, p. 21, for the peculiarity of Tiberius' tribunician dating). Though there is some inconsistency among the emperors of the first century AD in the day of assumption of the tribunician power after their accession, it can be stated as a general proposition that we can always date a document with reasonable precision if that document contains a statement of the emperor's tribunician number; and this will be seen many times in this selection of documents.

We may note that the actual powers and offices listed in the titulature of Augustus and Tiberius, together with the 'imperial salutations', are all of a 'Republican' character. Augustus was always anxious to emphasize the continuity of his regime with the Republic and thereby to conceal his extraordinary powers. As M. Hammond says (*The Augustan Principate*, Cambridge, Mass. 1933, p. 112): 'The titles employed by the Emperors illustrate the general tendency of the Principate. At first they indicated the Republican positions held by Augustus, his hereditary names, or special epithets, such as had not been unknown under the Republic. But they became formalized and regularized. Those which had been at first peculiar to Augustus himself were conferred on all who held his position, and hence come to denominate the legal monarchy into which the unofficial principate changed.' The titles of Augus-tus and Tiberius, as given on our inscription, are well worth studying. For, with variations of the positions of the powers and offices that follow 'Augustus' and with amplifications due to the assumption of victory-titles such as 'Germanicus', they form the basis of the official imperial titulature as it appears on all official documents of the period covered by this selection.

23 (*ILS* 8781 = E&J 315)

In the 3rd year from the 12th consulship of the emperor Caesar, son of the deified, Augustus, on 6 March, the oath taken at

Gangra in the agora by the inhabitants of Paphlagonia and by the Romans conducting business among them.

I swear by Zeus, Earth, Sun, all the gods and goddesses and Augustus himself that I will be well disposed towards Caesar Augustus and his children and descendants for all the time of my life both in word and in deed and in thought, considering as friends whomsoever they consider as friends and regarding as my personal enemies whomsoever they themselves judge (to be enemies); and that I will spare neither body nor soul nor life nor children on behalf of their interests, but will endure any and every danger, in any and every manner, on behalf of the things that are their concern; and that if I perceive or hear of anything being said or devised or done contrary to them, I will inform about this and will be an enemy to the person saying or devising or doing any of these things; and that whomsoever they judge to be their enemies, these I will pursue and punish by land and by sea, with arms and with steel. If I do anything contrary to this oath or not in accordance as I have sworn, I myself invoke against myself and my body and soul and life and children and all my family and interests total and utter destruction and upon every successive generation of my own and of all who spring from me; and may neither earth nor sea receive the bodies of my family or of those who spring from me nor may they bear fruits for them.

There also swore in the same words all the inhabitants of the country in the temples of Augustus in each administrative subdivision, by the altars of Augustus. Similarly the Phazimonites who inhabit what is now called New Town swore en masse in the temple of Augustus, by the altar of Augustus.

The inscription, which is in Greek, is from the town of Neapolis (= 'New Town') in Paphlagonia, a district which in 6 BC was added by Augustus to the province of Galatia. The year of the inscription can be obtained from the statement that the oath was taken in the third year from the twelfth consulship of Augustus. Augustus' twelfth consulship was in 5 BC; thus the year is 3 BC, this being the third year from that date. From the method of dating used by the Paphlagonians it would appear that they had begun a new 'era', a 'commencing year' (see OGIS 583 = E&J 134 = **74**), with Augustus' twelfth consulship. In this same year or the next year the neighbouring principalities of Amasia and Sebastopolis were incorporated in the province of Galatia and began new 'eras' with Augustus' thirteenth consulship, i.e. 2 BC. The day on which the oath was taken, 6 March, was probably deliberately chosen because of its special religious significance for Augustus and hence the Roman world. We know from other inscriptional evidence, namely the Calendars, that on this day Augustus was elected pontifex maximus, head of the Roman state religion. The oath itself was probably sworn on this occasion for the first time by the people of the new provincial district; hence its engraving as a permanent record. On the accession of a new emperor the armed forces and entire civilian population of the empire swore an oath of allegiance to him and renewed this oath annually on the anniversary of his accession. Tacitus, *Annals* 1.7, tells us that on the death of Augustus, 'Sextus Pompeius and Sextus Appuleius, the consuls, were the first to swear allegiance to Tiberius Caesar, and in their presence the oath was taken by Seius Strabo and Gaius Turranius, respectively the commander of the praetorian cohorts and the superintendent of the corn supplies. Then the Senate, the soldiers and the people did the same' (translated Church and Brodribb). The institution of this oath of allegiance probably goes back to the oath of allegiance sworn by the whole of Italy and the western provinces to Augustus in 32 BC: 'The whole of Italy voluntarily took an oath of allegiance to me and demanded me as its leader in the war in which I was victorious at Actium. The same oath was taken by the provinces of the Gauls, the Spains, Africa, Sicily and Sardinia' (*RG* 25). At another part of the *RG* Augustus implies that this oath of allegiance gave him a legal right to the supreme power which he exercised for years afterwards: 'having attained supreme power by universal consent' (*RG* 34). Constitutional lawyers may well dispute and have disputed this clause; but there is no doubt that this demonstration of solid unanimous support was a key aspect of the position of Augustus both before and after the campaign of Actium. The oath, it should be noted, is not taken to the head of state, but to Augustus as a person; and historians are agreed in emphasizing the 'personal' aspect of his power, as compared with formal, legal powers conferred upon him. Augustus and his successors were in a very special relation-ship with the peoples of the empire, an intimate and reciprocal relationship whereby the people are regarded as unanimously supporting the emperor's rule and the emperor guarantees to protect and benefit the people. This protective, personal aspect is well seen in the title 'father of his country' or, with a different emphasis, in the words of Galba in Tacitus, *Histories* 1.16 that, 'Under Tiberius, Gaius and Claudius, we were, so to speak, the inheritance of a single family'. We do not know the wording of the first oath of allegiance, establishing this personal relationship between emperor and people, the oath sworn in 32 BC; but this oath sworn by the Paphlagonians to their new ruler may have been very similar. For the swearer of the oath maintains to uphold, not the Roman state, but the person of Augustus and his family in perpetuity.

24   (*SEG* XI 923 = E&J 102(b))

Letter of Tiberius. Tiberius Caesar, son of the deified Augustus, Augustus, pontifex maximus, of tribunician power for the 18th time, sends greetings to the ephors and the city of Gytheum. The envoy who was sent by you to me and to my mother, Decimus Turranius Nicanor, gave me your letter in which had been written the legislation passed by you for the revering of my father and the honouring of ourselves. Whilst I praise you for this, I think that it is befitting that all mankind in general and your city in particular should preserve as exceptional the honours appropriate to gods, in keeping with the greatness of the benefits conferred by my father on all the world. For myself, I am satisfied with the more modest honours appropriate to men. My mother, however, will send her reply when she has learned from you your decision about the honours concerning her.

The inscription, which is in Greek, was found at Gytheum in Laconia. Two stones were discovered, the first of which contains provisions for the placing of images of Augustus, Tiberius and Livia in the theatre, the conducting of sacrifices for the welfare of the rulers, and the performance of theatrical celebrations in their honour. The second stone contains penalties for anyone whose proposals violate a cult, presumably the imperial cult, and then the letter of Tiberius. The letter, which can be dated to AD 15 or 16 by the conjectural restoration of Tiberius' tribunician numbering, contains a politely worded refusal by Tiberius of the offer of divine honours by the people of Gytheum, and illustrates well two aspects of the imperial cult in the provinces: firstly, the desire of many communities, particularly in the Greek East, to establish a cult of the reigning emperor and members of the imperial family; and secondly, Tiberius' own reluctance to accept such honours, though recognizing their appropriateness in the case of Augustus (who was now officially a god of the Roman state). Suetonius, *Tiberius* 26, says that Tiberius 'forbade the voting of temples, flamens and priests in his honour, and even the setting up of statues and busts without his permission; and he gave this only with the understanding that they were not to be placed among the likenesses of gods, but among the adornments of the temples' (Loeb translation). Tacitus tells us (*Annals* 4.15) that in AD 23 the cities of Asia voted a temple to Tiberius, Livia and the senate, and permission was given to build it; but two year later, when the province of Further Spain asked permission to build a temple to Tiberius and Livia, Tiberius refused the honour with the words, 'It would be a vain and arrogant thing to receive the sacred honour of images representing the divine throughout all the provinces, and the homage paid to Augustus will disappear if it is vulgarized by indiscriminate flattery. For myself, senators, I am mortal and limited to the functions of humanity, content if I can adequately fill the highest place' (*Annals* 4.37 and 38, translated Church and Brodribb). But Tiberius was powerless to check the spread of cult of himself and we find priests of Tiberius in many towns and cities. The present letter, however, is interesting as being an official statement of Tiberius, at the start of his reign, on this matter. It is also interesting to note the emperor's deference to his mother at this stage; Livia, in the letter, is left to make up her own mind whether or not to accept divine honours. Nine years later Tiberius has no hesitation in refusing the honour for both himself and his mother.

25 (*ILS* 206 = S 368)

In the consulship of Marcus Junius Silanus and Quintus Sulpicius Camerinus, on 15 March, at Baiae, in the imperial headquarters: the edict of Tiberius Claudius Caesar Augustus Germanicus, which is inscribed below, was published.

Tiberius Claudius Caesar Augustus Germanicus, pontifex maximus, of tribunician power for the 6th time, saluted as victorious commander 11 times, father of his country, designated as consul for the 4th time, declares:

Since, as the result of ancient disputes, which were of long standing even in the times of my uncle Tiberius, who had sent Pinarius Apollinaris to settle them — although, as far as I recall from memory, they were only between the people of Comum and the Bergaleans — and since he (Apollinaris), at first because of the obstinate absence of my uncle, and then, in the principate of Gaius, because he was not asked to report on the situation, not foolishly neglected to do so; and since after this Camerius Statutus reported to me that several fields and woodlands were under my jurisdiction; I sent to meet the present situation Julius Planta, my friend and councillor. And since he, after consulting my procurators, both those who were in the rest of

the region and those who were in the immediate neighbour-
hood, has investigated and inquired into the matter with the
utmost care, with regard to all other matters I permit him to
make decisions and to give pronouncements according as they
have been demonstrated to me in the memorandum composed
by himself.

But as far as the status of the Anauni and the Tulliassies and
the Sinduni is concerned, some of whom the informer is said to
have proven to be attributed to the Tridentini, and some of
whom not even to be attributed: even though I notice that that
class of men do not have a very secure basis for Roman
citizenship; nevertheless, since they are said to have been in
possession of it as a result of long usage and to be so
intermingled with the Tridentini that they cannot be separated
from them without serious harm to the distinguished municipality, I permit them, by my benefaction, to remain in that legal
condition in which they have believed themselves to be; and I
do this all the more gladly, because several of that class of men
are even said to be serving in my Praetorian Guard, several
indeed also to have attained positions of command, and some
to have been enrolled in the jury panels at Rome and to be
judging cases.

I so confer this benefaction on them that, whatever they have
done or acted as if Roman citizens, either amongst themselves
or with the Tridentini or with others, I order these acts to be
valid; and I shall permit them to have those names which they
had previously as though they were Roman citizens.

The inscription, which is in Latin, is preserved as a bronze tablet
found at the modern Trento (ancient Tridentum) in the Italian
Alps. It is an edict of the emperor Claudius and can be dated
accurately, by means of the date given in the text, the tribunician
year of the emperor and the consuls, to 15 March AD 46. Note that
Claudius, like all the successors of Augustus till the end of Nero's
reign, does not use the *praenomen imperatoris*, i.e. the title of
'emperor' before his first name. The document has several points
of interest. In the first half of the edict, which deals with
long-standing disputes between two communities in North Italy
(the subject of these disputes is not specified, but, from the fact that
the emperor's own domains were found to be affected, they
probably concerned community boundaries), we can see how
difficult it could be to obtain a judicial decision if there was not a
firm and conscientious ruler at Rome. These particular disputes
had been dragging on since the reign of Tiberius; and Claudius is

implicitly claiming the credit for rapid and efficient action to solve the matter by delegating powers of decision to one of his intimate advisers, sent specifically to investigate the situation. The second part of the edict shows the emperor himself making a decision, that can only be called humane and sensible, in a matter that seems to have been reported by an informer, no doubt hoping for financial gain. The situation is that the tribes mentioned in the text, believing or claiming to believe that they were members of the municipality of Tridentum, had all assumed Roman citizenship. The informer is said to have produced proof that none of the tribes in fact were entitled to the citizenship – some were 'attributed' to Tridentum, i.e. subject to the jurisdiction of the municipality but not entitled to full civic rights, while others had no connections at all with Tridentum. Claudius, while recognizing the probability that the informer is correct, balances this against several other factors (the length of tenure of this usurped citizenship; the fact that some of the tribesmen were soldiers in the Guard and some were serving on the jury panels) and decides that the wisest course is to legalize the *de facto* situation by conferring the citizenship on the tribespeople. The document thus affords us evidence not only of Claudius' concern to extend the Roman citizenship, but also of his prudent humanity and concern for equity and fair dealing in the government of the empire. It was, of course, a decision that laid him open to the charge, so often levelled against him, of indiscriminate lavishing and consequently cheapening of the Roman citizenship. The decree also gives us a good insight into the mind of Claudius as expressed in his style of speaking and writing. Note throughout the document, but particularly in the first half, the tortuous, involved and laboured expression. Claudius frequently forgets how his sentences begin and gets himself tangled up in a maze of subordinate clauses and parentheses. The translation tries to reproduce the clumsiness of the Latin as closely as possible.

26 (*IG* VII. 2713 = S 64)

The emperor Caesar declares: Since I wish to reward the most noble Hellas for its good will and sense of duty towards me, I order as many as possible from this procuratorial district to be present at Corinth on 28 November.

When the crowds had gathered in assemble, he made the proclamation which is written below:

Unexpected, men of Hellas, is the gift which I bestow on you —
even though there is nothing which may not be hoped for from
my magnanimity — a gift so great that you were incapable of
asking for it. All Hellenes inhabiting Achaea and what was up
to now the Peloponnese, receive liberty and immunity from
taxation, which not all of you had even in your most prosperous
times. For you were slaves either to foreigners or to each other.
If only I could be making this gift whilst Hellas was still
flourishing, in order that more people might enjoy my benefactions! For this reason I reproach the passage of time, which has
squandered in advance the greatness of my benefactions. And
yet even now it is not through pity that I benefit you, but
through goodwill; and I make requital to your gods, whose
constant care for me, both by land and sea, I have always
experienced, because they have granted to me to make such a
great benefaction. For other rulers have freed cities, but [only
Nero] has freed a province.

The chief priest of the Augusti for life and of Nero Claudius
Caesar Augustus, Epaminondas, son of Epaminondas, moved:
that the following draft resolution of his be put before the
Council and the People: Since the lord of all the world, Nero,
greatest emperor, of tribunician power for the 13th time,
designated, father of his country, a new Sun that has shone on
the Hellenes, in choosing to benefit Hellas and in requiting and
revering our gods who ever stand by him with a view to his
forethought and safety, has given and bestowed the liberty that
is through all time native and indigenous and which was taken
away from the Hellenes, thus alone and uniquely the greatest
and most philhellenic emperor, [Nero] Zeus, the god of Freedom; and since he has also added to this great and unexpected
gift immunity from taxation, which none of the previous
Augusti gave in its entirety; for all these reasons be it resolved
by the magistrates, the councillors and the people to dedicate
immediately the altar next to the altar of Zeus the Saviour,
inscribing on it
          'To Zeus, god of Freedom, Nero, forever'
and to set up in the temple of Ptoian Apollo along with those
of our native gods statues of [Nero] Zeus, god of Freedom, and
of the goddess Augusta [Messalina], in order that by the
execution of these things our city too may be seen to have
fulfilled every honour and act of loyalty towards the lord
Augustus [Nero's house]. Be it further resolved that the decree
be set up in copies by the altar of Zeus the Saviour in the agora,
on a stone pillar, and in the temple of Ptoian Apollo.

This very famous inscription, which is in Greek, is from the Greek town of Acraephia (modern Karditza) in Boeotia. It is in three parts: firstly, a decree of Nero, ordering all the Greeks to assemble at Corinth; secondly, a speech of Nero to the assembled Greeks in which he proclaims the freedom of the province; and thirdly, a decree of the Acraephians, conferring certain honours upon Nero and his wife, in gratitude for the benefit conferred by Nero on Greece (the translation 'Hellenes' has been retained throughout). In the inscription the names of Nero and his wife − probably Messalina − have been systematically erased, due to the *damnatio memoriae*, or condemnation of his memory, which the senate decreed against Nero after his death. These erasures are in square brackets in the text. The date of the speech of Nero is given as 28 November; the decree of Nero would have been published sometime earlier in the year and the decree of Acraephia shortly afterwards. The year is AD 67, as we know from our literary sources, which date his Greek tour to the years AD 66–7. Suetonius tells us (*Nero* 24.2) that 'on his departure (i.e. late AD 67), he presented the whole province with freedom and at the same time gave the judges Roman citizenship and a large sum of money. These favours he announced in person on the day of the Isthmian Games, standing in the middle of the stadium' (Loeb translation).

The speech of Nero is very important, since it is one of few genuine examples of that emperor's style of discourse. It shows Nero's strong taste for the dramatic and theatrical and, especially, his deep passion for things Greek, a passion dwelt on with much venom by the literary sources. The speech is boastful and egotistic, but it cannot be denied that Nero genuinely wants to benefit a people for whom he has a great admiration, even though this admiration is coloured by a romantic yearning for 'the glory that was Greece'. The obvious sincerity of Nero's gratitude to the gods of Greece also contradicts what Suetonius has to say about his attitude towards religion (*Nero* 56): 'He utterly despised all cults, with the sole exception of the Syrian Goddess, and even acquired such a contempt for her that he made water on her image . . .' (Loeb translation). The reference, however, to 'what was up to now the Peloponnese' makes one suspect that he had decided to rename it 'the Neronese', which would be in line with what Suetonius says at ch. 55 of the *Nero*: 'He had a longing for immortality and undying fame, though it was ill-regulated. With this in view he took their former appellations from many things and numerous places and gave them new ones from his own name. He also called the month of April Neroneus and was minded to name Rome Neropolis' (Loeb translation).

The decree of the Acraephians, moved by the priest in charge of the imperial cult, sets up an altar to Nero in the town and statues of Nero and Messalina to be set up in the temple of Apollo, along with the statues of the other native gods. Its language is extravagant and adulatory; but there is no need to doubt its sincerity. Nero *was* popular with the Greeks and this was a great benefit that he was conferring on them. Nero is frequently associated by the Greeks with their own gods, including Apollo and, on here, Zeus, the king of the gods. A coin of Nero, struck about this time, probably at Corinth, has on its front side a laureate head of Nero, with the legend 'the emperor Nero Caesar Augustus', and on its reverse side a depiction of Jupiter (= Zeus) seated on a throne, holding a thunderbolt and a long sceptre, with the legend 'Jupiter the Liberator' – an obvious reference to Nero's action in Greece.

We may note that in this inscription it is not possible to use the emperor's tribunician year to assign a date. In the month of November, AD 67, Nero was of tribunician power for the fourteenth time, not the thirteenth, as the inscription states. Nor does the word 'designated', which follows the tribunician number, have any meaning: there was no 'designation', i.e. appointment in advance, for the tribunician power; and there is no evidence that Nero, at this time, was designated for a consulship. We must assume that Epaminondas, the drafter of the decree, has made two errors in his attempts to render Nero's Roman titulature.

27   (*ILS* 244 = M&W 1)

... that he be permitted to make a treaty with whomsoever he wishes, just as the deified Augustus, Tiberius Julius Caesar Augustus and Tiberius Claudius Caesar Augustus Germanicus were permitted:

And that he be permitted to hold a meeting of the senate, to make and refer proposals to it, and to have made decrees of the senate by proposals and divisions for voting, just as the deified Augustus, Tiberius Julius Caesar Augustus and Tiberius Claudius Caesar Augustus Germanicus were permitted;

And that, whenever in accordance with his wish, authorization, order or command, or in his presence, a meeting of the senate be held, all business there transacted be regarded and upheld as legal, just as if the meeting of the senate had been normally proclaimed and held;

And that whomsoever seeking a magistracy, position of authority, position conferring the right to issue commands, or commissionership in any matter, he recommends to the senate

Document 27   The so-called law on Vespasian's imperial powers.
Reproduced by courtesy of Licinio Capelli.

and Roman people, and to whomsoever he gives or promises his vote, extraordinary consideration be given to these people at each and every election;

And that he be permitted to move forward and advance the boundaries of the *pomerium*, whenever he considers it to be in the state's interest, just as Tiberius Claudius Caesar Augustus Germanicus was permitted;

And that whatever he considers to be in the interest of the state or in accordance with the majesty of things divine, human, public, private, there be the right and power for him so to do, just as there was for the deified Augustus and for Tiberius Julius Caesar Augustus and Tiberius Claudius Caesar Augustus Germanicus;

And that by whatever laws or plebiscites it was enacted that the deified Augustus and Tiberius Julius Caesar Augustus and Tiberius Claudius Caesar Augustus Germanicus be not bound, the emperor Caesar Vespasian be absolved from these laws and whatever in accordance with each law or enactment it was proper that the deified Augustus or Tiberius Julius Caesar Augustus or Tiberius Claudius Caesar Augustus Germanicus do, the emperor Caesar Vespasian Augustus be permitted to do all these things;

And that whatever before the passage of this law was done, performed, decreed, ordered by the emperor Caesar Vespasian Augustus or by anyone at his order or command, those things be as regular and as binding as if they had been done by order of the people or the plebs.

Sanction
If anyone because of this law has acted or shall have acted contrary to laws, enactments, plebiscites or decrees of the senate, or if because of this law he shall not have done what he ought to do in accordance with a law, enactment, plebiscite or decree of the senate, let that not be a cause of harm to him and let him not for that reason have to pay any penalty to the people and let no one take legal action or institute a judicial inquiry about that matter and let no one permit legal action to be taken before him on that matter.

The inscription, which is in Latin, is engraved on a bronze tablet and is to be found in the Capitoline museum at Rome. It is the last part of a law whereby the imperial powers were bestowed on the emperor Vespasian, probably early in AD 70; hence the title usually given to it by modern scholars, 'The Law on Vespasian's Imperial Powers'. It must be stated straightaway that the interpretation of the law, both in its entirety and in its several parts, has long been the subject of great controversy among scholars; and it is not proposed to enter here into all the technical arguments, but merely to try to indicate some of the more general points of interest to the student of Roman history.

Firstly, it is a very important document because it is the only one of its kind that has been discovered, and the question obviously arises: was this a law passed at the accession of every emperor, or was it a unique piece of legislation passed at the accession of Vespasian? If the latter is the case, what is the law trying to achieve? Is it trying to limit the hitherto undefined powers of the emperor by defining them, with the citation of precedents, or is it trying, by gathering together all the accumulated powers of past emperors and conferring them *en bloc* on Vespasian, to make stronger the position of a new emperor, who, as Suetonius puts it (*Vespasian* 7.2), 'was lacking in prestige and, so to speak, a certain majesty', compared with the tremendous prestige of his Julio-Claudian predecessors? If, however, a law of this kind was passed at the accession of every new emperor (with, consequently, a constant accumulation and increase of powers to each successive ruler), then the law does throw some light on the constitutional procedures that were followed. The literary sources, particularly Tacitus, imply that it was the senate that conferred his powers on a new emperor. Thus, on the accession of Otho in January AD 69, Tacitus says (*Histories* 1.47): 'The senators hastily assembled and conferred by decree upon Otho the tribunician power, the name of Augustus and every imperial honour'; later, in March of the same year, at the accession of Vitellius, 'In the senate all the customary honours which had been devised during the long reigns of other emperors were straightaway decreed'; and in December of this year, at the accession of Vespasian himself, 'the senate, delighted and full of confident hope, decreed to Vespasian all the honours traditionally bestowed on emperors' (*Histories* 2.55 and 4.3).

But, if this law was passed for each new emperor, we can see that, though the initiative for the conferring of the imperial powers may have come from the senate, the powers were not legally conferred, i.e. the emperor was not legally emperor, until the Roman people, meeting in its legislative assembly, had passed legislation to confer these powers. Indeed, other inscriptional evidence (the Acts of the Arval Brothers) shows us that separate meetings of the electoral-legislative assembly (*comitia* in Latin) were held to confer the tribunician power, the imperial power, the office of pontifex maximus and all other priestly offices on a new emperor; and it seems not unreasonable to assume that a similar procedure was adopted to confer on him any special powers not covered by the imperial power ('imperium' in Latin) and the tribunician power. If this is the case, then our present law is one of these pieces of legislation; though to which specific power the extant clauses refer is not clear. At any rate, we can say, if this kind of law was passed for every new emperor, that at least the fiction of popular participation in legislation was maintained by the emperors – fiction, because there can be no doubt that the popular legislative action amounted to nothing more than formal approval of a text presented to the assembly in the form of a senatorial decree. The present law, indeed, is phrased, with the exception of the final 'Sanction', not in the imperative language of a law, but in the advisory language of a senatorial decree; each clause, it must be understood, being prefaced with some such words as 'we advise that . . .' or 'we recommend that . . .'. The 'Sanction' at the end, which absolves any person from guilt if, by obeying this law, he should contravene another existing statute, was a regular part of any Roman law and would not form part of the senatorial decree. Hence it is couched in the imperative language of a law ('let him', 'let no one' etc.). We can, however, see from the 'advisory' phrasing of this law, which merely 'rubber stamps' the senatorial decree, that the legislative process is well on the way to the situation that would come into force from the time of Hadrian, whereby senatorial decrees acquired the validity of laws.

Two specific points may be noticed. Firstly, only Augustus, Tiberius and Claudius are cited as precedents for particular powers (and Claudius, it should be observed, is not referred to as 'the deified'). This is because the other two Julio-Claudian emperors, Gaius and Nero, suffered from *damnatio memoriae*, or condemnation of their memory. Secondly, we may note the final, 'retrospective' clause, conferring legality on any official action of Vespasian's before the passage of the law. This was probably a standard clause, if this law was passed for every emperor, since there was always an interval of time between the passage of the senatorial decree and the meeting of the legislative assembly which legally conferred the power; but in the case of Vespasian it was particularly necessary, since at least six months had elapsed between his proclamation in the East on 1 July AD 69 and the passage of this law early in AD 70.

28 (*IGRR* III. 133 = M&W 237)

The emperor Caesar Vespasian Augustus, pontifex maximus, of tribunician power for the 7th time, saluted as victorious commander 14 times, consul 6 times, designated for the 7th time, father of his country, censor, and the emperor Titus Caesar, son of Augustus, of tribunician power for the 5th time, consul 4 times, designated for the 5th time, censor, and Domitian Caesar, son of Augustus, consul 3 times, designated for the 4th time, strengthened these fortifications for Mithridates, King of the Iberians, son of King Pharasmenes and Iamaspus, friend of Caesar and friend of the Romans, and for the people of the Iberians.

The inscription, which is in Greek, was discovered at Harmozica (near Tiflis, in the modern Soviet Republic of Georgia), the capital of the state of Iberia. From the combination of the tribunician and consular numbering for Vespasian and Titus the document can be dated with precision to between 1 July and 31 December AD 75: from 1 July of this year Vespasian was in his seventh year of tribunician power and Titus in his fifth; and from 1 January AD 76 he was consul for the seventh time and Titus for the sixth. The inscription throws light on both the 'constitutional' policy of the Flavian family and their policy on the eastern frontier of the empire. The naming of the father and his two sons is in keeping with Vespasian's consistent policy of stressing the dynastic capabilities of his family. But the strict gradation of seniority within this dynastic framework is seen by the differences in the offices and powers held by the three men. Titus, the elder son, who was both the designated successor and virtually co-emperor with his father, differs from Vespasian only in the absence of the name Augustus (the sign of the ruling emperor), of the 'military salutations' (though he frequently receives these in official documents) and the title 'father of his country'. (But note that he does not normally have the title 'emperor' on official documents, this being a prerogative of his father, the 'senior' emperor.) Domitian, however, the junior of the sons, has merely the number of his consulships stated. In the field of foreign policy, the inscription throws light on Vespasian's reaction to a problem which had recently made itself felt in the neighbouring countries of Armenia and Parthia – the invasion of Sarmatian Alans from the Russian steppes across the Caucasus mountains. The Parthian king, about this time, asked Vespasian to join him in punitive measures against these Alans, since their plundering expeditions threatened the Roman provinces of Asia Minor as well as Armenia and Parthia. Vespasian refused this request, but, as the inscription shows us, built fortifications in the client-state of Iberia, which stood directly on the main invasion-route over the Caucasus and from where such invasions could be repelled. The fortifications so built were also strategically situated to the north of Armenia; and it may be that Vespasian was also trying to establish a stronghold here in order to make up for the loss of direct Roman influence in Armenia, caused by Nero's settlement with the Parthians. Corroboration of this view may perhaps be seen in the fact that under the reign of Domitian another inscription proves that Roman troops were operating even further east in the Caucasus area, in the client-kingdom of Albania. The inscription (M&W 369) found at Mt Beiouk-Dagh, near Baku, simply says, 'Under the emperor Domitian Caesar Augustus Germanicus, Lucius Julius Maximus, centurion of the legion 12 Fulminata'. The appearance of 'Germanicus' in Domitian's titles shows that the inscription is to be dated to AD 84 or later; and 12 Fulminata was one of the legions forming the garrison of Cappadocia, the nearest armed province to the Caucasus region.

29   (*ILS* 6092 = M&W 461)

The emperor Caesar Vespasian Augustus, pontifex maximus, of tribunician power for the 8th time, saluted as victorious commander 18 times, consul 8 times, father of his country, greets the members of the College of Four and the town councillors of Sabora. Since you point out that your weakness is burdened by many difficulties, I permit you to build the town under my name, as you wish, on level ground. The revenues, which you say you received from the deified Augustus, I maintain intact; if you wish to add any new ones, you will have to approach the proconsul concerning these; for I can make no decision when there is nobody to put the other side of the case. I received your decree on 25 July; I dismissed your envoys on the 29th of the same. Farewell.

The duovirs, Gaius Cornelius Severus and Marcus Septimius Severus, had this inscribed on bronze at public expense.

The inscription is from the town of Sabora (modern Canete) in southern Spain, the district known as Hispania Baetica, and is in Latin. It is an example of an imperial rescript, or letter of the emperor in reply to a petition sent to him by the town council of Sabora. The townspeople had evidently asked permission to move their town from high ground to the plain, in order to acquire more productive land; to add, as a municipality which had recently received Latin status, the emperor's family name to its official designation, thus making it the 'Flavian municipality of Sabora'; to retain, after the moving of the town, the revenues that they had enjoyed since the time of Augustus; and to collect new, additional revenues. Vespasian, in his reply, grants all the requests except the last one. This, he states, he cannot grant because he has had no opportunity of hearing appeals and complaints against the suggested new revenues. Hence the decision must be made by the senatorial proconsul of Baetica, who can hear all aspects of the proposal. The inscription throws valuable light on aspects of Roman provincial administration at the end of the first century AD. We see from it one of the most common forms of local government in provincial towns whose constitutions were modelled on the pattern of the Italian municipalities: the executive college of four, consisting of two senior magistrates (duovirs), an aedile and a quaestor, and a town-council or decurions. From other documents we know that all these magistrates and councillors were elected from the wealthy aristocracy of the district. The inscription also indicates Vespasian's concern for the well-being of the towns and peoples of the provinces of the empire, though at the same time it is a good example of an ever-increasing phenomenon: the encroachment of the emperor upon the areas of administration that belonged traditionally to the senate. Baetica was a senatorial province, governed by an annually appointed proconsul of praetorian rank, yet the people of Sabora appeal not to their proconsul but to the emperor, and the emperor has no hesitation in giving a decision on these matters. Direct imperial intervention at this level of government, while it might show an interest in provincial affairs, could only lead eventually to a stifling of local enthusiasm and initiative. The style of the letter is worth noting: brisk, crisp and to the point; whether this is actually Vespasian's own composition or a letter drafted by one of the imperial secretaries for his signature is impossible to say. Other incidental information obtainable from the inscription concerns Vespasian's official title and the dating of the document. The reply to the petition was given on 29 July; the year is given by the tribunician power. Vespasian's tribunician power began on 1 July AD 69, and increased by a figure of one on each successive 1 July. The eighth year of tribunician power begins, therefore, on 1 July AD 77 and runs to 30 June AD 78. In the list of titles we may notice the resumption by Vespasian of the *praenomen imperatoris*, i.e. the title of 'emperor' replacing the normal Roman first name (e.g. Titus, Gaius). Vespasian was the first emperor since Augustus to adopt this practice on a regular, official basis, though it became common with his successors. Note too the sequence of offices and titles which follows the name Augustus – this is the normal sequence on official documents of Vespasian, though often the title of censor appears in the list of titles, usually after the number of consulships.

30   (*ILS* 264 = M&W 53)

The senate and Roman people, to the emperor Titus Caesar, son of the deified Vespasian, Vespasian Augustus, pontifex maximus, of tribunician power for the 10th time, saluted as victorious commander 17 times, consul 8 times, father of his country, their prince, because on the instructions of his father and by his advice and under his auspices he subdued the race of the Jews and destroyed the city of Jerusalem, which had been either attacked in vain or completely unattempted by all commanders, kings and peoples before him.

The inscription is from Rome, on an arch in the Circus Maximus, and is in Latin. The arch was set up, as the inscription says, by the senate and people of Rome to commemorate Titus' victory in the Jewish war and his capture and destruction of Jerusalem in AD 70. The inscription gives a good indication of Titus' official title, in which we may note the *praenomen imperatoris*, i.e. the title of 'emperor' at the beginning of the personal names, a practice resumed by his father. We may note two ways in which Titus' title differs from his father's: firstly, he retains his own first name, Titus, after 'emperor'; secondly, he is called 'son of the deified Vespasian', this being the result of Vespasian's deification after his death. Before his accession to sole power, whilst he was still his father's colleague and junior partner, Titus' title on official documents had run 'Titus Caesar, son of Augustus (i.e. Vespasian), Vespasian, pontifex, saluted as victorious commander x times, of tribunician power for the nth time, consul y times'. Often, both before and after his accession the office of censor appears in the list of titles, usually after the number of consulships. Titus' years of tribunician power began on the same day as his father's (1 July), but two years later (AD 71). Hence the tribunician year 10 runs from 1 July AD 80 to 30 June AD 81. The victory in the Jewish war was the proudest military achievement of Vespasian and Titus and was celebrated by a splendid triumph in AD 71 and by several issues of coins. Josephus, *Jewish War* 7.122–56 (given in abridged form in Lewis and Reinhold II, pp. 91–2), gives a description of the triumph of Vespasian and Titus. M&W 44 (= *BMC* II, p. 131, no. 604 = **11** above), is an *as* of AD 71 commemorating the capture of Judaea. M&W 45 (= *BMC* II, p. 81, no. 397) is an undated *aureus* of Vespasian, which has on the reverse a picture of Vespasian in a triumphal carriage with Victory crowning him. In front of the horses of the carriage is a captive, escorted by a soldier. The legend says 'The Triumph of the Augustus'. The two men wished to make out their victory to be as great and glorious as any achieved by their Julio-Claudian predecessors, and the language of the inscription reflects this 'official' point of view. We might note too another aspect of Flavian propaganda: family unity and solidarity. The victory was a joint effort of father and son, with the father providing the prudent guidance of the elder statesman and the son the vigorous leadership of youth.

31a   (*ILS* 6089 = M&W 453 – Selections)

THE CHARTER OF SALPENSA

Magistrates to Obtain Roman Citizenship

XXI. .... All persons who become duovirs, aediles, or quaestors in accordance with this charter shall be Roman citizens on laying down the magistracy at the end of the year, together with their parents and wives, and children born in lawful wedlock and subject to the father's power, and in like manner grandsons and granddaughters on the male side subject to the father's power, provided that no more shall be Roman citizens than the number of magistrates who are to be elected in accordance with this charter.

Persons Obtaining Roman Citizenship to Remain under the Legal Dominion, Marital Control, or Parental Power of the Same Persons

XXII. .... All persons, male or female, obtaining Roman citizenship in accordance with this charter or in accordance with an edict of the emperor Caesar Augustus Vespasian or the emperor Titus Caesar Augustus or the emperor Caesar Augustus Domitian, father of his country, shall be under the parental power or marital control or legal dominion of that person who becomes a Roman citizen by this charter and under whose control they would properly belong if the change to Roman citizenship had not taken place; and the said persons shall have the same right of choosing a legal guardian that they would have had if they had been born of a Roman citizen and had not changed their citizenship.

Persons Obtaining Roman Citizenship to Retain Rights over Freedmen
XXIII. All persons, male or female, obtaining Roman citizenship in accordance with this charter or in accordance with an edict of the emperor Vespasian Augustus or the emperor Titus Caesar Vespasianus Augustus or the emperor Caesar Domitian Augustus, shall have the same rights and status in respect to freedmen and freedwomen, whether their own or their fathers' (such freedmen and freedwomen not having come into Roman citizenship), and also in respect to the property of these persons and to the services imposed as a consideration for their freedom as would have existed if the said persons had not changed their citizenship.

Concerning the Oath of the Duovirs, Aediles, and Quaestors
XXVI. The incumbent duovirs with judicial power in this municipality, likewise the aediles and quaestors now holding office in this municipality, each of them within the five days next following the promulgation of this charter, and likewise the duovirs, aediles, or quaestors who shall henceforth be elected in accordance with this charter, each of them within the five days next following their entrance upon the office of duovir, aedile, or quaestor, and before a meeting of the decurions or *conscripti* is held, shall in a public meeting take oath by Jupiter, by the deified Augustus, by the deified Claudius, by the deified Vespasian Augustus, by the deified Titus Augustus, by the genius of Domitian Augustus, and by the (municipal) tutelary gods, that they will properly perform whatsoever they believe to be in accordance with this charter and in the public interest of the citizens of the municipality Flavia Salpensa, and that they will not knowingly and with malice afore-thought act contrary to this charter or the public interest of the citizens of the said municipality, and that they will as far as they can prevent others from so doing; and that they will neither hold nor allow any meeting of the decurions nor express any opinion except such as in their judgement is consistent with this charter and the public interest of the citizens of the said municipality. Any person who fails to take such oath shall be condemned to pay to the citizens of the said municipality 10 000 sesterces, and may be sued or prosecuted for that amount at will by any citizen of the said municipality who has the legal right to do so in accordance with this charter.
(Translated by Lewis and Reinhold, II, pp. 321–3)

31b (*ILS* 6090 = M&W 454 — Selections)

THE CHARTER OF MALACA
On the Nomination of Candidates

LI. If, up to the day when declaration of intention (to be a candidate) must be made, declaration is made either in the name of no one or of fewer persons than the number which must be elected, or if, out of those persons in whose name a declaration of intention has been made, those who may properly stand for election in accordance with this charter are fewer than the number which must be elected, then the person responsible for conducting the elections shall post, in a place where they may be plainly read from level ground, the names of as many persons, qualified by this charter to stand for the said offices, as are required to make up the number which must be elected by this charter. Each of those whose names are so posted shall, if he so desires, go before the magistrate who is to conduct the said elections, and nominate one additional person of his own status; in like manner each of the persons so nominated by the aforesaid shall, if he so desires, go before the same magistrate and nominate one additional person of his own status. And the said magistrate, before whom such nomination is made, shall post the names of all the aforesaid persons in a place where they may be plainly read from level ground and shall likewise conduct the elections in respect to all the said persons exactly as though, in accordance with the clause in this charter 'On Candidature of Office', declaration of intention had been made in their names within the prescribed time, and as though they had of their own accord in the first instance stood for the said offices and had not withheld their candidacy.

On Those Whose Candidature May Properly Be Considered
at the Elections

LIV. The person responsible for conducting the elections shall first see to the election of duovirs with judicial power from that category of freeborn persons already specified and set forth in this charter; then in succession he shall see to the election of aediles and likewise of quaestors from that category of freeborn persons already specified and set forth in this charter, provided that, in the case of candidates for the duovirate, he does not allow any person to stand for election who is less than twenty-five years of age or has held that office within five years; likewise, in the case of candidates for the aedileship or the quaestorship, he shall not allow consideration of any person who is less than twenty-five years of age or who is subject to any impediments whereby, if he were a Roman citizen, he could not lawfully become a member of the decurions or *conscripti*.

On the Casting of Votes

LV. The person conducting the elections in accordance with this charter shall summon the citizens to cast their votes by *curiae*, issuing a single call to vote to all the *curiae*, in such manner that the said *curiae*, each in a separate voting booth, may severally cast their votes by means of tablets. He shall likewise see to it that three citizens of the said municipality are placed at the ballot box of each *curia* who do not themselves belong to that *curia*, to guard and count the ballots; and that before performing such duty each of them shall take oath that he will handle the counting of the ballots and make report thereon in good faith. Furthermore, he shall not hinder candidates for an office from placing one watcher each at every ballot box. And the said watchers, both those placed by the person conducting the elections and those placed by candidates for office, shall each cast his vote in that *curia* at whose ballot box he is placed as a watcher, and the votes of the said watchers shall be just as lawful and valid as if each had cast his vote in his own *curia*.

On the Course to be Taken in the Case of Those Who Have an Equal Number of Votes

LVI. The person conducting the said elections, according as any candidate has more votes in each *curia* than the others, shall declare the person who is ahead of the rest as chosen and elected with reference to that *curia*, until the number to be elected is made up. If in any *curia* two or more candidates have the same number of votes, he shall prefer a married man or one with the rights of a married man to an unmarried man without children or without the rights of married men, a man with children to a man without children, and a man with more children to a man with fewer children, and shall declare the former (elected). In such matter, two children lost after the ceremony of naming or one boy lost after puberty or one girl of marriageable age lost shall be counted as equivalent to one surviving child. If two or more candidates have the same number of votes and are of the same qualifications he shall submit their names to choice by lot and shall declare the person whose name is drawn by lot to be ahead of the rest.

No Person to Destroy Buildings Except with a View to Restoration

LXII. No person shall unroof or destroy or cause to be demolished any building in the town of the municipality Flavia Malaca or any buildings in the environs of the said municipality except by resolution of the decurions or *conscripti*, passed when a majority of the same is present, unless he intends to restore the said building within the year. Any person acting in contravention of this shall be condemned to pay to the citizens of the municipality Flavia Malaca a sum of money equivalent to the value of the said property and may be sued or prosecuted for that amount at will by any citizen of the said municipality who has the legal right to do so in accordance with this charter. (Translated by Lewis and Reinhold, II, pp. 323–5)

Both of the inscriptions, of which selections are given above, are in Latin and both were found near the town of Malaca (modern Malaga), or, to give it its official name, 'the Flavian municipality of Malaca'. The fragments that remain are good examples of municipal charters, i.e. laws conferring a certain legal status on a community. The towns in question are Malaca and Salpensa (or, to give it its official name, 'the Flavian municipality of Salpensa') and both were situated in the senatorial Spanish province of Baetica. It will be noticed that the fragment of the law of Salpensa consists of subsections 21 to 29, and that of Malaca consists of subsections 51 to 69. It is highly probable that, with the appropriate changes having been made, the surviving parts of the Malaca charter would have been found in the Salpensa charter and vice versa (though we may note that subsection 26 of the Salpensa charter appears as subsection 59 of the Malaca charter). We learn from the elder Pliny (*Natural History* 3.30) that Vespasian, as censor in AD 73–4, conferred Latin status, i.e. the 'half-way' status between foreign status and that of full Roman citizens, on the whole of Spain; and it is highly probable that the same basic charter would be given to each new Latin municipality. Hence we are justified in regarding the provisions of each charter as having a general application for all the Spanish municipalities. It will be noticed that there is frequent mention in the Salpensa charter of Domitian as emperor. Hence the charters can be dated to between AD 81 and AD 84, because Domitian is not given the title of Germanicus, which he assumed in the latter date. The fact that the charters are only now being promulgated, at least seven and possibly ten years from the conferment of Latin status by Vespasian, is an indication of the length of time that can elapse between the announcing of a reform and the executing of it.

The charters are of great interest to the historian because they show us the administrative details of the broad policy-decision of the emperor and because they give us many insights into the principles and working of the Roman system of provincial administration. In general the Romans preferred to use the city as the basic unit of local government in the provinces; and, within the city organization, to have a government that was in the hands of the usually pro-Roman aristocracy. Democracies were not favoured. The cities were allowed a considerable degree of local autonomy, perhaps on the principle that the vigorous city-life, so important to the central government, could only be maintained if the citizens of the community – or, at least, those of them qualified to hold office – had some responsibility for their city's welfare and were not simply the tools of a remote bureaucracy. Where the city had traditionally been the way of life, as in the Greek East, the Romans were content to leave the already existing structure; but in areas where there was little or no tradition of city life, as in the western provinces, the general policy was to encourage the development of cities and towns with an administrative structure like those of Italy. The cities were to be Romano-Italian in structure and the citizens were to be encouraged to gain Roman citizenship by adopting a life-style like the Romans.

In the case of cities given the Latin status, all the citizens could hope eventually to become full citizens of Rome by an upgrading of their community's status at a later date; but in the meantime an incentive was given to the upper classes of the community by the granting of Roman citizenship to all office-holders (and, at a later date, to all members of the town council). In the Salpensa charter we see a provision to this effect in the first surviving subsection, XXI, 'Magistrates to Obtain Roman Citizenship'. But in the first extant clause of the Malaca charter, L, 'On the Nomination of Candidates', we can see that pride in holding office and the attaining of Roman citizenship could be counterbalanced or even outweighed by another consideration – the expense in which the holder of a municipal office was inevitably involved. These expenses became even greater in the second century AD, so much so that in many municipalities it was impossible to find sufficient wealthy men willing to stand as candidates. Because the efficiency of the administration of the provinces depended largely on the efficient running of the local municipalities, the central government at Rome was forced to resort to compulsion in the filling of municipal offices; and this section of the Malaca charter is one of the earliest pieces of evidence that we have for this compulsion.

Other clauses of interest in the Malaca charter are LV, 'On the Casting of Votes', which indicates a desire for avoiding electoral corruption, and LVI, 'On the Course to be Taken in the Case of Those Who Have an Equal Number of Votes', which shows that the central government, almost a century after Augustus' famous social and moral legislation, was still concerned with promoting family life and an increase in the birthrate among Roman citizens or potential citizens. The clause LXII, 'No Person to Destroy Buildings Except with a View to Restoration', is also of contemporary interest, dealing as it does with the subject of property speculation. There are two decrees of the senate, from the time of Claudius and Nero, cited in Lewis and Reinhold, II, pp. 211–12, which show that the clause in the Malaca charter is not an isolated example of the concern of the central government to prevent property speculation. The texts of the two charters are also cited by Jones, II, pp. 212–23, nos 93 and 94.

32 (*SIG*³ 838 = S. *N–H* 72)

The emperor Caesar, son of the deified Trajan Parthicus, grandson of the deified Nerva, Trajan Hadrian Augustus, pontifex maximus, of tribunician power for the 13th time, 3 times consul, father of his country, to the magistrates and Council of the Ephesians, greetings. Lucius Erastus states both that he is a citizen of yours and that he has frequently sailed the sea and that he has been as useful to his country as is possible from this profession and that he always conveys the governors of the country. He has twice sailed with me, the first time when I was going to Rhodes from Ephesus, and now when coming to you from Eleusis; and he desires to become a member of your Council. I myself leave the examination of his qualifications in your hands, but, if nothing stands in his way and he is worthy of the honour, I shall give the money, which Councillors give, for his election to office. Farewell.

The inscription, which is in Greek, comes from the city of Ephesus, on the coast of Asia Minor. From the reference to Hadrian's tribunician numbering it can be dated to between 10 December AD 128 and 9 December AD 129. The titulature of Hadrian is, as always, simple and straightforward, as compared with the grandiose military titles assumed by his adoptive father, Trajan. The inscription itself is a letter sent by Hadrian to the magistrates and town council at Ephesus, requesting them to elect a certain Ephesian, Lucius Erastus, to membership of the council. Hadrian himself has been asked by Erastus for his support in the matter. The letter, then, is a letter of recommendation, and though no obligation is put on the council to elect Erastus, it is obvious that with the emperor both recommending him and promising to pay on his behalf the customary sum of money paid by office-holders as a necessary prerequisite to holding office, Erastus would undoubtedly have been made a councillor of Ephesus. The letter would appear to have been written during Hadrian's second visit to the Greek East, early in AD 129, shortly before his departure from Eleusis to Asia Minor and the Levant, where he intended to spend the summer at Antioch in Syria. The inscription gives us the information that he made his way firstly to Ephesus, before proceeding inland and then southwards to Antioch. It was his second visit to Ephesus, as the inscription says. The first visit occurred during his first eastern tour of AD 123–6; and it was from that city that he then departed to return, by way of the Aegean islands, to Athens. This is the voyage 'to Rhodes from Ephesus' referred to in the inscription. On both occasions Hadrian travelled in boats owned and operated by Lucius Erastus, who seems to have enjoyed a monopoly of the conveyance of dignitaries to and from the province of Asia ('governors of the country' refers to the proconsuls of Asia). The letter is interesting in that it demonstrates clearly how deeply Hadrian, the philhellene emperor, was prepared to involve himself in the affairs of these ancient and beautiful cities. To Athens he showed a deep devotion and respect, but Ephesus enjoyed many marks of his esteem, and it is likely that a citizen of Ephesus who enjoyed the emperor's favour would be held in great respect by his city.

33   Selections from the Acts of the Arval Brothers

The priesthood of the Arval Brothers, which was devoted to the worship of the agricultural goddess Dea Dia and was of very great antiquity, was revived from its obsolescence by Augustus. Its membership included the most noble families of the state, including the emperor himself, and numbered twelve. The college met regularly in a grove of its own near Rome, where it offered sacrifices especially for the safety and well-being of the emperor and his family. The record or minutes of these meetings were engraved on marble tablets and set up in the grove. Though in a fragmentary condition, these minutes extend from the year 21 BC to AD 241 and often contain incidental information which is of great help to the historian. The following extracts illustrate both

the character of the records and the sort of information that can
be obtained from them.

a (S 9, AD 39)

On 27 October (AD 39), because of the discovery of the wicked
plot of Gnaeus Lentulus Gaetulicus against Gaius Germanicus,
Lucius Salvius Otho, priest and deputy master, sacrificed in the
name of the college of the Arval Brothers . . .

Dio Cassius, 59.22, relates that when Gaius was in Germany in
AD 39 'he put to death Lentulus Gaetulicus, who had an excellent
reputation in every way and had been governor of Germany for
ten years, for the reason that he was endeared to the soldiers.
Another of his victims was Lepidus, that lover and favourite of his,
the husband of Drusilla (his sister) . . . whom he kept declaring he
would leave as his successor to the throne' (Loeb translation).
Suetonius, *Claudius* 9.1, connects the two murders and makes
Gaetulicus and Lepidus the leading partners in a plot to remove
Gaius. Gaius left Rome for the north in September AD 39, and this
minute shows us that Gaetulicus at least, and probably Lepidus
also, had been executed by the middle of October, since we may
allow at least a week for the news to reach Rome and for the
college to assemble to perform the sacrifice stated in the text.

b (S 13, AD 43)

On . . . January (the fragmentary state of the Latin text makes it
impossible to be more specific than 6 to 12 January) a sacrifice
was held to Jupiter because Tiberius Claudius Caesar Augustus
Germanicus was called 'father of his country': on the Capitol
(the college sacrificed) to Jupiter an ox, to Juno a cow, to
Minerva a cow, to Prosperity a cow, to the deified Augustus an
ox, to the deified Augusta a cow . . . There were present . . . (8
names follow).

This minute shows us the approximate date on which Claudius
accepted the title of 'father of his country' – almost exactly two
years after his accession. This was intended to indicate an attitude
of modesty and deference to the senate, unlike that of his
predecessor, Gaius, and in keeping with the modest practice of
both Augustus, who only accepted the title in 2 BC, and Tiberius,
who refused to accept it at all. In the list of sacrifices made to
honour the occasion, it will be noted that 'the deified Augusta' is
included. This is Livia, Augustus' wife, who became Julia Augusta

by the terms of Augustus' will. Suetonius, *Claudius* 2.2, says that
Claudius, in order to show this family devotion (*pietas*) 'had divine
honours voted his grandmother Livia and a chariot drawn by
elephants in the procession at the Circus, like that of Augustus'
(Loeb translation).

c (S 16, AD 55)

In the consulship of Gnaeus Lentulus Gaetulicus and Titus
Curtilius Manca, on 11 December, on the Sacred Way, Publius
Memmius Regulus, deputy master of the Arval Brothers, in
accordance with an edict of Nero Claudius Caesar Augustus
Germanicus, prince and parent of the commonwealth, in front
of the house of the Domitii, (sacrificed) an ox on account of the
memory of Domitius, his father.

The first piece of information we can obtain from this minute is
its date. From other evidence we know that the two men
mentioned as consuls held the office at the end of AD 55. Secondly,
the minute affords clear proof of what the literary sources
emphasize: Nero's family devotion (*pietas*) towards the memory of
his natural father after becoming emperor. Nero, it will be
remembered, was the son of Agrippina the Younger by her first
marriage to Gnaeus Domitius Ahenobarbus, consul AD 32, and
was called Lucius Domitius Ahenobarbus before his adoption by
Claudius in AD 50. Suetonius, *Nero* 9, says that at the start of his
reign, Nero 'paid the highest honours to the memory of his father
Domitius'. Britannicus, Claudius' own son, is said to have won
Nero's hatred by continuing to call him Ahenobarbus after his
adoption; but from Suetonius, *Nero* 41.1, we learn that when in AD
68 the rebel Julius Vindex referred to him as Domitius Ahenobarbus, rather than Nero Caesar, thus implying that Nero was no real
Caesar, Nero 'declared that he would resume it (i.e. his family
name) and give up his adoptive name' (Loeb translation). Tacitus,
Annals 13.10, tells us that in AD 54, the year of his accession, Nero
asked the senate for a statue to be set up to his father Domitius.
The sacrifice was repeated on 11 December every year during
Nero's reign, as the records of the Arval Brothers show, where
they still exist for this date (e.g. AD 57, 58, 59). Suetonius, *Nero* 8,
says that on the day of his accession Nero refused only one of the
many high honours voted him, the title of 'father of his country',
and this because of his youth. This, as with Claudius, was an
instance of his modest bearing towards the senate. He did not
accept the title until the end of AD 55. The present minute uses

the phrase 'parent of the commonwealth', which may be a flattering way of conferring on the emperor the attributes of the normal title, shortly before Nero allowed the real title to appear on his coins.

d   (M&W 2, AD 69)

In the same consulship (of Lucius Verginius Rufus, for the second time and Lucius Pompeius Vopiscus), on 14 March, vows were pronounced for the safety and return of [Vitellius] Germanicus the emperor, with Lucius Maecius Postumius leading the recitation, in the mastership of [Vitellius] Germanicus the emperor and the deputy mastership of Maecius Postumius, in the name of the college of the Arval Brothers (then follows a list of the deities to whom sacrifices are promised).

This minute gives a fascinating glimpse into the confusion caused in a totalitarian state when revolution and anarchy throw up a series of new masters in rapid succession. From Tacitus, *Histories* 1.90, we learn that on 14 March AD 69, the emperor Otho set out from Rome to the theatre of war in the north of Italy, where, a month later, he was defeated by the armies of Vitellius and committed suicide. Shortly after this, Vitellius was declared emperor by the senate. The college of the Arval Brothers was here guilty of falsifying their minutes. The vows pronounced on 14 March were for the safety and return of the departing Otho. By the time the college got around to having its minutes inscribed on stone, more than a month later, the situation had altered drastically. Otho was dead and Vitellius, his enemy, now emperor. It would have been most imprudent now to set up in a public place a record of vows undertaken for Otho's safety; and so the college altered its minutes and substituted the name of Vitellius for that of Otho. About seven months later the college was placed in an equally embarrassing position. Vitellius was dead and his memory condemned and Vespasian was now emperor. The minutes, with their falsified vows for Vitellius, were already inscribed and set up; and so the college did the only thing possible in the circumstances – they chiselled out the condemned name of Vitellius, hence its appearance in the translation in square brackets. A similar falsification occurs with the mastership of the college: the emperor was normally the master and on 14 March Otho was still emperor.

e   (S. N–H 1, AD 101)

In the consulship of Quintus Articuleius Paetus and Sextus
Attius Suburanus, on 25 March, on the Capitol, the Arval
Brothers pronounced vows for the safety and return and
victory of the emperor Caesar Nerva Trajan Augustus Germanicus in these words which are written below: Jupiter, greatest
and best, we pray, beseech and entreat you to bring about, in
prosperity and felicity, the safety, the return home and victory
of the emperor Caesar, son of the deified Nerva, Nerva Trajan
Augustus Germanicus, our prince and parent, pontifex maximus, of tribunician power, father of his country – him, who we
feel is speaking to us – from those places and provinces to
which he will go by land and by sea; and to give to him a goodly
outcome of those matters which now he is executing or is about
to execute; and to preserve him in that condition in which he
now is, or in one better than that; and to bring him back and
restore him in safety and victory to the city of Rome at the
earliest possible time. And if you so do this, we vow in the name
of the college of the Arval Brothers that you shall have a gilded
ox (then follow similar vows to Queen Juno, Minerva and
several other deities).

This minute of the college records the vows made by the college
for the safe return and victory of the emperor Trajan as he set out
from Rome in the spring of AD 101 for his first Dacian war and is
of interest as recording not only the gods to whom prayers were
offered, but also the actual words of the prayer. From other
evidence we know that Quintus Articuleius Paetus was ordinary
consul with Trajan in AD 101; hence the dating of the document,
which also shows us – the unique piece of evidence for this – that
when Trajan retired from the office (his fourth consulship) in order
to go to the Dacian front, he was replaced by Sextus Attius
Suburanus. Three years later, in AD 104, Suburanus was to be
consul for the second time, on this occasion for the whole year –
a very rare distinction.

ii.   Minor Administrative Records

The following twenty-two inscriptions are all examples of documents that emanated from the emperor or from one of his
representatives. They consist of military discharge certificates
(diplomas), milestones, aqueducts, lead pipes, lead pigs, boundary
stones and legionary tiles. The information that can be gained

from each document is, once again, very varied in that they not only reflect general imperial policy but also provide precise information on many particular problems, both political (e.g. the composition of a large province, **45**) and social (e.g. the legal status of a soldier's children, **34**).

34 (*ILS* 1992 = M&W 399)

The emperor Caesar Vespasian Augustus, pontifex maximus, of tribunician power for the 5th time, saluted as victorious commander 13 times, father of his country, consul 5 times and designated for the 6th and censor;

to the cavalrymen and infantrymen who are fighting in 6 squadrons (I Flavia Gemina, I Cannenefatium, II Flavia Gemina, Picentiana, Scubulorum and Claudia nova) and 12 cohorts (I Thracum, I Asturum, I Aquitanorum veterana, I Aquitanorum Biturigum, II Augusta Cyrenaica, III Gallorum, III and IV Aquitanorum, IV Vindelicorum, V Hispanorum, V Dalmatarum and VII Raetorum), and are in Germany under the command of Gnaeus Pinarius Cornelius Clemens, who have served for 25 or more years, and whose names have been written below;

has granted to them, to their children and their descendants, citizenship and legal marriage with the wives they had when citizenship was granted to them or, if they were single, with the ones they might marry later, limited to one wife each.

21 May, in the consulship of Quintus Petillius Cerialis Caesius Rufus and Titus Clodius Eprius Marcellus, both consuls for the second time;

to the ordinary soldier Veturius, son of Teutomus, a Pannonian of the Scubuli squadron, whose officer is Tiberius Claudius Atticus, son of Spurius. An authenticated copy from the bronze tablet set up at Rome in the Capitol, on the left-hand side, as one enters, of the wall between two arches (the names of seven witnesses complete the document).

The inscription, which is in Latin, is from a military diploma found at Sikator in Upper Pannonia; it was issued on 21 May AD 74 to Veturius, a member of the auxiliary forces serving in Germany. A military diploma was a bronze tablet issued to all auxiliary troops and to members of the urban cohorts, praetorian guard, and imperial fleets at the time of their discharge or else on the completion of their term of service, and it contained the emperor's full official name, a list of all the units with members due for the award, the name of the individual soldier to whom the diploma was issued and various other pieces of information. Unfortunately, only a few hundred of these documents have survived; many of them have been collected by H. Nesselhauf in Volume XVI of *CIL*, whilst some have been translated into English by Lewis and Reinhold, II, pp. 521–4 and by Jones, II, pp. 158–61.

One of the more interesting features of this particular document is that, like Augustus' *RG*, it provides an indication of Vespasian's attitude to his own position in the state. His family had only recently become prominent, and so he felt that it was essential to convince the peoples of the empire that the new 'royal family' was as prestigious as its predecessor; for this purpose, an accumulation of honours and titles was deemed important. The relatively uncomplicated titles of the early emperors were now replaced by something far more elaborate, with Vespasian's development of a 'two-part' system, one imperial and the other Republican; in the first section appeared essentially imperial titles, either created by the emperors or perhaps developed by them from earlier prece-dents (*imperator*, 'Caesar', 'Augustus'), whilst those with Republican connotations follow ('consul', 'censor'). This order, established by the time of this diploma (May 74), was retained for centuries; it was to be the regular pattern of imperial nomenclature. For a discussion of the significance of the items *imperator*, 'Caesar', 'Augustus' and 'pontifex maximus', see **22** above. The following merit special attention:

'Of tribunician power for the 5th time'. This enables the diploma to be assigned to the period 1 July 73 to 30 June 74.

'Saluted as victorious commander 13 times'. See **22**. Vespasian accepted twenty salutations between 69 and 79, and, as this document indicates, more than half of them were awarded by May 74.

'Consul 5 times and designated for the 6th'. The Julio-Claudian emperors, with the exception of Gaius, were reluctant to hold the consulship regularly as it deprived senators of an honour which they still coveted. Once again, Vespasian's policy was different and, as the diploma shows, he had held five consulships and was already elected to yet another in the fifth year of his reign. But it was no longer the practice for a consul to hold office for an entire year. On the contrary, some emperors were in office for but a few weeks or even days, and were then replaced by a senator. In this case, the emperor would be referred to as the 'ordinary' consul, and his replacement(s) as 'suffect' consul(s); thus in 74 Vespasian was ordinary consul, and Cerialis Rufus and Eprius Marcellus two of the suffects. In one sense Vespasian tried to have the best of both worlds, for, by increasing the number of consulships to be awarded each year (there were seven consuls already by the month of June 74), he hoped to satisfy senatorial ambitions and, by restricting the ordinary consulship to members of this family, he intended to enhance the prestige and status of the new regime.

'Censor'. During the Republic, the censorship had been regarded as the culmination of a senatorial career. Relatively few censors, however, were appointed in its last decades, and so Augustus attempted to restore the office, as did Claudius in 47. Vespasian too was determined to revive it, holding it in 73–4 with his son Titus as his colleague; in addition, he retained the title on coins and inscriptions for the rest of the reign, even though the normal duration of the office was eighteen months.

The diploma then lists those units that contained men due for discharge and adds the details of the grant each soldier received.

'Squadrons . . . Raetorum'. There were three broad divisions of the Roman army – the legions (usually about thirty in number and each containing some five to six thousand men), the praetorian guard, urban cohorts and the fleet (all of which were stationed closer to Rome than the legions and were more directly under the emperor's control), and finally the auxiliary forces (probably as numerous as the legions). Our diploma deals solely with men in this latter category. The normal practice was for the auxiliary cavalry to be divided into groups of 500 troops, though sometimes units of double strength are found. They enjoyed higher status and pay than their counterparts in the infantry who were also grouped into units or cohorts of 500. Both were commanded by men of equestrian and not senatorial rank.

A good deal of information can be gleaned from the names of the auxiliary units stationed in a particular area at a known time. Often, some sort of an idea emerges of the imperial recruiting policy and of the extent to which the auxiliaries served in, or, more often, near their own areas. Again, by comparing various diplomas, all of which can be accurately dated, the degree to which units were transferred from one part of the empire to another can be ascertained; usually this has considerable bearing on the frontier policy of the time, a topic rarely mentioned by the literary sources.

In this diploma appear units from Spain ('Asturum', 'Hispanorum'), Holland ('Cannenefatium'), France ('Aquitanorum'), Germany ('Vindelicorum'), Cyrene ('Cyrenaica'), Dalmatia ('Dalmatarum'), Thrace ('Thracum') and Rhaetia ('Raetorum'), and, as they were serving in Upper Germany, one can note that it was the practice for auxiliaries to serve in areas fairly close to their homelands.

Other diplomas confirm this. More interesting, though, are the units 'Claudia nova', 'III Gallorum' and 'V Hispanorum'; by 82 they had been moved to Moesia (M&W 402), even though the other units were still in Germany. This is a clear indication of Domitian's foreign policy – consolidation in Germany, enabling forces to be freed for use further east, along the Danube. But as this diploma indicates, such a movement had not yet begun in 74.

'Germany'. One of the more important administrative changes made during the early empire was the division of Germany into two separate units, Upper and Lower: this change had not taken place in 74, but had done so by 27 October 90 as is shown by a diploma issued on that day (M&W 403) to units in 'Germania Superior' (Upper Germany).

'Gnaeus Pinarius Cornelius Clemens'. The diploma reveals that Cornelius Clemens was commander of the army stationed in Germany. So he was a senator, and also an ex-consul, since the overall command of the four legions located in this region was always assigned to a senator of consular status. We cannot determine precisely when he was consul, but, from the date of this diploma, one would assume that it was very early in Vespasian's reign, as there was usually a gap of some three or four years between the consulship and this position in Germany. Possibly he had been particularly loyal to the Flavian cause in the civil war, and the consulship was his reward.

'Have served for 25 or more years'. Auxiliary soldiers at this time enlisted for a period of twenty-five years; sometimes, however, they were retained in service after their time had expired, as apparently occurred in this instance – the omission of the phrase *dimissi honesta missione* ('having received an honourable discharge') suggests that Clemens' campaign was still in progress in May 74 and hence the auxiliaries due for discharge could not be released until strategic conditions allowed it.

'To them . . . citizenship and legal marriage'. At this period, Roman citizenship was a rare award, eagerly sought after. Citizens enjoyed certain legal and other privileges, not the least of which being the right to stand for office. By granting this privilege to the ex-soldiers of the auxiliary forces, the government would be assured of a consistent supply of volunteers for the army, and if the discharged troops took up permanent residence in the areas where they last served, the process of Romanization would be acceler-ated. Furthermore, it had long been impossible for soldiers to contract a legal marriage during their years of service; indeed marriages in existence before men enlisted were broken off. But, given that the men served for twenty-five years or even longer, this policy was unenforceable and unofficial unions were common. This led to a number of legal problems. Until the time of Claudius, for example, unofficially married soldiers were still liable to the legal penalties applicable to the unmarried. Again, their children were legally illegitimate and so could not, for example, inherit property in the usual way. If their father treated them in his will as he would non-relatives, then they were liable to the 5 per cent tax applied to property inherited by such persons. Sometimes an attempt was made to ensure the legal rights of a soldier's child by drawing up an unofficial attestation of the birth, signed by witnesses, so as to provide evidence for establishing the child's civic status after the father's discharge. Consider, for instance, the following document drawn up (in Latin) by Marcus Lucretius Clemens a few days after the birth of his son Serenus on 25 April AD 127:

(Witnesses): Gaius Antonius Maximus, keeper of weapons (in the unit) of Lucius Farsuleius; Marcus Arrius Antoninus from the squadron of Rufus; Gaius Barga, soldier (in the unit) of Lucius Farsuleius; Gaius Julius Marcellus, *cornicularius* ... ; Titus Marsias Bammogalis ...; Numerius Alexa son of Longus; Marcus Lucretius Clemens ... ;

Marcus Lucretius Clemens, cavalryman from Silvanus' unit in the 1st cohort of Thracians called those who are about to sign to bear witness to the fact that whilst on military service he had become the father, by Octavia Tamusta, of a natural son Serenus on 25 April in the eleventh year of the emperor Caesar Trajan Hadrian Augustus, and he took an oath by Jupiter Best and Greatest, by the divine majesty of the deified emperors and by the divine spirit of the emperor Caesar Trajan Hadrian (that this was so).

(This statement was made) so that, on the certification of his status as citizen after his honourable discharge, he would have proof that (Serenus) was his natural son.

Done in the winter camp of the 1st cohort of Thracians opposite Apollinopolis Magna in the Thebaid, on 1 May of the year mentioned above. (*AE* 1937, 112)

For these reasons, then, the grant of citizenship and legal marriage was most important, and a comparison of diplomas from various periods enables one to determine the changing imperial policy in this regard.

'Quintus Petillius Cerialis Caesius Rufus'. The diploma provides us with evidence that he was (suffect) consul for the second time in May 74. Rarely was an individual senator awarded more than one consulship, and an honour such as this is always quite significant. Perhaps it is to be explained by Tacitus' comment, that Petillius was 'closely related' (*Hist.* 3.59) to Vespasian; possibly he was the husband of the emperor's daughter, Domitilla. Furthermore, his first consulship was granted in 70, the first year of the new regime, and was a reward for his services to his father-in-law during the civil war.

'Titus Clodius Eprius Marcellus'. As the diploma indicates, he too received a second consulship in May 74. According to Tacitus (*Dial.* 8), he was one of the 'most powerful men in the state' under Vespasian as well as being one of his closest friends. After his unusually long tenure of the governorship of Asia — three years instead of the regular one — he was granted another (suffect) consulship, as our diploma indicates. However, he subsequently fell out of favour, and, in 79, was executed for his part in a plot against Vespasian. The diploma of 74, then, is a particularly valuable document, for it assists us to build up a composite picture of the careers of these Flavian officials.

'Veturius'. The recipient of this diploma was a native of Pannonia serving under a Greek officer (Tiberius Claudius Atticus) in an army commanded by an Italian (Cornelius Clemens). Apparently the Roman army had achieved a reasonable degree of ethnic integration by 74.

A variety of information, then, is contained in this one document. It is of considerable value to the historian of the early empire who would otherwise have little information on imperial policy in Germany under Vespasian, whilst, when used in conjunction with other epigraphical evidence, it assists in our knowledge of the careers of prominent Flavian officials, enabling us to determine precisely when they held important administrative posts. It provides an insight into the composition of the auxiliary units of the imperial army, and into various social problems, and not least of all, shows clearly the elaborate nomenclature of an emperor bent on establishing a new dynasty.

35   (*AE* 1961, 319)

The emperor Caesar, son of the deified Vespasian, Domitian Augustus Germanicus, pontifex maximus, of tribunician power for the 10th time, saluted as victorious commander 21 times, consul 15 times, perpetual censor, father of his country;

to the cavalrymen who are fighting in 3 squadrons (names listed) and to the infantrymen and cavalrymen who are fighting in 7 cohorts (names listed) which are in Syria under the command of Aulus Bucius Lappius Maximus, who have served for 25 or more years, having received an honourable discharge at the end of their period of service, and whose names have been listed below;

has granted ... one wife each (as in **34**).

12 May, in the consulship of Publius Valerius Marinus and Gnaeus Minicius Faustinus.

to the ordinary soldier Quelses, son of Bola, a Thracian of the Third Augustan squadron of Thracians commanded by Marcus Terentius Quirinalis, son of Marcus, of the Pollian Tribe (the location of the original bronze tablet in Rome completes the document).

The inscription, which is in Latin, is from a military diploma found at Suhozen in Bulgaria. It was issued on 12 May AD 91.

It indicates that Aulus Bucius Lappius Maximus was governing Syria in 91. Two years previously, a governor of Germany (whose name appears as Lucius Appius Maximus or Lucius Appius Maximus Norbanus in the literary sources) suppressed the revolt against Domitian led by Saturninus. As promotion to Syria from Germany was regular at this period, it is clear from this document that the name of the senator who suppressed the revolt was Aulus Bucius Lappius Maximus and also that Lappius must have been one of Domitian's most favoured consular legates, in that he governed two strategically significant provinces – Lower Germany and then Syria. Rome's thirty legions were stationed in about thirteen provinces, and, apart from two in Egypt, one in Judaea and one in Numidia, were under the control of senators of consular status. These 'consular legates' were perhaps the most important men in the empire after the emperor himself and their loyalty and support were vital to him. Those few who, like Lappius, governed more than one consular province in the course of their career were obviously regarded as particularly capable and reliable.

This document then enlarges our knowledge of the name and career of one of Domitian's most honoured supporters.

36   (*CIL* XVI = S. *N–H* 343)

The emperor Caesar, son of the deified Nerva, Nerva Trajan Augustus Germanicus, pontifex maximus; of tribunician power for the 4th time, father of his country, consul 3 times;

to the cavalrymen and infantrymen who are fighting in 3 squadrons and 21 cohorts (list of names), and are in Upper Moesia under Gaius Cilnius Proculus, who have served for 25 or more years and received their honourable discharge and whose names have been written below;

has granted . . . one wife each (as in **34**);

8 May, in the consulship of Titus Pomponius Mamilianus and Lucius Herennius Saturninus;

to the infantryman Sapia, son of Sarmosus, from Anazarbus, (member) of the 1st Antiochan cohort, commanded by Marcus Calpurnius Sabinus (the location of the original bronze tablet in Rome and the names of the witnesses complete the document).

The inscription, which is in Latin, is from a military diploma found at Siscia in Upper Pannonia; and since Mamilianus and Saturninus were consuls in 100, it must have been issued on 8 May in that year.

One of the interesting points connected with this diploma is the identity of the Upper Moesian governor. A senator named Gaius Cilnius Proculus had long been attested as suffect consul in 87, and it would be unusual, though not completely unprecedented, for thirteen years to elapse between the consulship and a post of this nature. Some scholars have explained the difficulty by assuming that Proculus fell out of favour before Domitian's death in 96, only to be rehabilitated on Trajan's accession. But that hypothesis, based on flimsy evidence, was demolished in 1972 by the discovery of the complete consular list for the year 100, for it revealed the existence of another Gaius Cilnius Proculus, consul for the first time in that year, just before the Mamilianus and Saturninus of this document. Clearly we are dealing with two Cilnii, father and son. The father is known to us only as consul in 87, whereas the son, consul in 100 (possibly in absence, since it was possible for those favoured by the emperor to hold a suffect consulship at the same time as a post in the provinces), went on to govern the consular province of Upper Moesia, as this diploma shows.

37 (*CIL* XVI 160 = S. *N–H* 344)

The emperor Caesar, son of the deified Nerva, Nerva Trajan Augustus Germanicus Dacicus, pontifex maximus, of tribunician power for the 14th time, saluted as victorious commander 6 times, consul 5 times, father of his country;

to the infantrymen and cavalrymen who are fighting in the 1st Ulpian cohort of Britons, 1000 strong, decorated with the (ceremonial) collar, loyal and true, Roman citizens, which is in Dacia under Decimus Terentius Scaurianus and whose names have been written below;

has granted Roman citizenship for loyal and true service in the Dacian campaign, before completion of their period of service;

11 August, at Darnithithis, in the consulship of Lucius Minicius Natalis and Quintus Silvanus Granianus;

to the infantryman Marcus Ulpius Novantico, son of Adcobrovatus, from Leicester (the location of the original bronze tablet in Rome and the names of the witnesses complete the document).

The inscription, which is in Latin, is from a military diploma found at Porolissum in Dacia; and since Natalis and Granianus were consuls in 106, it must have been issued on 11 August in that year. Trajan held his fifth consulship in 103 and his sixth in 112, his sixth salutation is recorded in 106 but his seventh not before 114, whilst he did not hold tribunician power for the fourteenth time until 109, from 10 December 109 to 9 December 110. There is, then, a discrepancy between the emperor's tribunician year (109/10) and Natalis' and Granianus' consular year (106), a discrepancy rarely found in documents of this type.

But it can be easily explained. Novantico had served the emperor with conspicuous success, as the diploma indicates ('for loyal and true service in the Dacian campaign'), and was rewarded by being discharged with a grant of citizenship some four years before he had completed his agreed period of service. It is more than likely that he had signed on until 110, for a diploma that can definitely be assigned to that year refers to the regular discharge of other members of the same British unit:

The emperor Caesar, son of the deified Nerva, Nerva Trajan Augustus Germanicus Dacicus, pontifex maximus, of tribunician power for the 14th time, saluted as victorious commander 6 times, consul 5 times, father of his country;

to the infantrymen and cavalrymen who fought in 4 squadrons and 18 cohorts (list of names) which are in Dacia under Decimus Terentius Scaurianus, having served for 25 or more years and received their honourable discharge and whose name have been written below;

has granted . . . one wife each (as in **34**);

2 July, in the consulship of Gaius Erucianus Silo and Lucius Catilius Severus;

to the infantryman Marcus Ulpius Longinus, son of Saccus, from the Belgae, and to Vitalis, his son, (serving) in the 1st Ulpian cohort of Britons, 1000 strong, decorated with the (ceremonial) collar, Roman citizens, and commanded by Marcus Aemilius Bassus (the location of the original bronze tablet in Rome and the names of the witnesses complete the document). (*CIL* XVI 163 = S. *N–H* 357)

This military diploma was also found at Porolissum and was issued on 2 July in the consulship of Silo and Severus, i.e. in AD 110. Note that in S. *N–H* 344 and also in *CIL* XVI 163 the emperor is recorded as having held five consulships and six salutations in the fourteenth year of his reign – 110; only the (suffect) consular years are at variance. The Longinus of *CIL* XVI 163, however, had served his full term unlike Novantico in S. *N–H* 344, and was granted citizenship at that time. Compare the tenses used in each diploma: 'to the infantrymen and cavalrymen who are fighting' (S. *N–H* 344) and 'to the . . . who fought' (*CIL* XVI 163) and also the comment in S. *N–H* 344 that Novantico (and the others who were being similarly honoured) were receiving the citizenship 'before completion of their period of service'. It is clear, then, that the discrepancy was not accidental but rather intended to indicate the extent of the honour Novantico had received, and since he had won the rare distinction of being made a Roman citizen before completing his full term of service, the formula common to most diplomas ('has granted to them, to their children . . . one wife each') is omitted in S. *N–H* 344 and an appropriate substitution made.

There is an interesting copying error towards to the end of S. *N–H* 344. The Latin reads *M. Vlpio Adcobrovati f. Novanticoni Ratis*, 'to M(arcus) Ulpius, son of Adcobrovatus, Novantico, from Leicester', but the *-ni* of *Novanticoni* was added later and above the line, between the *-o* and the *R* of *Ratis*. The explanation is that *Novantico*, being a rare name, was at first assumed by the copyist to be the dative case of some such word as 'Novanticus'; when he realized that *Novantico* was in fact nominative and not dative, and that

Novanticoni was the form required, he could then do little but
squeeze in the additional letters above the line.

Even though Novantico was born in Britain, he apparently
preferred to spend his retirement in the area where he had so long
served, since it was here that his copy of the diploma was found.

38   (*CIL* XVI 69 = S. *N–H* 347)

The emperor Caesar, son of the deified Trajan Parthicus,
grandson of the deified Nerva, Trajan Hadrian Augustus,
pontifex maximus, of tribunician power for the 6th time, consul
3 times, proconsul;

to the cavalrymen and infantrymen who fought in 13 squadrons (names listed) and 37 cohorts (names listed) which are in
Britain under Aulus Platorius Nepos, having served for 25 years
and received their honourable discharge from Pompeius Falco
and whose names have been written below;

has granted . . . one wife each (as in **34**);

17 July, in the consulship of Tiberius Julius Capito and Lucius
Vitrasius Flamininus;

to the *sesquiplicarius* Gemellus, son of Breucus, a Pannonian of
the squadron I Pannoniorum Tampiana, commanded by
Fabius Sabinus (the location of the original bronze tablet in
Rome and the names of the witnesses complete the document).

The inscription, which is in Latin, is from a military diploma found
in 1930 at O-Szöny on the Danube, in Roman Brigetio (western
Hungary), and is now in the British Museum; it was issued on 17
July 122. After securing the throne in 117, Hadrian proclaimed
himself the adopted son of Trajan – and thereby the grandson of
Nerva; hence the first lines of the diploma. Most of his 'father's'
hastily acquired and ill-secured gains were soon lost, and in Britain
the Romans were forced to retreat to the line of the Solway and
Tyne. But by the sixth year of his reign, as the document shows,
Hadrian had taken decisive action, with the capable Pompeius
Falco, a senior consular, commanding a huge auxiliary force – few
diplomas indeed list fifty regiments. The composition of these units
is interesting in itself, for they contained relatively few soldiers
from Gaul and Spain, the normal recruiting areas in the first
century of the empire; instead, the majority came from the
Rhineland and Danubian areas, a situation indicative rather of the
third century. The document also reveals that Gemellus (and other
troops who had served their twenty-five years) were given their

honourable discharge by Pompeius Falco, but that, before the diplomas had been registered in Rome, Falco had been replaced by Hadrian's personal friend Platorius Nepos, the man who was to superintend the building of the famous wall. It was also in this year, probably, that Hadrian visited Britain.

Of greater significance is the reference to Pompeius Falco who held many important posts under Trajan and Hadrian. His full name and career are revealed in two inscriptions, *ILS* 1035 and 1036: 'To Quintus Roscius, son of Sextus, of the Quirinian tribe, Coelius Murena Silius Decianus Vibull(i)us Pius Julius Eurycles Herclanus Pompeius Falco, consul, member of the college of 15 for the performing of sacrifices, proconsul of the province of Asia, legate with the rank of propraetor of the emperor Caesar Trajan Hadrian Augustus of the province of Britain, legate with the rank of propraetor of the emperor Caesar Nerva Trajan Augustus Germanicus Dacicus of the province of Lower Moesia, commissioner of the Trajanic Way, and legate of the emperor with the rank of propraetor of the province of Judaea and of the legion 10 Fretensis, legate with the rank of propraetor of the province of Lycia and Pamphylia, legate of the legion 5 Macedonica, presented in the Dacian War with military gifts . . .' (*ILS* 1035 = S. *N–H* 231). The other inscription, *ILS* 1036, adds his praetorship and pre-praetorian posts, including that of tribune of the people. His career might be summarized as follows:

tribune of the people : *c.* 97 (see below)
praetor : ? 100
legate of 5 Macedonica : between 100 and 108
governor of Lycia and Pamphylia : between 100 and 108
governor of Judaea and legate of 10 Fretensis : between 100 and 108
commissioner of Via Traiana : between 100 and 108
consul : ? 108
governor of Lower Moesia : between 116 and 117 (see below)
governor of Britain : 17 July 122
proconsul of Asia : after 122
member of college of 15 : ?

ILS 1035 indicates that Falco was one of the very few senators ever recorded as governing more than one imperial praetorian province (Lycia-Pamphylia and Judaea). Note that, so long as Judaea was a praetorian province (from Vespasian's reign until *c.* 130), the position of governor was assigned to the commander of the legion stationed there, the 10 Fretensis, who regularly appears on inscriptions as holding both posts. Despite his extensive military experience before the consulship, Falco seems to have seen comparatively little service during the last ten years of Trajan's reign, apart from his post of governor of Lower Moesia where he is first attested in 116/17 (*CIL* III 7537: Trajan is recorded as holding tribunician power for the twenty-first time). His origin may well have counted against him, for he was apparently born in Cilicia, and although senators of Eastern origin had been admitted for some time to commands of considerable military significance, it may well have been that some opposed the practice, feeling that a halt should be called and preference given to Italians and Westerners. These two inscriptions, however, do not provide positive reasons for his apparent loss of imperial favour and, in any case, Falco's career after 108 can be explained in other ways; he may, for instance, have accompanied Trajan as some sort of staff officer during the protracted series of wars in the East.

His extensive name is not without parallel at this period and is presumably to be explained by adoption – it was not unusual for the person adopted to assume some (see Sejanus in **4**) or all of the names of the adopting parent. Again, one of his names, Murena, poses an interesting problem. In a letter that can be assigned to approximately AD 97, Pliny refers to a tribune of the people named Murena (*Ep.* 9.13.19), and, if this is Falco, it would seem that he, like other Easterners, must have been admitted to the senate two or three years before, by Domitian and not by Nerva.

Although a number of senators were put to death in 117 on Hadrian's accession, Falco apparently enjoyed his favour. He is next recorded in Britain; in *AE* 1957, 336 he appears as 'legate of Augustus with the rank of propraetor of Lower Moesia, legate of Augustus with the rank of propraetor of Britain'. According to some scholars, this suggests that he passed directly from Lower Moesia to Britain, and, if this is so, his term there was longer than the normal three years.

In *ILS* 1035 Falco appears as governor of 'Brittannia', a not unparalleled error, cf. S. *N–H* 206 = M&W 309, where Javolenus Priscus holds a post in 'Brittannia': in S. *N–H* 217 the spelling becomes 'Brittania', but M&W 315 records the correct 'Britannia'. Apparently the Roman stonecutters were far from familiar with the name of this remote province.

The diploma is important in that it provides a definite date for one post in Falco's career (not even the year of his consulship is absolutely certain: a . . . *ius F* . . . appears as consul in 108 [S. *N–H*, p. 5], and that fragmentary name is assumed to be his) and assists in the reconstruction of the career of a prominent senator who is almost entirely neglected in the literary sources.

39   (*ILS* 100)

Father of his country, the emperor Caesar, son of the deified (Julius Caesar), Augustus, pontifex maximus, consul 12 times and designated for the 13th, saluted as victorious commander 14 times, of tribunician power for the 21st time.

The inscription, which is in Latin, is from a milestone on the road from the Cottian Alps to Arles in southern France, and is of some significance in dating Augustus' assumption of the title *pater patriae* ('father of his country'). In his *RG* he states that, 'Whilst I was holding my 13th consulship, the senate and equestrian order and the entire Roman people gave me the title "father of my country", and decreed that this should be inscribed in the porch of my house and in the Curia Julia and in the forum of Augustus, under the chariot which was set up in my honour by decree of the senate' (*RG* 35.1). But the milestone bears an earlier date than this, i.e. it was set up before he entered into his thirteenth consulship. His twenty-first tenure of tribunician power extended from 27 June 3 BC to 26 June 2 BC; he was consul for the twelfth time in 5 BC and for the thirteenth in 2 BC. So the evidence provided by the milestone contradicts Augustus' statement in his own autobiography; but the explanation is not hard to find. The position of the title 'father of his country' on the milestone is most unusual, and it could well be that the milestone had been prepared by the end of 3 BC but not erected; then, when the emperor acquired his new title early the following year, it was inserted in the only space available, which was also the position of honour. Certainly it is highly irregular to find 'father of his country' so prominent in the imperial titulature. For the other items in Augustus' titulature, note the comments on the Ariminum inscription (**22**).

In general, inscriptions on milestones provide valuable information on the topography and geography of Rome and the provinces, and also on broad aspects of imperial strategy; for the direction of a road or even the construction of one, whilst not mentioned in the literary sources, is an important indication of government policy, showing, amongst other things, conquests either successful or intended. Many thousands have been found throughout the empire; usually they bear the emperor's name and the distance between two towns. The latter has not survived on this particular milestone. Sometimes they record the name of the provincial governor. They are of various shapes and sizes – one of the earliest (*ILS* 5807) is a rectangular block four feet by two, whilst many of Augustus' are cylindrical. For further examples of this type of document, see Lewis and Reinhold, II, pp. 153–5 and Jones, II, pp. 198–9.

40   (*CIL* XIII 9145 = S 340)

Tiberius Claudius, son of Drusus, Caesar Augustus, Germanicus, pontifex maximus, of tribunician power for the 4th time, saluted as victorious commander 8 times, designated to a 4th consulship, father of his country. 59 miles from Moguntiacum.

The inscription, which is in Latin, is from a milestone found at Koblenz, on the road from Colonia Agrippina (Cologne) to Moguntiacum (Mainz). It can be assigned to the period 25 January 44 to 24 January 45. Claudius held his third consulship in 43 and his fourth in 47. Thus the consular number is of little assistance to us, and since his eighth salutation is usually combined with his fourth tenure of tribunician power, it is from the latter alone that a date can be assigned to the milestone.

   Claudius' policy on the Rhine was much more positive than Tiberius'. He founded the colony that subsequently became Cologne, and, in general, strengthened the Rhine defences. Behind the Rhine, in Gaul, he reorganized the entire road system, and a number of milestones attest to this, i.e. S 335a and S 335b (two roads from Nemausus) and S 336, S 337 and S 339 (three roads from Lugdunum). Between Cologne, his new colony, and Mainz, a road was constructed providing not only an excellent line of communication for the legions behind their Rhine defences but also a useful commercial route.

41   (S 343)

27 (miles) from Turris. Tiberius Claudius Caesar Augustus Germanicus, pontifex maximus, of tribunician power for the 6th time, father of his country, saluted as victorious commander 11 times, designated to his 4th consulship (built this road) when Lucius Aurelius Patroclus was prefect of the province of Sardinia.

The inscription, which is in Latin, is from a milestone erected in Sardinia between the towns of Turris and Carales, and it can be assigned to the period 25 January 46 to 24 January 47, during Claudius' sixth tenure of tribunician power. Since he held his third consulship in 43 and his fourth in 47, the designation referred to in the inscription is of little assistance in dating it.

Sardinia's status was altered on a number of occasions – see **42** for the details. It is clear, however, that in 46 it was an imperial province, ruled by an equestrian prefect Aurelius Patroclus.

42   (*CIL* X 8024 = M&W 337)

56 miles from Turris. The emperor Caesar Vespasian Augustus, pontifex maximus, of tribunician power for the 5th time, saluted as victorious commander 13 times, father of his country, consul 5 times and designated for the 6th, censor, repaired and restored the road when Sextus Subrius Dexter was procurator and prefect of Sardinia.

The inscription, which is in Latin, is from a milestone (the fifty-sixth) on the road from Carales to Turris in Sardinia; since Vespasian's fifth consulship was held in 74, whilst his fifth tribunician year extended from 1 July 73 until 30 June 74, it is clear that the milestone is to be assigned to the first six months of 74.
The provinces of the Roman empire were regarded as either imperial or senatorial, and the former were further subdivided into consular, praetorian and equestrian provinces: in each case the governor's title indicates the province's status. Sardinia was a senatorial province (i.e. governed by a proconsul) until AD 6, when it came under the emperor's control. It retained that status for the next sixty years and thus in 46–7 was governed by the equestrian Aurelius Patroclus (**41**). However, when Nero proclaimed the liberation of Greece in 67 (**26**) and Achaea passed from the control of the proconsul of Macedonia, the senate was given Sardinia once again in order to compensate it for the loss of the Achaean section of Macedonia. Hence in *ILS* 5947 = M&W 455 = S 392, Lucius Helvius Agrippa appears as 'proconsul of Sardinia' (dated March 69). This milestone, however, indicates that, by 74, Sardinia was no longer governed by a man of that rank and the Vespasian had assumed control officially of the former senatorial province, appointing as governor a man of equestrian status, Sextus Subrius Dexter.

43   (*CIL* VIII 10119 = M&W 419)

In the 5th consulship of the emperor Titus Caesar Vespasian, son of Augustus, saluted as victorious commander 10 times, priest, of tribunician power for the 5th time, and in the 4th consulship of Caesar, son of Augustus, Domitian, and when

Quintus Egnatius Catus was legate of the emperor with the rank of propraetor of the legion 3 Augusta. 20 (or 31) miles.

The inscription, which is in Latin, is from a milestone found between Theveste and Hippo Regius in North Africa, near modern Duvivier. Since Titus' fifth tenure of tribunician power extended from 1 July 75 to 30 June 76, whilst his fifth and his brother's fourth consulships were held at different times during the first months of 76, the inscription can be assigned to the first half of that year.

It provides an indication of the relative constitutional positions of Titus and Domitian during the reign of Vespasian. Titus had already received tribunician power and, in many documents such as this one, the *praenomen imperatoris* (e.g. **45** but cf. **50**), awards that were not granted to Domitian even during Titus' reign. On the other hand, Vespasian had no intention of neglecting his younger son since, at the age of twenty-five (the normal time of entry into the senate), he is recorded as holding a fourth consulship.

This is one of the large number of inscriptions from the Flavian era that have been found in North Africa; when collated they assist in the determination of imperial policy and achievements in an area only occasionally mentioned by the literary sources. The Flavians expended considerable money and effort in consolidating the province and it was under them that the first African obtained a consulship: 'To Quintus Aurelius Pactumeius, son of Publius, of the Quirinian tribe, Fronto, adlected into the senate amongst the ex-praetors by the emperor Caesar Vespasian Augustus and by Titus, emperor, son of Augustus, priest, fetial, prefect of the military treasury, first consul from Africa, Pactumeia . . . gave (this) as a gift to her excellent father' (M&W 298).

The commander of the legion stationed in Numidia (3 Augusta) was a very senior legionary legate, and his post was equivalent to that of a governorship of an imperial praetorian province: compare the status of a commander of the 10 Fretensis in Judaea such as Pompeius Falco (**38**). Egnatius Catus is known to have commanded a legion already, the 15 Apollinaris, early in Vespasian's reign. His tenure of Numidia can be accurately dated, then, thanks to this and the many other milestones that have survived from his governorship.

44   (*ILS* 8904 = M&W 86)

In the 7th consulship of the emperor Vespasian Caesar Augustus, pontifex maximus, of tribunician power for the 7th time, saluted as victorious commander 14 times, father of his

country; and in the 5th consulship of Titus Caesar, son of
Augustus; and in the 4th consulship of Domitian Caesar, son of
Augustus: and when Gnaeus Pompeius Collega was legate of
the emperor with the rank of propraetor. 3 miles.

The inscription, which is in Latin, is from a milestone found at
Melik Scherif in Lesser Armenia. The imperial consulships mentioned were held in 76, whilst Vespasian's seventh tenure of
tribunician power is to be dated between 1 July 75 and 30 June 76:
the milestone, then, can be assigned to the first six months of 76.

  Lesser Armenia was one of the many divisions of Roman Asia
Minor, which, under Nero, consisted largely of a collection of
unarmed provinces under client kings; Tacitus attests to Lesser
Armenia's status at that time — 'It was entrusted to Aristobulus'
(*Annals* 13.7: similarly *Annals* 14.26). But by 80 it was clearly part of
the new complex, Cappadocia-Galatia, as a milestone indicates (**45**).
The reorganization was basically the work of Vespasian, who not
only assumed full control of the various client kingdoms, but also
strengthened his position by establishing two legionary fortresses
in the area, at Melitene and Satala. The legion 12 Fulminata was
stationed at Melitene in Cappadocia and divisions from this legion
have been found close to the Caspian Sea (see **28**); the other, the
16 Flavia Firma, was posted to Satala in the heart of Lesser
Armenia. The three Flavian emperors saw to the construction of
a network of military roads spreading in all directions.

  In this milestone the consular legate Pompeius Collega is
attested at work at Melik Scherif (modern Carsaga) in the area of
Satala. In the *Journal of Roman Studies*, 64, 1974, pp. 165–6, T. B.
Mitford has described the area's significance: 'Satala commanded
the strategic cross-roads of north-eastern Anatolia. . . . Immediately below the fortress lay the intersection of the natural and
historic routes that lead east and west from Persia to the Aegean,
and north and south from the Black Sea to the Euphrates valley
and Syria. . . . (Satala) was the key to control traffic and resist
invasion, or to mount and support offensive operations into
Armenia and the Caucasus. Its site illustrates . . . the strategic
judgement of Roman commanders. In terms of the issues and
forces at stake, it is perhaps the most crucially placed legionary
fortress in the Empire.' His comment on the road from Melik
Scherif is also worth noting: '(Its) course . . . is clear . . . It crossed
the high range . . . by a now disused pass, leading in two days from
Melik Scherif directly towards . . . the fortress at Satala. From its
use by Russian troops in 1917, it is still known at Satala as the "eski
Rus yol" (old Russian road).'

45 (*ILS* 263 = M&W 105)

The emperor Titus Caesar, son of the deified Vespasian,
Augustus, pontifex maximus, of tribunician power for the 10th
time, saluted as victorious commander 15 times, consul 8 times,
censor, father of his country, and Caesar [Domitian, son of the
deified] (Vespasian), consul 7 times, Leader of the Youth, by
means of Aulus Caesennius Gallus, legate with the rank of
propraetor, built the roads of the provinces Galatia, Cappadocia, Pontus, Pisidia, Paphlagonia, Lycaonia and Lesser
Armenia. 71 miles.

The inscription, which is in Latin, was found on a milestone on the
road from Ancyra to Dorylaeum in Roman Asia Minor. It provides
some quite useful information. One of the problems of the
imperial administrative system is the difficulty of determining the
precise status of each province; Sardinia, for instance, was at one
time under the senate's control and at another under the
emperor's – see **42**. Much more complicated is the area of Roman
Asia Minor, part of which was administered by the senate, part by
the emperor, and part by client kings. Vespasian's activities in
uniting this vast complex have been considered under **44**. We can,
however, be sure that by Titus' reign it consisted of the seven areas
referred to in the inscription, that its governor was of consular
status, and that it was administered by the emperor. The consular
years of Titus and Domitian enable the milestone to be assigned
to 80, whilst the emperor's tenth tribunician power limits it to the
latter half of the year. It also reveals the name of the governor of
the area, the somewhat enigmatic Aulus Caesennius Gallus. He
commanded a legion in 66 during the conquest of Galilee
(Josephus, *Jewish War*, 2.510–13), and since he seems to have been
related to the Lucius Caesennius Paetus who married Vespasian's
niece, one might have expected him to receive a consulship early
in the Flavian era rather than around the year 76, which would be
the usual time for a legate of 66. Had he done so, one would then
expect him to have governed an imperial consular province well
before Vespasian's death. However his consular year is not
recorded, and one wonders why a relative of Vespasian (if such he
was) had to wait for some fourteen years from his legionary
command before being appointed to the Cappadocia-Galatia
complex; compare Trajan's father who had commanded a legion
two years after Caesennius Gallus yet governed Cappadocia-
Galatia nine years before him.

Once again, Domitian's constitutional position is shown to be
substantially inferior to that of Titus (**43**), in that he still lacks the

praenomen imperatoris and tribunician power, even though Titus had them both when Vespasian was emperor. But at that time, when four emperors had died violently in the space of eighteen months, Vespasian clearly felt, at the age of sixty, the need to strengthen his position by associating Titus with him in his official powers. But the situation was quite different for the forty-year-old Titus a decade later, in a time of relative peace. Domitian is listed as 'Leader of the Youth', a title equivalent to that of heir apparent. It is interesting to note that Titus had retained the title of 'censor', even though he held it for a period of only eighteen months in 73–4 with his father. His motives for still using it are open to dispute. When Domitian was declared 'perpetual censor' in 85, it was regarded as highly unconstitutional, yet it is difficult to name any specific additional power it gave him, any he did not already possess in his role of *imperator*. Titus' retention of the title does not appear to have provoked any hostile reaction – which may be an indication of the attitude of the literary sources to the last two Flavian emperors.

It would seem that, after Domitian's death in 96, his name was erased from the milestone. Further examples of this *damnatio memoriae* can be seen in **59** and **60**. Note that, in the translation, the conjectural restoration of his name has been indicated by its inclusion in square brackets.

46 (*ILS* 5866 = S. *N–H* 408a)

The emperor Caesar, son of the deified Nerva, Nerva Trajan Augustus Germanicus Dacicus, pontifex maximus, of tribunician power for the 13th time, saluted as victorious commander 6 times, consul 5 times, father of his country, built the road and the bridges from Beneventum to Brundisium at his own expense.

The inscription, which is in Latin, is from a milestone found on the Via Traiana between Beneventum and Aequum Tuticum. Trajan held his fifth consulship in 103 and his sixth in 112. A narrower limit is provided by his tribunician year, i.e. December 108– December 109. As well as his massive public works in the capital itself (see **17**), the emperor interested himself in Italy, an area that was theoretically under the senate's control. Roads and bridges, as the milestone indicates, together with aqueducts and ports, were provided, most of them around this part of the reign. No doubt the recently completed Dacian campaign provided the finance. It is interesting to note that the Via Traiana was one of the few Roman roads to be commemorated on the coinage. An *aureus* of Trajan minted in Rome *c.* 112 bears the following legend: 'To the emperor Trajan Augustus Germanicus Dacicus, pontifex maximus, of tribunician power, consul 6 times, father of his country' (Obverse): 'the senate and the Roman people to the Best of Rulers. The Via Traiana' (Reverse: *BMC* III, p. 98, no. 484 = S. *N–H* 408c).

47 (*SEG* IX 252 = S. *N–H* 59)

The emperor Caesar, son of the deified Trajan Parthicus, grandson of the deified Nerva, Trajan Hadrian, pontifex maximus, of tribunician power for the 2nd time, consul 3 times, restored the road, which had been ripped up and ruined in the Jewish revolt, by means of the soldiers of the ... cohort.

The inscription, which is in Latin, is from a milestone on the Cyrene–Apollonia road in North Africa. Since Hadrian held his third consulship in 119, and tribunician power for the second time from December 118 until December 119, the milestone can be assigned to 119. The road was constructed only twenty years before by a detachment of local recruits, as an earlier milestone on the same road indicates: 'The emperor Caesar, son of the deified Nerva, Nerva Trajan Augustus Germanicus, pontifex maximus, of tribunician power for the 4th time, consul 3 times, father of his country, constructed the road by means of the recruits chosen from the province of Cyrene' (S. *N–H* 424: the inscription is in both Latin and Greek, facilitating the reading of the fragmentary sections). Trajan held his third consulship in 100 and his fourth in 101, whilst his fourth tenure of tribunician power extended from December 99 until December 100. The road had been constructed, then, in 100.

After an economic decline in the first century BC, Cyrene experienced something of a recovery under Augustus, and, by the end of the first century AD, not only were roads being built but the great baths were completed. An inscription provides the details: 'The emperor Caesar Nerva, son of the deified (Nerva), Trajan Augustus Germanicus, pontifex maximus, of tribunician power, father of his country, consul twice, built the bath and the hot baths through the agency of Gaius Memmius ...' (S. *N–H* 399). The completion of this huge complex was a definite indication of Cyrene's economic recovery, but, like the Apollonia–Cyrene road, it also suffered in the revolt of 115, and had subsequently to be restored by Hadrian. An inscription attests to his activity: 'The emperor Caesar, son of the deified Trajan Parthicus, grandson of

the deified Nerva, Trajan Hadrian Augustus, pontifex maximus, of
tribunician power for the 3rd time, consul 3 times, ordered the
restoration for the community of Cyrene of the bath with its
colonnades, tennis courts and other adjoining (buildings) which
had been torn down and burned in the Jewish revolt' (S. *N–H* 60).
It can be assigned to the period December 119/December 120,
when Hadrian held tribunician power for the third time. The
Jewish revolt referred to began in 115, and in Cyrene the Jews
quickly gained control. According to Dio (68.32.2), they killed over
220 000 of their opponents, and whilst his figures are no doubt
exaggerated, the inscriptions cited above provide an accurate
indication of its ferocity and of the economic reversal suffered by
Cyrene – buildings and even roads were destroyed and the
province was reduced to ruins. The revolt had spread as far as
Egypt and Cyprus, and order was not restored until 116, but
because of Trajan's preoccupation with the Parthian campaign it
was left to Hadrian to repair the physical and economic damage.

48   (*ILS* 218 = S 309)

**Tiberius Claudius, son of Drusus, Caesar Augustus Germani-
cus, pontifex maximus, with tribunician power for the 12th
time, consul 5 times, saluted as victorious commander 27 times,
father of his country, undertook at his own expense the
extension into the city of the Claudian aqueduct, from its
springs called the Caerulean and Curtian, from the 45th
milestone, and again of the New Anio, from the 62nd milestone.**

The inscription, which is in Latin, was one of three found in Rome
at the Praenestine Gate, now the Porta Maggiore, where the
Claudian aqueduct entered the city. It can be assigned to the period
25 January 52 to 24 January 53 from Claudius' tribunician number;
however his fifth consulship is of no real assistance in dating the
inscription since he held it, his last consulship, in 51, and
mentioned it on the coins and inscriptions of the last four years of
his reign. There is also a reference to his father Drusus (stepson of
Augustus and brother of Tiberius) and to his brother Germanicus,
whose popularity in Rome, even thirty years after his death, was
still great. For the significance of the title 'Germanicus' when used
by later emperors, see **16**. Note also that Claudius, like Tiberius,
Gaius and Nero, does not use the title *imperator* ('emperor') in the
initial position of his titulature.
   Imperial Rome was justly proud of the excellence of her water
supply, attested to by writers of every race and persuasion, from

Marcus Aurelius' doctor Galen to the sixth-century monk Cassiodorus. The most authoritative account is that of Sextus Julius Frontinus who, in the last quarter of the first century AD, governed three consular provinces (Britain, ?Germany and Asia) and was granted the rare honour of three consulships. Most important of all, though, for our present purpose, was his post of *curator aquarum* ('Commissioner of the Water Supply') a very senior and responsible position which he held only after his three governorships and two of his consulships. This eminent politician, soldier and administrator wrote a technical treatise on Rome's water supply (*On the Aqueducts*), a subject for which he was obviously well qualified, indicating how the aqueducts were built, the routes followed, the natural problems to be overcome and the officials appointed to supervise it all. But even his detailed account can be supplemented by inscriptions such as this from the aqueducts themselves and also from the lead pipes which conveyed the water to individual consumers (**49**).

In his attempt to beautify the capital, Claudius inaugurated a massive building programme which included the completion of two aqueducts, the Claudian and the New Anio, that Gaius had begun in 38. When finished in 52, they brought an enormous volume of water into Rome from the Sabine mountains to the west. According to Suetonius, 'he brought into Rome on stone arches the cool and abundant founts of the Claudian aqueduct, one of which is called the Caerulean and the other Curtian and Albudignan, and at the same time the spring of the New Anio, distributing them into many beautifully ornamented pools' (*Claudius* 20.1: Loeb translation, adapted). Frontinus' account was similar: 'Claudius completed (the aqueducts begun by Gaius) on a very magnificent scale and dedicated them in 52.... One which had its source in the Caerulean and Curtian springs was called the Claudian and is next to the Marcian in excellence. The second came to be called the New Anio, so as to enable the two Anios that had now begun to flow to the city to be more readily distinguished, with the former one being named the Old Anio' (*On the Aqued.* 1.13: Loeb translation). He also provided details of the length of both structures, the number of arches in each, and so on, adding, 'With such a variety of essential structures carrying so much water, one might compare the useless Pyramids or other pointless, though famous, works of the Greeks'.

Frontinus' eulogistic account must, however, be corrected, for the Claudia had to be repaired on two separate occasions only thirty years after its completion. An inscription from Vespasian's reign notes that 'the emperor Caesar Vespasian Augustus, pontifex maximus, of tribunician power for the 2nd time, saluted as victorious commander 6 times, consul 3 times and designated for the 4th, father of his country, restored at his own expense for the benefit of the city the Curtian aqueduct and the Caerulean aqueduct which had been built by the deified Claudius but had been afterwards neglected for nine years and allowed to fall into disrepair' (*ILS* 218 = M&W 408a). Since Vespasian was consul for the third time in 71, and held tribunician power for the second time from 1 July 70 until 30 June 71, the inscription noting the first repairs can be assigned to the first six months of 71. Then, some ten years later, further extensive restoration was necessary: 'The emperor Titus Caesar, son of the deified (Vespasian), Vespasian Augustus, pontifex maximus, of tribunician power for the 10th time, saluted as victorious commander 17 times, father of his country, censor, consul 8 times, arranged that the Curtian aque- duct and the Caerulean aqueduct, built by the deified Claudius and afterwards repaired for the benefit of the city by his own father, the deified Vespasian, should be completely rebuilt at his own expense to a new design as they had collapsed from their source through age' (*ILS* 218 = M&W 408b). Titus held his eighth consulship in 80, and commemorated it in 81, whilst his tenth tenure of tribunician power extended from 1 July 80 to 30 June 81; however, his sixteenth and seventeenth salutations are not recorded before 81. Consequently the inscription noting the second series of repairs can be assigned to the first six months of 81. One notes with interest that the Flavian emperors preferred to name the aqueduct after the springs from which it originated, even though it was officially called the Claudian – the statements of Suetonius and Frontinus (both of whom wrote after Titus' death) and also of S 309 of AD 52 are quite precise on this point. Frontinus (*On the Aqued.* 1.13) and Suetonius (*Claudius* 20.1), unlike Claudius in S 309, acknowledged Gaius' role in the construction of these aqueducts. On the other hand, Claudius sometimes disparaged his nephew's work officially: 'Tiberius Claudius, son of Drusus, Caesar Augustus Germanicus, pontifex maximus, with tribunician power for the 5th time, saluted as victorious commander 11 times, father of his country, designated to a 4th consulship, completely renewed and restored the Virgo aqueduct that had fallen into disrepair because of Gaius Caesar' (*ILS* 205 = S 308b). This inscription, which is in Latin, is from the arch of the Virgo aqueduct, found near the Trevi fountain in Rome. The aqueduct was one of Agrippa's works and brought water to Rome from the north. Claudius restored it as part of his beautification programme during the fifth year of his reign, according to the inscription, i.e. during the period 25

January 46 to 24 January 47. A more precise date cannot be assigned to the restoration, even though the inscription records the fact that he was designated to a fourth consulship and saluted as victorious commander by his troops for the eleventh time; the former title appeared on his coins and inscriptions for some time (he held his third consulship in 43 and his fourth in 47) whilst the latter is no more helpful. Apparently the Aqua Virgo had been neglected by Gaius – hence the disparaging reference to him. On the other hand, Rome's water supply was so efficient that, when all eight aqueducts were functioning, 1000 million litres of water per day would reach the capital (T. Ashby, *The Aqueducts of Ancient Rome*, Oxford 1935, p. 30). It would appear, then, that Gaius' inaction was not so reprehensible, as no serious loss of water would have resulted.

49 (*CIL* VII 1201 = S 317)

Tiberius Claudius Caesar Augustus, pontifex maximus, of tribunician power for the 9th time, saluted as victorious commander 16 times. From Britain.

The inscription, which is in Latin, is from a pig of lead (i.e. an oblong mass of the metal) found on the Mendip Hills. Since it contains a reference to Claudius' ninth tribunician year, it can be assigned to the period between 25 January AD 49 and 24 January AD 50.

One of the motives behind his invasion of Britain was the island's reputed mineral wealth. But although precious metals were rare, a considerable quantity of lead was discovered, and, as this inscription shows, quickly mined. Enormous quantities must have been exported, for a number of lead ingots ('pigs') have been discovered, rare survivors from the few that were presumably lost in transit to Rome. Normally, all minerals were the property of the state, and hence the ingots bear the emperor's name. This particular example indicates that the British mines were in production within six years of Claudius' arrival.

50 (*ILS* 8710 = M&W 439)

The emperor Vespasian Augustus, consul 5 times; Titus, emperor, consul 3 times. (From the country of the) Deceangli.

The inscription, which is in Latin, is from a pig of lead found near Chester. The consular years of Vespasian and Titus enable it to be assigned to AD 74. Of some interest is the position of the word *imperator* ('emperor') in Titus' titulature. Normally, he appears in official documents as virtually co-emperor with his father (see the discussion in **43**), but in this instance his subordinate role is clearly indicated.

According to Tacitus (*Annals* 12.32), the Deceangli lived in the region of Cheshire, and so it would seem that these northern mines were in operation and exporting lead fairly early in Vespasian's reign.

51   (*CIL* XIII 12168 (7))

The legion 8 Augusta, under the command of Lappius.

The inscription, which is in Latin, is from a legionary tile found in Upper Germany. Legionary tiles have been discovered in most areas of the Roman empire, wherever a legion was stationed for any period of time. On them are usually inscribed the unit's name and number together (sometimes) with that of its commander, whilst their precise geographical location is excellent evidence for the legion's position at a certain period.

Lappius is known to have held his first consulship in 86 (M&W, p. 8); if he had advanced normally in his career, he would therefore have been praetor fairly early in Vespasian's reign and com-mander of a legion (a fairly senior praetorian post) towards the end. So the tile indicates that the 8 Augusta was stationed in Upper Germany towards the end of Vespasian's reign and that it was then commanded by Lappius who was to become one of Domitian's most powerful generals.

52   (*AE* 1967, 355)

Gaius Petillius Firmus, military tribune of the legion 4 Flavia (Felix), appointed as an arbitrator on the authority of the emperor Vespasian by ... tius Pegasus, legate of the emperor Vespasian Augustus with the rank of propraetor, fixed the boundaries ...

The inscription, which is in Latin, is from Zadar in Yugoslavia, on a boundary stone (*cippus*) now in the garden of the unoccupied St Demetrius monastery and probably brought there from the nearby hinterland during the Italian occupation of the city in World War II.

It is part of a boundary settlement and records the decision of Gaius Petillius Firmus who had been appointed as arbitrator of a number of conflicting claims by the consular legate, Pegasus.

Petillius' legion was a new formation by Vespasian on his accession
to the throne, and it remained in Dalmatia until 86: this is of some
assistance in dating the document and the career of Pegasus.

The tribune Petillius may well have been related to Vespasian's
famous general and son-in-law Quintus Petillius Cerialis, recorded
in **34**. More important is the identity of the legate, who must be
the eminent Flavian jurist Pegasus. All previous references to him
are in the literary and legal sources, with only the unusual 'Pegasus'
being preserved from his names. The new document, unfortunately, notes only the last letters of his gentile name '. . . tius';
however, it has been shown that the three missing letters before
'tius' must be 'Plo' (E. Champlin, 'Pegasus', *Zeitschrift für Papyrologie
und Epigraphik*, 32, 1978, pp. 269–78): no other combination of
three letters before 'tius' is known. Hence Pegasus could well be a
brother of D. (?L.) Plotius Grypus, suffect consul in 88.

Little is known of Pegasus' career. His consulate must have
occurred early in Vespasian's reign, and he was appointed to the
senior consular post of prefect of the city before its end. In addition,
an ancient commentator on the poet Juvenal claims that Pegasus
governed many provinces before becoming city prefect: the
inscription enables us to identify one of them, Dalmatia. Presumably, then, Pegasus moved from the consulate to Dalmatia, thence
to a second, more important consular province (such as Moesia)
and finally to the city prefecture.

53   (*ILS* 8704a = M&W 283)

(This pipe was laid) in the 9th consulship of the emperor
Vespasian and in the 7th of Titus, emperor, and when Gnaeus
Julius Agricola was legate of the emperor with the rank of
propraetor.

The inscription, which is in Latin, was found on a lead pipe
unearthed in Eastgate Street, Chester, in 1899, and now in the
Grosvenor Museum there. It is of considerable importance since it
contains one of the very few non-literary references to Agricola,
governor of Britain from *c.* 77 to 83 and father-in-law of the
historian Tacitus; and also since it is the earliest piece of datable
evidence we possess for the existence of the legionary fortress at
Chester, even though the inscription itself does not mention the
legion concerned.

Agricola's extraordinarily long tenure of Britain (twice the
normal period) indicates the high opinion held of his abilities by
the Flavian emperors, though this point is not stressed by Tacitus

in his biography of his father-in-law; but the fact that very little epigraphic evidence survives to attest to his existence is significant only in so far as it indicates the magnitude of the problems facing the ancient historian.

The reference to the consular years of Vespasian and Titus permit the inscription to be assigned to 79. There is the possibility that Agricola founded the fortress at Chester not long after his arrival in Britain, where he succeeded Frontinus (**48**) as governor, but, since piped water was available in the fortress by 79, it is more likely that the fortress was founded some years before, by Frontinus, for such an amenity would not be readily available in the early stages of construction. Two tombstones make it clear that it was the legion 2 Adiutrix that was brought to Chester as its first garrison force and that it came from Lincoln: *RIB* 258 (which is the inscription from the tombstone of Titus Valerius Pudens, a soldier of the legion 2 Adiutrix, who died in AD 76 and was buried at Lincoln) and *RIB* 475 (from the tombstone of Gaius Calventius Celer of the same legion, who was buried in Chester during the period 77–8).

54   (*ILS* 8682a)

Of the emperor Domitian Caesar Augustus Germanicus, under the control of Caec(ina) Paetus, Articuleius Paetus and Ninius Hasta.

The inscription, which is in Latin, is from a lead pipe found in Rome. Claudius' additions to Rome's system of aqueducts resulted inevitably in an increase in the number of officials needed to maintain them. Frontinus (*On the Aqued.* 2.116–18) remarks that Claudius set aside some 460 of his own slaves to help service them: in so doing he managed to complicate the bureaucratic process since there were already 240 state-owned slaves who performed this task. Claudius' additional men, however, remained his property; he was solely responsible for their upkeep and they were under his control. Again, more slaves meant more supervisors, and so he appointed one of his freedmen to control the new staff. His title was *procurator aquarum*; he did not replace the *curator* but rather assisted him – whilst all the time being responsible only to the emperor in person. By the time of Domitian, as our inscription shows, even more officials were needed. He preferred to adopt a different policy from Claudius', in that he co-opted senior senators to undertake the task of supervision. It would appear that Caecina Paetus, Articuleius Paetus and Ninius Hasta were given the title of *adiutores* (or 'assistants'), but there is some dispute on this point. All were of consular rank and, since the emperor is styled 'Germanicus' in the inscription, a title he did not use before 84, it is certain that these three held office in the period 84 to 96, a time when the *curator aquarum* was the senator Acilius Aviola. Obviously, then, they did not hold that post as some have argued. But whilst their precise function is not certain, we can be sure that men of their status had a fairly responsible position in the expanded hierarchy.

55 (*RIB* 1499, 1762 = S. *N–H* 321 b & i)

(From) cohort 6, the century of Lusius Suavis (built this).

(From Legion) 20 Valeria Victrix, cohort 10, the century of Julius Florentinus (built this).

These two centurial stones, with their Latin inscriptions, have been assigned to the sectors of Hadrian's wall near Milecastle 28 (cohort 6) and Turret 44b (cohort 10). Each British legion seems to have divided the length of wall assigned to it between its cohorts, and then subdivided each cohort's allocation among its constituent centuries. The century, the cohort and the legion marked each end of their lengths by the erection of an inscription. An examination of the hundreds of these so-called centurial stones that survive (either in the wall itself or perhaps in nearby farmhouses and other buildings) enables historians to determine the sections assigned to each unit. Construction of the 70-mile long structure began around AD 122, under the supervision of Platorius Nepos (**38**). Three legions and a large number of auxiliary units were employed; even a section of the fleet was involved. An inscription found in 1937 on the granary at Benwell attests to the work of the latter:

For the emperor Caesar Trajan Hadrian Augustus, a detachment of the British fleet (built this) when Aulus Platorius Nepos was legate of the emperor with the rank of propraetor. (*RIB* 1340 = S. *N–H* 317)

B.   Tributes to Particular Persons

The following twenty-one documents are all examples of inscriptions set up by private individuals or official bodies (e.g. town
councils) in honour of a person or to commemorate someone after
death. The selection falls into four parts, the first of which (**56** to
62) contains inscriptions dealing with senators; the second (**63** to
69) inscriptions dealing with men of equestrian status; the third (**70**
to **72**) inscriptions dealing with persons of the freedman class; and
finally (**73** to **77**) a brief miscellany illustrating several historical
facts and aspects. Whilst the inscriptions dealing with senators,
equestrians and freedmen contain much general and particular
historical information, to which we have drawn attention, one of
the most significant aspects of inscriptions of this kind is that they
are important pieces of data which help us to build a picture of the
growth and structure of an elaborate system of 'public service',
especially at the senatorial and equestrian levels, in the service of
the emperor. Each inscription that records a senator's or an
equestrian's public career is a piece of information that helps us to
create a general pattern both of the sort of official posts that
existed in the emperor's service and of the career structure
whereby a person progressed through the grades and offices. This
is one of the most important types of information that we can
obtain from inscriptions dealing with individual persons and
relating their official career; and we have tried to bring this out
clearly in our comments. The collections of Lewis and Reinhold
(vol. II) and Jones (vol. II) contain further examples of senatorial
and equestrian careers. Senatorial careers are to be found in Lewis
and Reinhold, section 30, and in Jones, ch. IV; equestrian careers
are in section 31 of Lewis and Reinhold and ch. IV of Jones; section
66 of Lewis and Reinhold contains a selection of freedmen
inscriptions, but, unfortunately, none of them records offices held
in the emperor's service. Jones, ch. V, however, does contain three
documents (nos 44–6) dealing with freedmen in the emperor's
service.

56   (*ILS* 966 = S 233)

To Titus (?) Domitius, son of Titus, of the tribe Voltinia,
Decidius, member of the college of three responsible for the
execution of justice, chosen by Tiberius Claudius Caesar
Augustus Germanicus to be the first quaestor to be in charge
of the treasury of Saturn for a three-year period without
selection by lot, praetor.

The inscription is from a monument at Rome and is in Latin. The subject, Titus (?) Domitius Decidius, has two claims to fame. Firstly, he was the father-in-law of Julius Agricola, the future governor of Britain, and secondly, he was, as the inscription tells us, chosen by the emperor Claudius to be the first quaestor to be in charge of the treasury of Saturn for a three-year period without selection by lot. The inscription thus becomes one of those instances in which the documentary evidence corroborates the literary sources. Suetonius, *Claudius* 24.2, says that Claudius, 'depriving them (the quaestors) of their official duties at Ostia and in Gaul, (he) restored to them the charge of the treasury of Saturn, which had in the meantime been administered by praetors, or by ex-praetors, as in our time' (Loeb translation). Tacitus, *Annals* 13.29, when speaking of administrative changes introduced by Nero in AD 56 to the Treasury of Saturn, says: 'The arrangement of this business had been variously and frequently altered. Augustus allowed the Senate to appoint commissioners; then, when corrupt practices were suspected in the voting, men were chosen by lot for the office out of the whole number of praetors. This did not last long, as the lot strayed away to unfit persons. Claudius then appointed quaestors, and that they might not be too lax in their duties from fear of offending, he promised them promotion out of the usual course. But what they lacked was the firmness of mature age, entering, as they did, on this office as their first step, and so Nero appointed ex-praetors of approved competency' (translated Church and Brodribb). Cassius Dio 60.24, under the year AD 44, says, 'He (Claudius) also did away with the praetors in charge of the finances, putting the business in the hands of quaestors, as it had been of old; these quaestors, however, were not annual magistrates . . . but the same two men attended to the business for three whole years. Some of these quaestors secured the praetorship immediately afterward and others drew a salary according to the estimate placed upon their administration of the office. The quaestors, then, were given charge of the finances in place of governorships in Italy outside of the city (for Claudius abolished all the latter positions)' (Loeb translation).

The inscription thus corroborates the literary sources on this administrative innovation of Claudius, whereby the emperor gained a tighter control over the often inefficient management of the public treasury, and confirms the statement of Dio that the quaestors were not only chosen by the emperor, but were appointed for a three-year period of office. Though Decidius is referred to as 'the first quaestor', we may assume that this is an abbreviated way of saying 'a member of the first college of two quaestors'.

The career of Domitius Decidius is given in ascending order, beginning with his vigintivirate office. It should be noted that no military service is recorded, nor, though he was of plebeian origin, did he hold either the tribunate of the plebs or the aedileship between the quaestorship and the praetorship; this may be the result of the 'promotion out of the usual course' mentioned by Tacitus. Domitius apparently did not reach the consulship. The inscription may have been set up during Claudius' lifetime, as that emperor is not referred to as 'the deified'.

Another inscription may be cited here, which demonstrates the same administrative reform of Claudius. This inscription (*ILS* 967 = S 234) is from the town of Suasa, in Umbria, is a dedicatory inscription and is in Latin.

To Lucius Coeidius, son of Lucius, of the Aniensian tribe, Candidus, military tribune of the legion 8 Augusta, member of the college of three responsible for the execution of justice, quaestor of Tiberius Caesar Augustus Germanicus, quaestor of the treasury of Saturn, commissioner for public records. This man, on his return from military service, Tiberius Claudius Caesar Augustus Germanicus presented with military gifts: a golden crown, a mural crown, a rampart crown, an untipped spear; and, since he had him amongst his own quaestors, in the same year he also ordered him to be quaestor of the treasury of Saturn. Set up at public expense.

The subject of this inscription appears to have taken part in Claudius' invasion of Britain in AD 43 as military tribune of the legion 8 Augusta and to have been decorated by Claudius on his return. The favour that he enjoyed from that emperor can be seen from the fact that he calls himself the emperor's quaestor, a very privileged position for a young man at the start of a career in the senate. The career on the inscription, however, mentions no senatorial offices after the quaestorship, and it may be that Coeidius either disgraced himself or died a premature death. It is also possible that the inscription was set up soon after his tenure of the office by his fellow citizens of Suasa from pride at this achievement of one of their local men.

57   (*ILS* 984 = M&W 97)

To ... legate with the rank of propraetor of the province of Moesia, commissioner for the Gallic census, prefect of the city for the second time. To this man the senate, on the proposal of the emperor Caesar Vespasian, his brother, set up a shield, after deferring legal suits for the sake of the honour, resolved a funeral appropriate to a man of censorial rank, and decreed that his statue should be placed in the forum of Augustus.

The inscription is from Rome, in Latin, and probably formed the base of the statue mentioned at the end. It is an interesting example of how inscriptions and literary sources can frequently both confirm and supplement each other and apparently contradict each other. The inscription is in a very mutilated state and the name of the person to whom the dedication is made is missing. However, the words 'Vespasian, his brother' are pretty certain; and therefore we can say, with equal certainty, that the dedicatee is none other than Vespasian's elder brother, Flavius Sabinus, who for a long time overshadowed his younger brother in public life and who played such an important part in the disturbed events of the year AD 69, before meeting his death at the hands of the troops of Vitellius. Some passages from Tacitus' *Histories* may be cited to illustrate the honours and offices given by the inscription.

Histories 3.75 (the 'obituary notice' after Sabinus' death): 'Such was the end of a man in no wise contemptible. In five and thirty campaigns he had served the State, and had gained distinction both at Rome and abroad. His blamelessness and integrity no one could question. He was somewhat boastful; this was the only fault of which rumour accused him in the seven years during which he had governed Moesia, and the twelve during which he was prefect of the city' (translated Church and Brodribb).

Histories 1.46 (immediately after the accession of Otho): 'Flavius Sabinus they (i.e. the Praetorian Guard of Otho) appointed prefect of the city, thus adopting Nero's choice, in whose reign he had held the same office, though many in choosing him had an eye to his brother Vespasian' (translated Church and Brodribb). From another source, Plutarch, *Otho* 5.4, we also learn that Galba had removed Sabinus from his office of prefect of the city and this is confirmed by Tacitus, *Histories* 1.14, where Ducennius Geminus is named as prefect of the city. The appointment by Otho, maintained by Vitellius, may have been Sabinus' appointment for the second time, as the inscription says.

Histories 4.47 (at a meeting of the senate early in AD 70): 'After this, on the motion of Domitian, the consulships conferred by Vitellius were cancelled, and the honours of a censor's funeral were paid to Sabinus; great lessons both of the mutability of fortune, ever

bringing together the highest honours and the lowest humilia-
tions' (translated Church and Brodribb). (The funeral, given at
state's expense, of a censor was especially splendid and spectacular
and may be compared with a Royal funeral in Britain.)

The documentary and the literary sources thus confirm and
supplement each other in many details. The inscription, moreover,
as restored, gives us a further piece of evidence concerning Flavius
Sabinus' career: between his tenure of the Moesian command and
that of prefect of the city, Sabinus held the important office of
commissioner for the census return of AD 61 of the Gallic
provinces, a consular appointment. This, indeed, raises problems,
since (i) Tacitus, *Annals* 14.46.2, gives the names of the three
consulars who carried out the Gallic census at this time and
Sabinus is not one of them; (ii) even if Sabinus held this position
and was then appointed at the end of AD 61 to the city prefecture,
there is not time between then and his death in AD 69 for the
twelve-year tenure of the office mentioned by Tacitus at *Histories*
3.75; (iii) any attempt to date Sabinus' appointment to the city
prefecture to before AD 61 and then to assume that he interrupted
his tenure temporarily with the Gallic census commission is made
difficult by the statement of Tacitus, *Annals* 14.42, that in AD 61
Pedanius Secundus, the city prefect, was murdered by his slaves.
The most recent attempt to solve these problems is that of J.
Nicols, *Vespasian and the Partes Flavianae*, pp. 26–30 (*Historia Einzelschrift* 28, Wiesbaden 1978). The essence of Nicols' argument is
that Sabinus was appointed to the city prefecture after his return
to Rome from Moesia around AD 56. For some unknown reason,
he resigned this post in about AD 58. In AD 61 he was appointed
to the Gallic census commission, but, on the death of Pedanius
Secundus, was reappointed city prefect and hence did not take up
the Gallic commission, one of the three men named by Tacitus
being appointed to replace him. Sabinus then continued as city
prefect during the rest of Nero's reign. After his dismissal from the
office by Galba, which, not surprisingly, the inscription does not
mention specifically, he was reappointed by Otho early in AD 69
and continued in office until his death in December AD 69. By
means of this reconstruction, it is possible to reach a total tenure
of twelve years for the prefecture, though, strictly speaking, it was
by means of *three* distinct appointments, whereas the inscription
says that he was prefect for the second time. Perhaps Vespasian,
who controlled the senate and the state at the time of the erection
of this inscription, refused to regard Sabinus' dismissal by Galba as
a legal act and therefore looked on his reappointment by Otho as
a reinstatement in a position which he had legally never vacated.

On this interpretation, Sabinus would indeed only have had *two* appointments to the office. The inscription also gives us the information, not recorded by Tacitus, that the censor's funeral was not the only honour accorded to Sabinus after his death; for a shield was set up in his honour, perhaps in the senate-house (the conjectural deferring of legal cases would emphasize the honour either of the shield or the funeral), and a statue was erected in the forum of Augustus. The shield may have been similar in style to that which Augustus describes in his *RG*, ch. 34: 'a golden shield was fixed in the Julian senate-house. The inscription of that shield testified that it was given to me by the senate and Roman people because of my uprightness and clemency and justice and sense of duty.' It should also be noted that, whereas Tacitus, *Histories* 4.47, says that the honorific motion was moved by Domitian, the inscription says that the mover was Vespasian himself. There is, perhaps, no conflict here, as the motion was probably moved by Domitian in the name of his father, who was still absent from Rome.

58   (*ILS* 986 = S 228)

To Tiberius Plautius, son of Marcus of the Aniensian tribe, Silvanus Aelianus, pontifex, priest of Augustus, member of the college of three for the casting and striking of bronze, silver and gold coinage, quaestor of Tiberius Caesar, legate of the 5th legion in Germany, urban praetor, legate and staff officer of Claudius Caesar in Britain, consul, proconsul of Asia, legate with the rank of propraetor of Moesia. Into this province he brought across more than 100 000 from the number of the Transdanubians, along with their wives and children and princes or kings, in order to pay tribute. He suppressed an incipient disturbance of the Sarmatians, even though he had sent a large part of his army to the expeditionary force in Armenia. He brought across to the river bank which he was protecting kings hitherto unknown or hostile to the Roman people, in order that they might pay homage to the Roman standards. To the kings of the Bastarnae and the Rhoxolani he sent back their sons and to the king of the Dacians his brothers; these had been captured or rescued from the enemy. From some of these kings he received hostages. By these measures he both secured and extended the peace of his province, also removing from the siege of Chersonesus, which is beyond the Borysthenes, the king of the Scythians. He was the first to relieve the grain supply of the Roman people by means of a great amount of wheat from that province. After he had been sent to Spain as legate and then recalled to the prefecture of the city, the senate honoured him during his prefecture with triumphal decorations, on the motion of the emperor Caesar Augustus Vespasian, in words which are written below from his oration:

'He was governor of Moesia in such a way that the honour of his triumphal decorations should not have been delayed to my time; except that as a result of the delay a greater honour befell him in his capacity of prefect of the city.'

The emperor Caesar Augustus Vespasian made him consul for the second time during the same tenure of the prefecture of the city.

The inscription, which is in Latin, is from the family tomb of the Plautii, near Tibur (modern Tivoli). There are several indications in the inscription which help us to date it and the career of its subject. Thus, from the fact that he was quaestor of Tiberius, his career began before AD 37; the fact that he accompanied Claudius to Britain in AD 43 as a staff-officer of praetorian standing (the career is given in ascending chronological order) means that he must have been over thirty years old in AD 43; and the fact that Vespasian is not referred to as 'the deified' would indicate that the inscription was set up after AD 70 (the year of Vespasian's return to Rome) and before AD 79 (the year of Vespasian's death). From other inscriptional evidence we know that the subject's first consulship was in AD 45, which would suggest a year early in the first decade AD for his birth, and that his second consulship was in AD 74 (held either with Vespasian's son, Domitian, or as suffect for Vespasian himself), at which date he would have been about seventy years old. Since the usual interval between consulship and proconsulship of Asia or Africa was ten to twelve years in the first century AD, his Asian proconsulship would have fallen in the middle to late 50s AD, i.e. under Nero's years. His governorship of Moesia probably extended from about AD 60 to AD 67 (in which year we know the name of another Moesian governor). The wording of the inscription suggests that his office of legate in Spain and his prefecture of the city were both conferred by Vespasian; and we can say definitely that he was still prefect of the city in AD 74, the year of his second consulship, in itself one of the rarest and highest distinctions open to a senator. A rough chronology of Plautius' career would perhaps run as follows:

> born : *c.* AD 5 (if plebeian) or *c.* AD 12 (if patrician)
> college of three etc. : *c.* AD 23 or *c.* AD 30

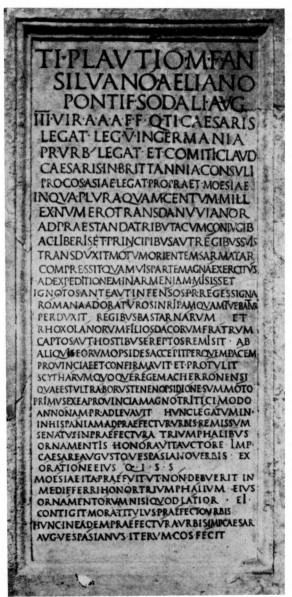

Document 58 The sepulchral inscription of Tiberius Plautius Silvanus. Reproduced by courtesy of Licinio Capelli.

quaestor of Tiberius : *c.* AD 30 or AD 37 (normal minimum age
  of *c.* 25)
legate of 5th legion : *c.* AD 32 or *c.* AD 39
urban praetor : *c.* AD 35 or *c.* AD 42 (normal minimum age of
  c. 30)
legate etc. of Claudius : *c.* AD 43–4
consul : AD 45 (normal minimum age of *c.* 42 for plebeians)
proconsul of Asia : *c.* AD 55
governor of Moesia : *c.* AD 60–7
legate in Spain : *c.* AD 70–*c.* AD 73
prefect of the city : *c.* AD 73–at least AD 74
consul II : AD 74 (with Domitian and as suffect for Vespasian)
died : before AD 79

Three points may be noted in this career: firstly, Plautius makes no
mention of an initial period of military service as a 'broad-stripe',
i.e. senatorial, tribune of a legion before his quaestorship; secondly,
his tenure of a legionary command before his praetorship is not
unusual at this date; and thirdly, Plautius makes no mention of
having held either the tribunate of the plebs or the aedileship
between his quaestorship and praetorship. This may suggest that
Plautius was of patrician status, patricians being exempted from
this step in the official career; and, indeed, it has been suggested
that he was the son of the patrician L. Aelius Lamia (consul in
AD 3) and had been adopted into the Plautius family, which at this
period was plebeian. If he were a patrician, it would be necessary
to raise the dates of his birth and of his offices as far as the
praetorship by several years, since patricians normally reached the
consulship at a much lower age than non-patricians. It may be,
however, that Plautius simply chose to omit this not very prestigious office from the record of his career. It is worthy of note that,
though Plautius was obviously a man of great distinction under the
Julio-Claudian emperors and Vespasian, there is only one mention
of him in our literary sources. Tacitus records, at *Histories* 4.33, that
the leading role in the ceremony initiating the work on the new
temple of Jupiter Capitolinus was taken by the pontifex Plautius
Silvanus, in the absence from the capital of the emperor. Moreover, the literary sources contain no reference to Plautius'
obviously important exploits on the Danube during his tenure of
the governorship of Moesia. In fact, there is no mention at all of
events on the Danube under the reign of Nero in our literary
sources. The inscription, therefore, is important to the historian in
two ways. Firstly, it is the record of the career of a highly
distinguished member of the Roman nobility in the service of the

state and the emperor. Secondly, and more importantly, it becomes our major source for events on the important Moesian sector of the Danube under Nero's reign. The Danube was, under the Flavian emperors and their second-century successors, to become the major trouble-spot in Rome's system of defences. The inscription shows us that as early as Nero's reign the pressures from the peoples across from the southern bank of the river were becoming explosively dangerous. A glance at a map will show where the tribes mentioned in the inscription lived and will give some idea of the extent of Plautius' operations – operations carried out with a weakened garrison-army, since in AD 62 he had had to send one of his three legions to help the operations of Corbulo in Armenia (hence the reference in the inscription). Plautius' response to these pressures was to try to syphon them off by 'transplanting' large numbers of the tribesmen, with their families, into the Roman province on the south bank of the river, in the hope that they would gradually learn to lead a settled life and to mingle with the local population. The fact that Vespasian proposed the award to him, several years after the event, of the triumphal decorations shows both Nero's jealous suspicions of his commanders towards the end of his reign and also the magnitude of Plautius' achieve-ments. It is interesting to note that another fragmentary inscrip-tion shows a governor of the neighbouring province of Pannonia carrying out similar operations to those of Plautius at about the same time and, again like Plautius, receiving triumphal decora-tions (perhaps also from Vespasian) for them. The inscription is M&W 274 (= *ILS* 985) and runs: 'To Lucius Tampius Flavianus, consul, proconsul of Africa, legate of the emperor with the rank of propraetor of Pannonia, commissioner for aqueducts . . . to him triumphal adornments . . . because he received hostages from the Transdanubians, investigated all the frontier-lines and brought the enemy across the river in order to pay taxes . . . Lucius Tampius Rufus.'

The inscription also shows us that the province of Moesia, originally a savage and primitive area of the Roman empire, was rapidly becoming settled and agriculturally prosperous. This is indicated by the fact that Plautius, as governor, was able to export wheat to help feed the population of Rome, which would mean that the province was now not only self-sufficient in grain production, but was even growing a surplus.

The Plautius Silvanus inscription is also cited by Lewis and Reinhold, pp. 115–16, and Jones, pp. 117–18.

59   (*ILS* 1005 = M&W 307)

To Lucius Funisulanus, son of Lucius, of the Aniensian tribe,
Vettonianus, military tribune of the legion 6 Victrix, quaestor
of the province of Sicily, tribune of the plebs, praetor, legate of
the legion IV Scythica, prefect of the treasury of Saturn,
commissioner of the Aemilian Way, consul, member of the
college of seven concerned with sacred banquets, legate with
the rank of propraetor of the province of Dalmatia, similarly of
the province of Pannonia, similarly of Upper Moesia, presented
[by the emperor Domitian Augustus Germanicus] in the Dacian
war with four crowns (mural, rampart, naval, golden), with four
untipped spears and with four pennants: to their patron (the
townspeople) gave as a gift.

The inscription is from Andautonia, in the province of Upper
Pannonia (modern Yugoslavia); it is in Latin.

This inscription is given mainly because it is a good example of
a distinguished senatorial career in the administration at the end
of the first century AD. Vettonianus was obviously a highly
talented and skilled administrator, whose career, after he had held
the vital office of praetor, was one of great distinction. The career
is given in ascending order, starting with the period of military
service and then progressing to and through the junior ranks
(quaestor, tribune of the plebs – the tribunate indicating that the
family was plebeian) of the official senatorial career. The praetorship, held normally in the early thirties, opened up the prospects
of holding administrative posts appropriate to a man of 'praetorian' standing (in Vettonianus' case, prefect of the main state
treasury and commissioner of one of Italy's arterial roads). The
consulship, usually held in the early forties, opened up the
prospects of the most senior administrative posts, which, in this
particular case, meant the governorship of a series of imperial
provinces containing large army groups. For a talented man, the
consulship was often accompanied by co-option into one of the
priestly colleges – a mark of great social distinction. Vettonianus
was co-opted into the college of seven with responsibility for sacred
banquets.

We may also note in the inscription an example of the workings
of *damnatio memoriae*, or condemnation of a dead person's memory. This was the fate suffered by 'bad' emperors (e.g. Gaius, Nero,
Domitian) and meant that their names were removed from all
official acts and records and usually from all private records. In this
case the 'condemned' emperor is Domitian, whose name has been
erased from the inscription; hence its appearance in square

brackets in the translation. In whichever of Domitian's Dacian wars it was that Vettonianus fought, he obviously distinguished himself, being decorated by the emperor no less than twelve times. We might also note that this inscription is one of the earliest records of the division into two of the important Danubian province of Moesia, a division probably caused by the large increase, under the Flavian emperors, of the legionary garrison of Moesia, which itself was caused by the ever-growing pressures on the province from across the Danube.

From other inscriptions which have been discovered concerning this man we can fill in further details of his public career. Thus we know that he began his career, before holding his military tribunate, as a member of the vigintivirate college. We also know that between his praetorship and consulship he held office as one of the commissioners for Rome's aqueducts and that after his consulship, as well as holding the provincial governorships mentioned in the inscription, he also was elected to membership of the priestly college of Augustus and was proconsul of Africa.

Some clues are available to help us date the inscription. The fact that Domitian's name has been erased makes it likely that it was put up before Domitian's death in AD 96. Since, from other evidence, the subject was probably consul in AD 78, he would have been proconsul of Africa about AD 92 or 93, there being usually a twelve- to fifteen-year interval between the posts. Since the proconsulate of Africa is not mentioned in our inscription, it seems likely that it was set up before that date, i.e. before AD 93, but after AD 86, the date of Domitian's first Dacian war. It was probably after his governorship of Moesia, but before his African proconsulate, that Vettonianus received the great distinction of a second priesthood. He appears to have died in May AD 98, and to have been buried near the Latin Way. This inscription is also cited by Lewis and Reinhold.

60 (*IGRR* III.551 = *TAM* II.563 = M&W 314)

To Publius Baebius, son of Publius, of the Ufentine tribe, Italicus, quaestor of Cyprus, tribune, legate of Gallia Narbonensis, praetor, legate of the legion 14 Gemina Martia Victrix, honoured in the war in Germany by the emperor with a golden crown, a mural crown and a rampart crown and with three untipped spears and three (?) pennants, legate with the rank of propraetor of the emperor Caesar [Domitian] Augustus [Germanicus] of Lycia and Pamphylia, benefactor and founder and holy giver of justice: the people of Tlos.

The inscription is from the town of Tlos in the province of Lycia and Pamphylia, in Greek, and from a statue set up to the subject by the townspeople of Tlos. It can be dated to before AD 90 because Baebius Italicus is known to have held the consulship in this year, and the inscription does not record the consulship. Hence the inscription was set up during Italicus' term as praetorian governor of Lycia and Pamphylia. The two names erased on the inscription from the titles of the emperor must be restored to 'Domitian' and 'Germanicus'; and the erasure took place after Domitian's assassination in AD 96 as a result of the *damnatio memoriae*, or condemnation of his memory. The inscription records Italicus' senatorial career in ascending order, though omitting any reference to a period of military service prior to his holding the first senatorial office, the quaestorship, during which he served in the senatorial province of Cyprus. After holding the tribunate of the plebs, thus indicating a plebeian senator, he served as legate (of the proconsul) of the senatorial province of Gallia Narbonensis, before holding the vital praetorship, which opened up to him the prospect of appointments in the administration at praetorian level. His first praetorian posting was as commander of the famous 14th legion and it was in this capacity that he served with distinction in Germany where 14 Gemina formed part of the garrison. The known date of Italicus' consulship makes it certain that the 'German war' was Domitian's war against the Chatti, fought in AD 83. After his legionary command, probably of three years' duration, Italicus was appointed to the praetorian imperial province of Lycia and Pamphylia and in this capacity he appears to have conferred some benefit on the city of Tlos, which set up in his honour the statue bearing this inscription, in which is recorded in highly flattering terms the gratitude of the citizens. It will be noticed that whereas Italicus' public career up to his praetorship was entirely in the traditional senatorial field, after the praetorship his public appointments are both in the emperor's service. No further administrative appointment is known for Italicus after his consulship; and we may regard him as one of the many capable senators whose administrative appointments were all at praetorian level and for whom the consulship represented the peak and closing point of their public career. We may note the extremely fulsome language of the inscription, which refers to Baebius Italicus as 'founder' and 'holy giver of justice'. This 'flowery' language is very common in inscriptions set up by Greek communities to their Roman masters.

61   (*ILS* 9485 = M&W 315)

To Gaius Caristanius, son of Gaius, of the Sergian tribe, Fronto, military tribune, prefect of cavalry of the Bosporan squadron, adlected into the senate among the ex-tribunes, promoted among the ex-praetors, legate with the rank of propraetor of Pontus and Bithynia, legate of the emperor, now deified, Vespasian Augustus of the legion 9 Hispana in Britain, legate with the rank of propraetor of the emperor, now deified, Titus Caesar Augustus and of the emperor Domitian Caesar Augustus of the province of Pamphylia and Lycia; to its patron, the colony (of Antioch in Pisidia).

Titus Caristanius Calpurnianus Rufus, because of his (sc. Fronto's) meritorious acts, looked after this.

The inscription is from Antioch in Pisidia, in Latin, and from a dedicatory statue set up by the citizens of Antioch in honour of the subject. It can be dated to before AD 90, because Fronto is known to have held in this year the consulship, not recorded in the inscription; but after AD 81, because both Vespasian and Titus are referred to as 'deified'. The fact that Domitian is not called Germanicus suggests that the inscription was set up before AD 84, the year in which Domitian assumed this title. The inscription has several points of interest. Caristanius Fronto is known to have been of Eastern origin, from the province of Galatia in Asia Minor. He was of an equestrian family, as is seen from his military career, which records the command of a squadron of auxiliary cavalry. He was adlected or enrolled into the senate, probably by Vespasian during his presence in the Eastern provinces in AD 70, among the senators who had held the office of tribune. He then received a further promotion within the senate to join the senators who had held the office of praetor; this probably took place during the joint censorship of Vespasian and Titus during the years AD 73–4. The power of adlection was one of the means whereby the emperor could incorporate talented men of non-senatorial background into the senate with a rank appropriate to their age, thus obviating the necessity of their going through all the junior grades of a senatorial career in competition with much younger men. By his adlection, firstly among the ex-tribunes and then among the ex-praetors, Fronto could be regarded as having fulfilled all the necessary preliminaries to holding the positions in the imperial administration, for which the praetorship was the qualificatory office. The first administrative post held by Fronto was as praetorian legate of the proconsul of the senatorial province of Pontus and Bithynia. This would probably have occurred about AD 75–6. The next posting was as legionary commander in Britain under Julius Agricola – a significant step on Vespasian's part in that he ventured to fly in the face of traditional Roman prejudice by appointing an Easterner to command Roman troops in the Western part of the empire. After Vespasian's death, Titus appointed him to the praetorian legateship of the imperial province of Lycia and Pamphylia, a position in which he was retained by Domitian on his accession. It was probably during his tenure of this office that the citizens of the colony of Antioch in Pisidia chose him as their official patron to represent their interests at Rome and this statue and inscription were set up in gratitude for some service to the colony performed by Fronto. The career of Fronto, which was crowned by the consulship in AD 90, is significant, because he is one of the first Easterners to enter the Roman senate and to find employment in the senatorial side of the imperial administration. This process, whereby Roman prejudices against Easterners was gradually overcome, was to continue to grow under the Flavian emperors and their successors. But it will be noted that Fronto's provincial governorships were both held in the Eastern provinces of the empire, not the Western provinces, where the presence of an Eastern governor might well have aroused hostile criticism. Note too that in this inscription the name of Domitian has not been erased, as was commonly done after that emperor's death.

For further examples of imperial adlection or enrolment, both into the senate and into the ranks of the patricians, see the career of Gnaeus Domitius ... Curvius Tullus, cited by Lewis and Reinhold, II, p. 123, and of Gaius Julius Cornulus Tertullus, cited by Jones, II, p. 126.

62   (*ILS* 1061 = S. *N–H* 225)

To Lucius Minicius, son of Lucius of the Galesian tribe, Natalis Quadronius Verus, consul, proconsul of the province of Africa, augur, legate of the emperor with the rank of propraetor of the province of Lower Moesia, commissioner for public works and sacred buildings, commissioner for the Flaminian Way, prefect of the alimentary system, legate of the emperor of the Legion 6 Victrix in Britain, praetor, tribune of the plebs as the emperor's candidate, quaestor as candidate of the deified Hadrian and at the same time legate of his father, the proconsul, of the Carthaginian diocese of the province of Africa, military tribune of the legion 1 Adiutrix Dutiful and Faithful, similarly of the legion 11 Claudia Dutiful and Faithful, similarly of the legion 14 Gemina Martia Victrix, member of the college of three for the casting and striking of bronze, silver and gold coinage, patron of the municipality, commissioner for the shrine of Hercules the Victor: the town councillors of Tibur dedicated this, from money that had been contributed, to an outstandingly exemplary member of the college of five.

The inscription, which is in Latin, is from the town of Tibur (modern Tivoli), near Rome. Some indications of dating can be obtained from the inscription and from other documentary sources. Thus, from the reference to 'the deified Hadrian' in the inscription, it must be after 10 July AD 138, the date of Hadrian's death. From other inscriptions we know that the subject was consul, perhaps in the year AD 139, and proconsul of Africa perhaps in AD 149–50. Another inscription, from Barcino (modern Barcelona) in the Spanish province of Tarraconensis, shows that his father may have been proconsul of Africa about AD 121–2. This enables us to assign a date to our subject's quaestorship, which he held whilst concurrently acting as his father's legate in Africa. From yet another inscription we know that he had held the office of praetor by AD 129 for it tells us that in this year he won the chariot race at the Olympic Games as a man of praetorian standing. We also know, from a further inscription, that the subject was born at Barcino. It would appear from our inscription that Minicius Natalis was chosen by the municipality of Tibur as their patron at Rome and was appointed by the Tiburtines as an honorary magistrate in the governing college of five.

The inscription is cited here mainly as a good example of a successful senatorial career in the imperial administration in the early and middle second century AD. The subject is a good illustration of the ever-growing number of men from the Western provinces, especially Spain, the birthplace of both Trajan and Hadrian, who made successful careers in the government of the empire. The career, after the consulship, the African proconsulate and the priesthood, is given in descending chronological order as far as his patronate of Tibur. The first public office was in the college of three responsible for the minting of coinage, which formed part of the vigintivirate. Members of this branch of the vigintivirate were often of patrician standing and marked out for a rapid and responsible career. After this office, held about the eighteenth or nineteenth year, the young Minicius served for at least three years as a 'broad-stripe' (i.e. senatorial) military tribune in the army. At about the age of twenty-five he was elected to the office of quaestor, which gave admission to the senate, and two years later to the office of tribune of the plebs. In both these offices he was marked out for preferential treatment by being 'Caesar's candidate', i.e. recommended by the emperor and therefore automatically elected. As quaestor he served on his father's staff in the senior senatorial province of Africa, governing one of the most important administrative districts of the province. His holding of the tribunate of the plebs shows that Minicius was not of patrician family. At about the age of thirty Minicius held the office of praetor, the key office which opened up the possiblility of holding responsible administrative posts appropriate to a man of praetorian standing. In Minicius' case these were three: the commissionership of one of the main roads of Italy; followed by the prefecture responsible for the administration of the system of state aid to the parents of poor children; and finally the command of a legion, usually for about three years. At about his forty-second year, Minicius was chosen consul, and probably about the same time given the great social distinction of membership of the priestly college of augurs. The consulship opened up to him the prospect of administrative employment at a higher level; and his consular appointments in the emperor's service were two: the governorship of the important armed province of Lower Moesia and the commissionership responsible for the public buildings and temples of Rome. About twelve years after his consulship, when he would be in his middle fifties, Minicius became eligible to draw lots with another consul of the same seniority for the proconsulates of Asia and Africa, whose tenure was, as with all senatorial provinces, for one year. Like his father, Minicius drew Africa. His career spans the reigns of three emperors: Trajan, Hadrian and Antoninus Pius.

63   (*ILS* 8995 = E&J 21)

Gaius Cornelius, son of Gnaeus, Gallus, Roman Knight, after the defeat of the monarchs by Caesar, son of the deified, first prefect of Alexandria and Egypt, victor in two battles of the revolt of the Thebaid within 15 days, in which he defeated the enemy, stormer of 5 cities: Boresis, Coptus, Ceramice, Great Diospolis, Ophieum. He captured the leaders of those rebellions; he took an army across the cataract of the Nile, into which place arms had not been carried before either by the Roman people or the kings of Egypt; he reduced the Thebaid, the common object of fear to all the kings; he received envoys of the king of the Ethiopians at Philae and accepted that king into his protection; he set up a monarch at Triacontaschoenus, a district of Arabia. He gives this gift to his native gods and to the Nile, his helper.

The inscription, which is in Latin (and immediately followed by a Greek translation), was found on the island of Philae, beyond the first cataract of the Nile, and is now in the Cairo Museum. The original stone was torn down from a temple wall and broken into two pieces. The upper part of the stone contains a picture of a horseman striking a prostrate foe and an Egyptian inscription of ten lines. This Egyptian inscription gives a precise date: 15 April 28 BC, i.e. in the very first year of direct Roman rule in Egypt. The lower part of the stone contains our inscription and its Greek translation. The subject of the inscription, and the person setting it up, is the famous Gaius Cornelius Gallus, the close friend of Augustus and his first appointment of a prefect of Egypt of equestrian rank. The rather tragic story of Gallus' prefecture and his disgrace and suicide is well known. The main cause of his disgrace seems to have been his arrogance and conceit. Dio Cassius, 53.23, says that he 'set up statues of himself in virtually the whole of Egypt and he inscribed all the deeds he had done on the Pyramids'. The present inscription, with its grandiose and boastful language, bears lucid testimony to Gallus' inflated opinion of himself and his achievements, though it should be noted that he is no more boastful than many members of the nobility had been in inscriptions of the Republic, and certainly not nearly as boastful as his former friend, Augustus, in the *RG*.

64   (*ILS* 1349 = S 258)

To Gaius Baebius, son of Publius, of the Claudian tribe, Atticus, member of the college of two for the administering of justice, senior centurion of the legion 5 Macedonica, prefect of the communities of Moesia and Treballia, prefect of the communities in the Maritime Alps, military tribune of the eighth praetorian cohort, senior centurion for a second time, procurator of Tiberius Claudius Caesar Augustus Germanicus in Noricum: the community of the Saevates and the Laianci.

The inscription, which is in Latin, comes from the town of Julium Carnicum, in the district of north-east Italy known as Venetia. The town was presumably the home of the subject and it is there that the dedication was made by the community of the Saevates and Laianci, both tribes of Noricum, where Baebius Atticus had been procurator. The inscription illustrates well the practice pursued by the early emperors of recruiting a capable municipal magistrate into the army with the rank of senior centurion and then employing him as prefect in charge of a number of still uncivilized tribal communities within a province, a post that would demand a man of toughness and ability. After holding two such posts, Atticus was moved to Rome as an officer in the Praetorian Guard and from there was transferred back to legionary service as senior centurion for a second time. On completion of this service Atticus, if he did not already possess it, was given equestrian rank by Claudius and made equestrian governor, or procurator, of the province of Noricum. We would thus be able to see in this career the beginnings of what is frequently called the 'praetorian career', whereby a man who is not of equestrian birth or rank acquires this by serving in a given sequence of posts in the army, passing from a legionary senior centurionate to tribunate in the armed forces at Rome, back to a second senior centurionate in the legions. He is then qualified to be employed in a series of administrative posts in the equestrian public service, including financial and administrative procuratorships. We might note that it was under the reign of Claudius that the title of equestrian governors of provinces became regularly 'procurator' instead of 'prefect'.

The career of Marcus Bassaeus Rufus, cited by Jones (no. 42), is a good example of a 'praetorian career'. Jones comments that, 'Ex-centurions normally held three military tribunates in the forces stationed at Rome (the *vigiles* or night watch, the urban cohorts under the city prefect and the praetorians) before rising to procuratorships and the higher prefectures. Then followed provincial procuratorships, then a ministry at Rome . . . and then the four great prefectures'.

65 (*ILS* 1447 = M&W 338)

To Sextus Caesius, son of Sextus, Propertianus, priest of Ceres, at Rome procurator of the emperor in charge of the patrimony and the department of inheritances and the department of petitions, military tribune of the legion 4 Macedonica, prefect of the Third cohort of Spaniards, presented with an untipped spear and a golden crown, member of the college of four for the administration of justice, member of the college of four appointed every five years: the townspeople set this up to their patron.

The inscription is from Mevania, in Umbria, and is in Latin. It is from a statue set up by the people of Mevania to their fellow citizen Sextus Caesius Propertianus. The official positions held by Propertianus are given in descending order of importance and of tenure, with the local municipal offices at the end.

The inscription is particularly interesting as it almost certainly records one of the first equestrian officials to head a major secretarial bureau in the imperial civil service. Tacitus, *Histories* I.58.1, says that Vitellius, on his elevation to the principate, distributed the civil service posts normally held by freedmen among Roman knights. He did this whilst still in his German province. The legion 4 Macedonica, which was Propertianus' last military posting before his imperial civil service positions, was one of Vitellius' legions in Germany and was disbanded by Vespasian soon after his accession. Hence it is certain that Propertianus was one of the equestrian officers appointed by Vitellius to head his imperial civil service bureaux; and the fact that the emperor was Vitellius will explain the absence of his name on the inscription. For Vitellius suffered the process of *damnatio memoriae* or condemnation of his memory. The scarcity of qualified equestrians on the German front may well explain the cumulation of positions held by Propertianus, who was put simultaneously in charge of three departments. The innovation of Vitellius was of great significance. It was obviously aimed at winning the support of the equestrian class; and, though Vespasian reverted to the Julio-Claudian practice of heading the bureaux with freedmen (see *ILS* 1519 = M&W 203), a precedent had been created, to which Domitian and his successors returned, thereby gradually creating the elaborate and powerful secretarial branch of the equestrian administration. Of Propertianus' further career we know nothing. He would have lost his positions on the downfall of Vitellius; for Vespasian, as we have seen, reverted to the Julio-Claudian practice of using Greek freedmen to head the secretarial bureaux. The fact that his fellow-citizens of Mevania continued to use him as their 'patron' – that is, to represent their interests with the emperor at Rome – would seem to indicate that Propertianus did not suffer any loss of personal influence with Vespasian, despite his allegiance to Vitellius. His career in public life had begun, as was frequent with men of equestrian origin, in the field of local, municipal administration, perhaps early in the reign of Nero, when he served as a member of Mevania's governing body of four and then on the town's quinquennially elected body of four, whose functions were similar to those of the censors at Rome. He then entered the imperial army as an equestrian officer, firstly commanding a cohort of auxiliary infantry, in which capacity he probably won the military decorations mentioned in the inscription, and then moving on to one of the equestrian military tribunates of the legion 4 Macedonica. It was whilst he was serving in this position in Germany that the downfall of Nero, the accession of Galba and the discontent of the German legions with this latter resulted in the rebellion that brought Vitellius to the throne. Why Propertianus did not continue his career in the normal way under Vespasian must remain a mystery. Perhaps Vespasian, while not holding this former Vitellian officer in disgrace, was reluctant to give him further employment; or perhaps Propertianus himself made the decision to retire from public life and live the life of a prosperous gentleman, either at Rome or in Mevania.

66   (*ILS* 9200 = M&W 372)

To Gaius Velius, son of Salvius, Rufus, senior centurion of the legion 12 Fulminata, prefect of detachments of the following nine legions: 1 Adiutrix, 2 Adiutrix, 2 Augusta, 8 Augusta, 9 Hispana, 13 Gemina, 20 Victrix, 21 Rapax, tribune of the 13th Urban cohort, leader of the African and Mauretanian army with the purpose of suppressing the tribes which are in Mauretania, presented with gifts by the emperor Vespasian and the emperor Titus in the Jewish war: with a rampart crown, neck chains, medallions and armlets; likewise presented with gifts: a mural crown, two spears, two banners, and in the war with the Marcomanni, Quadi and Sarmatians, against whom he made an expedition through the kingdom of Decebalus, king of the Dacians, (presented) with a mural crown, two spears and two banners, procurator of the emperor Caesar Augustus Germanicus of the province of Raetia with full judicial powers. He was sent to Parthia and brought back Epiphanes and Callinicus, the sons of King Antiochus, to the emperor Vespasian along with a considerable number of tribute-paying subjects. Marcus Alfius, son of Marcus, of the Fabian tribe, Olympiacus, standard-bearer and veteran soldier of the legion 15 Apollinaris (erected this).

The inscription is from Heliopolis (modern Baalbek) in Syria and is in Latin. It is from a statue set up to his former commander by an officer of one of the legions of the Pannonian garrison, 15 Apollinaris. The officer's *cognomen*, Olympiacus, would suggest that he is of Eastern, Greek birth. The career of the subject, Gaius Velius Rufus, which is set out in such detail, is a fascinating record of the life of a talented officer of non-senatorial status under the Flavian emperors. After serving in many parts of the Roman empire, in the course of which he was entrusted with several independent commissions, Rufus was transferred to the equestrian branch of the imperial administrative service in the emperor's provinces on the Danube. It is difficult to relate Rufus' military service, as the inscription does not record his postings in chronological sequence. His service appears to have started as senior centurion of the legion 12 Fulminata, in which capacity he served with distinction under Vespasian and Titus in the Jewish War. The legion 12 Fulminata formed part of the army assigned to the Jewish campaign. The inscription does not record any military service before the senior centurionate; and if this was his first post, it could be an indication that he was not originally of equestrian rank. His next posting would appear to have been the mission into Parthia, recounted at the end of the inscription, which was more of a diplomatic than a military operation. The story of the deposition of King Antiochus of Commagene and the incorporation of his kingdom into the province of Syria in AD 72 is narrated by Josephus, *Jewish War* 7, 7.243. From Josephus we learn that resistance to the Roman occupation was offered by Antiochus' two sons, Epiphanes and Callinicus, who fled for refuge to the Parthian king. Their extradition was demanded by Vespasian, and the Parthian king, pressed with problems elsewhere, agreed to this. The inscription confirms the evidence of the literary sources, which show that it was common practice to entrust diplomatic missions of this kind to centurions (see, for example, Tacitus, *Annals* 2.65, 13.9, 15.5; *Histories* 2.58). The 'considerable number of tribute-paying subjects' mentioned in the inscription refers probably to the supporters of Epiphanes and Callinicus, who fled along with the princes into Parthia. Their restoration to Commagene would put them in the class of Rome's tribute-paying provincial subjects.

Rufus' next posting would appear to have been his special command as leader of a force made up of detachments from nine legions, drawn from the provinces of Britain and Upper Germany. Neither the size of the detachments nor the purpose of the resulting force is stated, but it is tempting to associate it with Domitian's war against the Chatti, fought in AD 83. Note that the inscription only records in detail eight legions instead of nine. Carelessness on the part of the engraver has caused him to omit the legion 11 Claudia. We are similarly left in the dark concerning the size and date of the 'African and Mauretanian army', which again appears to have been a specially formed 'task force'; it is, however, tempting to associate it with Domitian's Mauretanian war, fought *c*. AD 84–5. This part of the inscription seems to run in chronological sequence; hence it seems that after his command of the detachments of the nine legions, Rufus was promoted to the command of the 13th Urban cohort, which, despite its name, was permanently stationed at Carthage in North Africa, and that during this posting he was put in command of the special force operating in Mauretania. About four years later we find him again leading a special expeditionary force, this time in Domitian's war against the transdanubian tribes of the Marcomanni, Quadi and Sarmatians. From our literary sources we know that this war broke out whilst Domitian's armies were fighting against those of Decebalus in Dacia in the years AD 88–9 and that Domitian was forced to sign a peace treaty with Decebalus in order to deal with this serious new threat. The conclusion of peace enabled Domitian to send this special force, drawn probably from the army that had been operating in Dacia, through the kingdom of Decebalus and so to attack the hostile tribes in the rear as well as from the front. Once again Rufus' service was rewarded with prestigious military decorations. His army career, which had taken him to the Eastern provinces, to Germany, to Africa and to the Danubian lands and which had extended over at least eighteen years, came to an end soon after this, when Domitian appointed him as financial officer, or procurator, of the provinces of Pannonia and Dalmatia, an area known generally as Illyricum. This post normally carried with it a salary of 200 000 sesterces a year. In this capacity Rufus was directly responsible to the emperor for the financial administration of this important area of the Roman empire. The final promotion in Rufus' career was to the equestrian governorship, also called a procuratorship, of Raetia, with full judicial powers, which included the power of capital punishment.

Rufus' long and distinguished career in the service of at least three emperors may be taken as a typical example of the use made by the emperors of equestrian army officers in the administration of the empire. The long and varied experience acquired in the army was regarded as qualifying a man for administrative positions in the emperor's provinces, in those areas in which military and civilian functions would frequently coincide. Rufus' army commands reveal a growing tendency to form special expeditionary forces by taking detachments from several legions, rather than move the legion itself from its permanent quarters; and is indicative, too, of a tendency for equestrian officers to assume functions which might traditionally be regarded as appropriate to a senator.

The increasing social mobility of the imperial age can be well illustrated by the career of Rufus. Himself, in all probability, of non-equestrian origin, he acquired equestrian status through his military achievements. His descendants were then able to progress upwards into the senatorial class, and we know of at least two senatorial descendants of Rufus, one of whom, Decimus Velius Rufus, was 'ordinary consul' in AD 178.

A word on the dating of the inscription: it was almost certainly set up during Domitian's lifetime, as it would be difficult to believe that the hated name would have been inscribed after AD 96 and that emperor's *damnatio memoriae*, or condemnation of his memory; that the name escaped erasure after AD 96 must be ascribed to chance. Since the last reasonably sure date in the inscription is the war of AD 88–9, we may say that the inscription was engraved between this date and AD 96, probably close to the latter date in view of Rufus' two intervening offices. One cannot say why M. Alfius Olympiacus, of the legion 15 Apollinaris, should erect this monument to Rufus at this time and in Heliopolis, unless he had previously served in the Jewish War in the legion 12 Fulminata under Rufus' command.

Finally, we might note that Rufus' military service, if it did in fact commence with the senior centurionate, has similarity to the so-called 'praetorian career', in that he advances from the senior centurionate to a tribunate in one of the 'urban' military units. He does not, however, hold the post either of tribune of a cohort of the praetorian guard or of senior centurion for the second time; perhaps he was exempted from these posts by his distinguished service in his independent commands.

This inscription is also cited by Lewis and Reinhold.

67   (*ILS* 1374 = M&W 336)

To Gaius Minicius, son of Gaius, of the tribe Velina, Italus, member of the college of four for the administration of justice, prefect of the 5th cohort of Gallic cavalry, prefect of the 1st cohort of Breucian cavalry of Roman citizens, prefect of the second cohort of Varcian cavalry, military tribune of the legion 6 Victrix, prefect of the 1st cavalry squadron of individual Roman citizens, presented by the deified Vespasian with gifts: a gold crown and an untipped spear, procurator of the province of Hellespont, procurator of the province of Asia which he governed on the emperor's command in place of the proconsul who had died, procurator of the provinces of Lugdunensis and Aquitania, likewise of Lactora, prefect of the grain supply, prefect of Egypt, priest of the deified Claudius: the town councillors decreed (this).

The inscription is from Aquileia in Northern Italy and is in Latin. It is from the marble base of a bronze statue set up in Italus' honour as the result of a decree passed by the town councillors of Aquileia. The text of this decree is inscribed on the side of the statue base and although it is in a rather mutilated condition, we can learn from it that Italus may have been a local man who had used the influence he possessed as a very senior equestrian official at Rome to obtain a favour from the ruling emperor, Trajan; and it was on this account that the statue was erected. The names of the consuls in office at Rome are appended to the decree, and from these names we can date it to AD 105.

The inscription itself is a very good example of a highly successful equestrian career in the imperial administration; the offices are given in ascending sequence of importance. After beginning his career in local government as a member of the governing body of four of Aquileia (cf. document 65), Italus entered the army as an equestrian officer, holding five different commands of the sort held by equestrian officers. His military service took place, mainly in Germany, under Vespasian, by whom he was decorated. After his military service, Italus was appointed as financial officer, or procurator, of the Hellespontine financial district. This was a new financial area created by Vespasian during his reorganization of the empire's finances. Italus probably held this post early in Domitian's reign. He was then appointed procurator in Asia. This province was traditionally the most jealously guarded area of the senate's administration, where ordinary revenues were administered by the proconsul's quaestor. Italus' position probably entailed the supervision of revenues that were of direct concern to the emperor's side of the government. The incident related in the inscription, in which Italus took over the government of the province on the death of the proconsul, may refer to the execution, whilst he was still in office, of Civica Cerealis, which was carried out on Domitian's orders *c.* AD 88. It is indicative of the emperor's ever-growing control of all spheres of government that his own representative was instructed to act as governor of the province instead of the senatorial quaestor. From Asia Italus was transferred to further financial procuratorships in the Gallic provinces, and from there he was promoted to one of the top positions in the equestrian administration, the prefecture responsible for the grain supply of the city of Rome. His next, and final, position was a further promotion, perhaps *c.* AD 100, to the prefecture of Egypt, which ranked second only to the prefecture of the Praetorian Guard in the equestrian service. A copy of a letter written by Italus during his tenure of Egypt is included as document **88** of this collection. It was probably at the time of his appointment as prefect of the grain supply that Italus received the honour of the priesthood of the cult of the deified emperor Claudius. Since Italus was already Prefect of Egypt when the inscription was set up in AD 105, his promotion to the first prefecture probably occurred under Nerva's reign or at the beginning of Trajan's. His career in the service of five emperors spanned a period of more than thirty years and shows both the variety of employment available to a talented official of equestrian rank and the continuity of administration from one emperor to another. His employment by Domitian, it will be noted, had no harmful effect on the course of his career under that emperor's successors.

68 (*ILS* 1448 = M&W 347)

Gnaeus Octavius Titinius Capito, prefect of a cohort, military tribune, presented with an untipped spear and a rampart crown, procurator in charge of correspondence and the patrimony, for a second time in charge of correspondence of the deified Nerva and on his instigation presented with the praetorian decorations in accordance with a decree of the senate, for a third time in charge of correspondence of the emperor Nerva Caesar Trajan Augustus Germanicus, prefect of the Watch, gave this as a gift.

The inscription is from Rome, in Latin, and is from a dedicatory offering set up by the subject, Titinius Capito. It is an inscription full of interesting pieces of information. Firstly, it can be dated between 25 January AD 98 and 8 August AD 117, because Nerva is referred to as 'the deified', showing that he is dead, whilst Trajan, by the absence of this distinction, is shown to be still alive. It will be noted that Capito served under three emperors, of whom only the last two are named (Nerva and Trajan). The first can only be Domitian, whose name is suppressed because of his suffering *damnatio memoriae*, or condemnation of his memory, after his death. The inscription shows us that Capito, after serving in the army as prefect of a cohort of auxiliary infantry and then (equestrian) military tribune of a legion and in the course of this service winning the highest military decorations, entered the secretarial side of Domitian's civil service in charge of the very important department of imperial correspondence (united, at this time, with the control of the imperial patrimony), a post in which he was retained by both Nerva and Trajan. As so often happens in a revolution, the political leaders may be swept away, but continuity of government is maintained within the administration.

Domitian's senior head of department was so valuable a public servant that he had to be retained in his post. We should note that the appointment by Domitian of the knight Capito to the senior secretariat is a reversion to the precedent created by Vitellius of replacing freedmen in the bureaucracy with men of equestrian status, a process that continues and increases under Domitian's successors. Note also that Capito, an equestrian, receives as a reward for good service the insignia (decorations of rank) of a senator of praetorian standing, on the motion of the emperor; this becomes the regular way of honouring senior members of the equestrian civil service. We should also note that Capito was finally promoted from the secretariat to one of the most senior equestrian offices, prefect of the *vigiles*, or 'watch', of the city of Rome. Within the ever-growing equestrian branch of the administration promotion to the top posts, the great prefectures of the Watch, the Grain Supply, Egypt and the Praetorian Guard, was by way of either the provincial procuratorships or the senior secretarial posts at Rome. It was possible for an equestrian to hold both a provincial procuratorship and a senior secretaryship during his career but the secretarial post at Rome was senior to the provincial procuratorship. Capito is mentioned several times in the letters of the Younger Pliny as a man of culture and a friend of literature.

69   (*ILS* 1339)

To Tiberius Claudius, son of Tiberius of the Palatine tribe, Secundinus Lucius Statius Macedo, senior centurion of the legion 4 Flavia Felix, tribune of the 1st cohort of the Watch, tribune of the 11th Urban cohort, tribune of the 8th Praetorian cohort, senior centurion for a second time, prefect of the legion 2 Trajana Fortis, procurator in charge of the 5 per cent tax on inheritances, procurator of the provinces of Lugdunensis and Aquitania, financial secretary of the emperor, prefect of the grain supply: Lucius Saufeius Julianus, to his most excellent friend.

The inscription, which is in Latin, comes from the city of Aquileia in Northern Italy. It was the home of the subject and it was there that the dedication was made by L. Saufeius Julianus. The inscription is a good illustration of the process seen in embryo in *ILS* 1349 (= S 258 = **64** of this collection) and M&W 372 (= **66** of this collection), the so-called 'praetorian career', which led to the acquisition by a soldier of the rank of senior centurion and of equestrian status and employment in the equestrian branch of the imperial administration. Statius Macedo, as well as serving as senior centurion for a second time in a legion, also spent some time as prefect of the legion 2 Trajana Fortis, one of the Egyptian legions. The Egyptian legions, unlike all other legions, which were commanded by senatorial legates of praetorian rank, were commanded by prefects of equestrian rank. In the same way, the governor of Egypt was a prefect of equestrian rank, directly appointed by and responsible to the emperor. From there he served in three different financial posts, firstly as procurator in charge of the 5 per cent inheritance tax, stationed in Rome; then he moved to the provinces as financial procurator of two of the three Gallic provinces; then he returned to Rome to head the most important of the civil service departments (with a salary of 300 000 sesterces per year), the financial branch; and finally he was promoted to one of the great equestrian prefectures, that of the grain supply. It is a very distinguished career in the equestrian administration and indicates the opportunities for advancement open under the empire to a man of talent from a provincial town. It also shows how it was possible to become a specialist in a particular department (in this case, finance) and to move from positions in the capital to positions in the provinces and back again. With respect to power and influence, the three financial positions of Macedo are in an ascending sequence; and the prefecture, with which he ends his career, while being of higher social prestige, was of less power than the position that preceded it. The inscription gives little help in the matter of dating, though the mention of the legion 2 Trajana Fortis tells us that the inscription is of at least Trajanic dating. We do, however, learn from another inscription that Statius Macedo was financial secretary to the emperor Antoninus Pius and, from another inscription, that he was a tribune under Hadrian's reign (probably after AD 129), though the type of tribunate is not specified.

70   (*ILS* 1546 = S 172)

To the divine spirit of Tiberius Claudius, freedman of the emperor, Saturninus, procurator in charge of the 5 per cent tax on inheritances of the province of Achaea: Saturnina, his faithful wife.

The inscription is from a funerary monument in Rome and is in Latin. The monument was set up by a wife to her dead husband and follows the fairly standard formulaic pattern. The main interest of the inscription for us is that the subject is a member of

the freedman (*libertus*) class of Roman society, and, more importantly, a freedman from the emperor's establishment of slaves.
The names 'Tiberius Claudius' would indicate that he was given his
freedom by the emperor Claudius, it being the practice for freed
slaves to take the name of their former master, who now became
their patron. Tiberius Claudius Saturninus was put by the emperor
in charge of the finanical department responsible for the collecting
of the tax of 5 per cent levied on inheritances in Achaea, or Greece.
This tax was put into the military treasury and used for paying
bonuses to the soldiers on their retirement. The inscription thus
gives us some insight into the elaborate civil service structure that
was gradually evolving among the emperor's own dependents,
particularly among the freedman class. The power gained by these
freedmen officials, especially under Claudius, was a matter of great
bitterness with the Roman aristocracy and traditional governing
class, and was not solved until the end of the first century AD and
the beginning of the second century AD, when the senior civil
service posts began to be filled by men of equestrian rank.

71   (*ILS* 2816 = S 182)

**To Tiberius Julius, freedman of the emperor, Xanthus, agent of
Tiberius Caesar and of the deified Claudius and subprefect of
the fleet of Alexandria: Atellia Prisca, his wife, and Lamyrus, his
freedman, both his heirs. He lived for 80 years.**

The inscription is from a funerary monument in Rome and is in
Latin. The monument was set up to the subject by his joint heirs,
his wife and freedman. Tiberius Julius Xanthus was a freedman,
whose name Xanthus indicated Greek birth. The names 'Tiberius
Julius' indicate that he was given his freedom by the emperor
Tiberius. He is therefore another example of a freedman from the
emperor's establishment of slaves, who serves his master in the
affairs of state. The fact that Claudius is called 'the deified' would
seem to indicate that the inscription was set up under the reign of
Nero or a later emperor. Xanthus thus served under at least three
emperors, firstly as a private agent of Tiberius and Claudius, and
then in an official capacity as subprefect of the fleet that was
permanently stationed at Alexandria. Under the Julio-Claudian
emperors, the commands of the various fleets were often in the
hands of imperial freedmen, usually of Greek descent; a good
example is Nero's freedman, Anicetus, who commanded the fleet
at Misenum. Later, after the Julio-Claudian emperors, the post of
prefect of the fleet was regularly held by a member of the

equestrian class. It is also worthy of note that it was possible for a freedman himself to own and manumit, or give freedom to, slaves, who thereby became the freedmen of a freedman.

72 (*ILS* 1519 = M&W 203)

To Titus Flavius, freedman of the emperor, Euschemon, who was in charge of correspondence and also procurator for the poll-tax of the Jews: his wife, Flavia Aphrodisia, made (this monument) for her patron and well deserving husband.

The inscription is from Rome, in Latin, and from a funerary monument. The dead man and his wife are, from their names (Euschemon and Aphrodisia), of Greek descent. Euschemon, who describes himself as 'freedman of the emperor', was a slave of the emperor Vespasian (or possibly Titus), by whom he was given his freedom; hence his assumption of his patron's names, Titus Flavius, while his wife became Flavia. Perhaps the most important piece of information given to us by this inscription is the fact that Euschemon was a very senior member of the emperor's civil service, holding the post firstly of secretary in charge of the emperor's correspondence and then of procurator of the department of the administration concerned with collecting the poll-tax on all practising Jews within the empire. It is well known how much the powerful Greek freedmen secretaries of the Julio-Claudian emperors were hated by the Roman governing class. Vitellius, in the civil war of AD 69, had made a revolutionary breakthrough when he appointed knights to senior secretarial positions. This inscription shows us that Vespasian reverted to the traditional Julio-Claudian practice of using highly trained Greek freedmen. However, the precedent had been set; and with Domitian knights reappear in the secretarial posts, becoming even more prevalent under succeeding emperors. The inscription also throws light on statements in our literary sources. Josephus, the Jewish writer, tells us (*Jewish War* 7.6.6) that Vespasian at the end of the Jewish War, 'imposed a tax on the Jews, wherever they were, ordering each one to pay two drachmas every year to the Capitol, just as in the past they used to contribute it to the temple at Jerusalem'. Suetonius, *Domitian* 12.2, says that Domitian levied the tax on the Jews with the utmost rigour; Euschemon may possibly be the procurator mentioned in this passage. The inscription shows us that Vespasian set up a special financial department, under a freeman procurator, to handle the collection of this Jewish poll-tax.

73   (*ILS* 8784 = E&J 77)

The people (honoured) Livia Drusilla, the wife of Augustus Caesar, as a goddess and benefactor.

The people (honoured) Julia, daughter of Caesar Augustus, as a benefactor, as were her forebears.

The people (honoured) Julia, daughter of Marcus Agrippa.

The inscription, which is in Greek, is from the north Aegean island of Thasos and forms part of an official dedicatory monument set up by the people of Thasos in honour of Augustus' wife, Livia, his daughter, Julia, and granddaughter, also called Julia. The occasion of the dedication is not stated; and it is perhaps not necessary to believe that it was a specific incident to which the title of 'benefactor', conferred on Livia and the elder Julia, refers, though this is possible. The interesting aspect of the inscription is the honouring of Livia as a goddess, which was perhaps right and proper in the case of the wife of the man who was widely honoured in the Greek East as a god during his lifetime. The admiration felt for Augustus and his family in the Greek East was certainly both deep and sincere; and the family was regarded as being divine – a belief and practice that was helped by the long tradition of ruler-worship in the Hellenistic states of the eastern Mediterranean. To the Greeks Augustus and his family were the legitimate successors of the Seleucids and Ptolemies. Jones, II, pp. 318–19, no. 164, 'Divine honours for Augustus in Asia', *c.* 9 BC, gives the text of a decree of the provincial assembly of Asia, whose preamble, written in highly fulsome language, gives an idea of the attitude of the Greeks of Asia to the cult of Augustus (= E&J 98). The decree of the people of Acraephia in Boeotia in honour of Nero, which is given as **26** of this collection (*IG* VII, 2713 = *S* 64), is written in the same sort of language. Nero is addressed as Nero Zeus, god of Freedom, and his current wife is referred to as the goddess Augusta Messalina.

Some idea of the dating of the inscription can be gained from its contents. We can say that the inscription must have been set up after 19 BC, the year of the younger Julia's birth from the marriage of Agrippa and the elder Julia, but before 2 BC, the year of the disgrace and banishment of both Julias. After this date it is difficult to imagine any community with any tact setting up a monument to the honour of the two women whom Augustus in his later years habitually referred to along with the younger Julia's brother, Agrippa Postumus, as 'my three boils'.

74   (*OGIS* 583 = E&J 134)

To Tiberius Caesar Augustus, god, son of the deified Augustus, saluted as victorious commander, pontifex maximus, of tribunician power for the 31st time, when Lucius Axius Naso was proconsul and Marcus Etrilius Lupercus his legate and Gaius Flavius Figulus his quaestor, Adrastus, son of Adrastus, Friend of Caesar, the hereditary priest of the temple and cult statue of Tiberius Caesar Augustus, which was set up in the gymnasium by him (i.e. Adrastus) at his own expense, the patriotic and most excellent and unpaid and voluntary gymnasiarch and priest of the gods in the gymnasium, built the temple and the statue from his own moneys for his own god (i.e. Tiberius), when Dionysius, son of Dionysius and Apollodotus, Friend of Caesar, was ephebarch. Adrastus, son of Adrastus, Friend of Caesar, dedicated (them), being assisted in the dedication by his son, Adrastus, Friend of Caesar, who is also unpaid and voluntary gymnasiarch of the boys, on the birthday of Tiberius on the 24th day of Apogonicus.

The inscription, which is in Greek, is from the town of Lapethus in Cyprus and may well be from the base of the cult statue of Tiberius mentioned in the text. The date of the inscription can be assigned to AD 29 on the basis of Tiberius' tribunician numbering. In a previous inscription (*SEG* XI 923 = E&J 102, **24** of this collection) it was seen how reluctant Tiberius was to accept divine honours from communities in the empire and it was stated that he was powerless to prevent the spread of this usually spontaneous expression of loyalty and enthusiasm for the imperial house. In this inscription we see a wealthy individual from Cyprus setting up a cult of Tiberius in his own city. The cult centre was the local gymnasium, the social meeting-place of any Greek city; and the man, Adrastus, must have had official approval from the town council to do this. The enthusiasm of the upper classes of the Eastern provinces for the imperial system and its individual head can be seen in the language used by Adrastus, who is 'friend of Caesar' and to whom Tiberius is 'his own god'. The inscription also throws light on the willingness of many of the wealthy citizens of the Greek cities to use their wealth to benefit their fellow citizens. Adrastus not only had incurred the expense of setting up the cult statue and temple of Tiberius, he has also made sure that the priesthood of Tiberius remains the hereditary – and expensive – property of his family. Moreover, both he himself and his son have voluntarily held the position of gymnasiarch, one of the most prestigious of municipal magistracies in the Greek cities and one that involved its holder in considerable personal expense, since, amongst other things, it was his duty to distribute olive oil to the citizens who used the gymnasium for exercising. The willingness of the wealthy to undertake costly public offices and expenditures is an indication of the flourishing state of the cities under the early emperors and of the civic pride engendered by this prosperity.

We may note the care with which Adrastus has dated this monument. Not only is Tiberius' tribunician year given, but also the name of the proconsul of Cyprus and his senior staff members and the names of the local annually elected ephebarchs, the magistrates responsible for the supervision of the young men of the community, who were being taught and trained at the gymnasium, the Greek equivalent of the modern high school. The ephebarch was an official subordinate to the gymnasiarch, who was 'always a very important person and sometimes "the foremost man in the city" ' (H. I. Marrou, *A History of Education in Antiquity*, London 1956, p. 110). A final date is given, specifying the day of the consecration of the statue and temple: the 24th of Apogonicus. Cyprus, like many other communities in the East, had begun a new 'era' with the accession to sole power of Augustus, i.e. it reckoned its years from a specific occasion connected with Augustus, which was regarded as year 1 of the new era. In Cyprus the years of the new era began from the day of Augustus' birth. Apogonicus was the second month in the new calendar and ran from 24 October to 22 November. The 24th of Apogonicus is thus 16 November, which we know from our literary sources to have been Tiberius' birthdate.

75   (*ILS* 158 = E&J 52)

To the divine power and providence of Tiberius Caesar Augustus and of the senate, in memory of that day which was 18 October. Publius Viriasius Naso, proconsul for the 3rd time, consecrated (this) from his own money.

The inscription, which is in Latin, is from the city of Gortyn in Crete and is from, probably, a shrine set up by the proconsul of the province in remembrance of a particular occasion. What was this event which took place on 18 October in one of the years of Tiberius' reign and which required that emperor's providence, or foresight? From another inscription, the Roman calendar from Ostia, we read the following under the year AD 31: 'On 18 October, Sejanus was throttled; on 13 October, Strabo, the son of Sejanus, committed suicide . . . of December (the day is missing) Capito

Aelianus (a relative of Sejanus) and Junilla, daughter of Sejanus, lay on the Stairs of Wailing'. Moreover Dio Cassius records, 58.12, that the senate decreed that the day on which Sejanus had died was to be celebrated by annual horse-races and other festivities. The monument, then, was set up by a loyal and zealous senator to express his gratitude for the deliverance of the state, as personified by the emperor, from a deadly peril. It will be noticed that the name of Sejanus does not appear on the inscription; this is because after his death Sejanus suffered a kind of *damnatio memoriae*, a condemnation of his memory, and his name was, as far as possible, removed or kept from all documents. Sejanus had been appointed ordinary consul for AD 31 by Tiberius, who was also ordinary consul. But the list of consuls for this year only gives Tiberius as ordinary consul. Another interesting point that arises from this inscription is the information that Naso was proconsul of Crete for the third time, i.e. for the third consecutive year – a most unusual procedure in a senatorial proconsulate, which was normally held for one year. Dio Cassius, 58.23, relates, under the year AD 33, that so many senators had been executed by Tiberius as a result of Sejanus' conspiracy that some of the proconsuls of praetorian rank got their provinces for six years. Naso, a proconsul of praetorian rank, confirms Dio's account at least in part.

76 (*ILS* 297 = S. *N–H* 101)

To the emperor Caesar, son of the deified Nerva, Nerva Trajan Optimus Augustus Germanicus Dacicus Parthicus, pontifex maximus, of tribunician power for the 18th time, saluted as victorious commander 7 times, consul 6 times, father of his country: the citizens of the municipality (dedicated this).

The inscription, which is in Latin, is from the town of Cisimbrium in the Spanish province of Baetica. The occasion of the dedication is not known. The inscription can be dated, on the basis of Trajan's tribunician numbering, to between the end of AD 113 and the end of AD 114. It was during this year that he received the name or title Optimus – 'the Best' – from a grateful, or flattering, senate, and the name appears on this provincial inscription. The main interest of the inscription perhaps lies in its demonstration of Trajan's love – even mania – for resounding and pompous names and titles which recall military victories. His successor, Hadrian, was to be much less vainglorious in this respect. It is to be noted, however, that Trajan was not officially voted the title Parthicus until the year AD 116; indeed, the Parthian war had only just commenced at the time that this inscription was set up. Hence we can say that the citizens of Cisimbrium, in their desire to express their loyalty, devotion and confidence in the emperor, have been somewhat premature in ascribing to him this title. It may be regarded as a statement of optimistic anticipation of future achievements.

77   (*ILS* 309 = S. *N–H* 64)

The senate and Roman people (dedicated this) to the emperor Caesar, son of the deified Trajan Parthicus, grandson of the deified Nerva, Trajan Hadrian Augustus, pontifex maximus, of tribunician power for the 2nd time, consul for the 2nd time, who first and alone of all emperors, by remitting 900 100 000 sesterces owed to the imperial treasuries, provided by this act of generosity for the security not only of his contemporary citizens but also for their posterity.

The inscription, which is in Latin, comes from Rome, where it was found in the Forum of Trajan. It can be dated accurately to the year AD 118 by the tribunician numbering – Hadrian's second year of tribunician power began on 4 December AD 117 – and the consular year, Hadrian being consul for the second time in AD 118. One is always struck by the fairly simple nomenclature of Hadrian as compared with the boastful, bombastic string of names and titles adopted by Trajan (cf. **76** and the coin of AD 116–17, which has 'the emperor Caesar Nerva Trajan Optimus Augustus Germanicus Dacicus Parthicus, pontifex maximus, of tribunician power, consul 6 times, father of his country'). The event referred to in this dedicatory inscription also finds confirmation and detailed explanation in the literary sources and coinage of Hadrian. A *sestertius* from Rome (S. *N–H* 50), datable to between AD 119 and 124/5, has on its reverse side a depiction of a lictor setting fire to a pile of debt-bonds in the presence of three citizens, and a legend which reads, 'The outstanding debts of 900 000 000 sesterces abolished. By decree of the Senate'. Dio Cassius, 69.8, says that Hadrian, 'having come to Rome, remitted the moneys that were owing to the imperial treasury and to the public treasury of the Romans, setting a period of 16 years from which and up to which this dispensation was to be observed'. The author of the *Life of Hadrian*, 7.6, also states that he 'remitted to private debtors in Rome and in Italy immense sums of money owed to the privy-purse or *fiscus* (i.e. the emperor's treasury) and in the provinces he remitted large amounts of arrears; and he ordered the promissory notes to be burned in the Forum of the Deified Trajan, in order that the general sense of security might thereby be increased' (Loeb translation). The measure referred to in these pieces of evidence is one of the many financial measures whereby Hadrian attempted to restore the chaotic state of the treasuries at the death of Trajan. It would have two major effects: firstly, it would restore confidence and give a fresh start to the debtors to the treasury, many of whom had been owing money for years; and secondly, it would remove an unrealistic sum of money from the credit side of the annual budget, for the outstanding debts would be carried over as a credit item from year to year, even though there was little chance of their ever being recovered. It is, moreover, highly likely that there were many senators among those who owed money to the imperial treasury. Hadrian, who was not popular with the senate at the start of his reign, could certainly hope to win over some senatorial support by such a measure, not to mention the goodwill of the non-senatorial debtors. Once again, we can see the evidence of the inscriptions confirming and even adding to the evidence of our literary sources. For the inscription and the coin not only tell us that Hadrian's act of generosity was commemorated by an honourary monument, of which this inscription formed part, set up by a formal measure of the senate and the people, assembled as a legislative body, but also give us the precise sum of money involved (the discrepancy of 100 000 HS is puzzling, but not significant), thus amplifying the biographer's vague 'immense sums of money'. It is, however, interesting to note, and helpful in putting the measure in some perspective, that the sum remitted by Hadrian is exactly the amount said to have been spent, fifty years before, by Vitellius, during his brief reign, on luxuries for the imperial table.

Part III
Papyri

The normal writing material of the ancient world was papyrus, manufactured from a marsh plant that grew abundantly in the Nile valley and elsewhere; only the Egyptian variety was suitable for conversion into paper. An excellent account of the manufacturing process is provided by the elder Pliny who wrote during the reign of Vespasian; for a translation, see Lewis and Reinhold, II, pp. 164–5. Because of the rainless climate in Egypt south of the Delta, many of these documents have survived in their original state, though often very fragmented. Inevitably those that we have deal in the main with Egypt. Many contain texts of ancient, usually Greek, authors, whilst others are concerned with a variety of matters, official and private, and although there is a concentration of documents written by officials stationed in Egypt, much of the material is directly relevant to the rest of the empire. By the first century AD, Roman government was firmly established in that area and the numerous documents on papyrus that deal with the army, for instance, are no doubt quite similar, if not identical, to those issued in other provinces. On the other hand, details of land and other taxes, marriage and divorce documents (and we have very many of these) provide excellent evidence for the history of Egypt but are far less relevant for an assessment of conditions elsewhere. In general, we must be careful not to generalize on the basis of papyrological evidence alone.

A. Official Documents

78 (*SP* 211 = E&J 320(b))

Proclamation of Germanicus Caesar, son of Augustus and grandson of the deified Augustus, proconsul: I acknowledge your good will, which you always display when you see me, but completely deprecate your acclamations, which are odious to me and such as are accorded to the gods; for your acclamations are appropriate only to my father and to his mother, my grandmother. My position is a reflection of their divinity, so if you do not obey me, you will force me not to show myself to you often.

This edict, which is in Greek, was issued in AD 19 by Tiberius' nephew and adopted son Germanicus on the occasion of his visit to Alexandria (see **91**). It has survived on a fragment of papyrus. Note the titulature of Germanicus: his adoption is indicated both by the title 'Caesar' and also by the reference to himself as Tiberius' son ('son of Augustus') and Augustus' grandson. Later in the edict he again mentions Tiberius ('my father') and also Livia, wife of Augustus and mother of Tiberius ('his mother, my grandmother').

So enthusiastic was his reception that he felt obliged to take some sort of action to limit any hostility or suspicion that it might inspire in the emperor, for the crowd had apparently hailed him as 'Augustus' in addition to the less politically dangerous 'God and Saviour'. Only the reigning emperor was allowed to be styled 'Augustus': even when Titus assumed the role of almost co-ruler with his father Vespasian in the period 70–9, he was always 'son of Augustus' but never 'Augustus'. Whilst such fine distinctions did not trouble the enthusiastic Egyptians, they were important to the constitutionally minded Tiberius who, as we know from Tacitus (see **91**), was far from pleased at his nephew's very presence in the country. For another edict issued in Egypt by Germanicus, see Lewis and Reinhold, II, p. 399.

79 (*P. Lond.* 1912 = S 370)

A. Proclamation by Lucius Aemilius Rectus: Since the whole population, owing to its numbers, was unable to be present at the reading of the most sacred and most beneficent letter to the city, I have deemed it necessary to display the letter publicly in order that reading it individually you may admire the majesty of our god Caesar and feel gratitude for his good will toward the city. Year 2 of the emperor Tiberius Claudius Caesar Augustus Germanicus, 14th of New Augustus.

B.   Greetings from the emperor Tiberius Claudius Caesar Augustus Germanicus, pontifex maximus, of tribunician power, designated to the consulship, to the city of the Alexandrians:

C.   Tiberius Claudius Barbillus, Apollonius son of Artemidorus, Chaeremo son of Leonidas, Marcus Julius Asclepiades, Gaius Julius Dionysius, Tiberius Claudius Phanias, Pasio son of Potamo, Dionysius son of Sabbio, Tiberius Claudius Archibius, Apollonius son of Aristo, Gaius Julius Apollonius, Hermaiscus son of Apollonius, your envoys, delivered your decree to me and discoursed at length concerning the city, directing my attention to your good will toward us, which from long ago, you may be sure, had been stored up to your advantage in my memory; for you are by nature reverent toward the emperors, as I have come to know well from many indications and in particular you have taken a warm interest — warmly reciprocated — in my house, of which fact (to mention the latest instance, passing over the others) the supreme witness is my brother Germanicus Caesar when he addressed you more frankly, by word of mouth. Hence I gladly received the honours given me by you, though I am not partial to such things.

D.   In the first place, I permit you to keep my birthday as an Augustan day in the manner you have yourselves proposed, and I agree to the erection by you in their several places of the statues of myself and my family: for I see that you were zealous to establish on every side memorials of your reverence for my house. Of the two golden statues, the one made to represent the Claudian Augustan Peace, as my most honored Barbillus suggested and persisted in when I wished to refuse for fear of being thought too offensive, shall be erected at Rome, and the other according to your request shall be carried in procession on my name days in your city; and it shall be accompanied in the procession by a throne, adorned with whatever trappings you wish. It would perhaps be foolish, while accepting such great honors, to refuse the institution of a Claudian tribe and the establishment of sacred groves after the manner of Egypt; wherefore I grant you these requests as well, and if you wish you may also erect the equestrian statues of Vitrasius Pollio my procurator. As for the erection of the statues in four-horse chariots which you wish to set up to me at the entrances to the country, I consent to let one be placed at the town called Taposiris, in Libya, another at Pharus in Alexan-

Document 79   A section of Claudius' letter to the Alexandrians.
Reproduced by courtesy of Licinio Capelli.

dria, and a third at Pelusium in Egypt. But I deprecate the appointment of a high priest for me and the building of temples, for I do not wish to be offensive to my contemporaries, and my opinion is that temples and the like have by all ages been granted as special honors to the gods alone.

E.   ... As for which party was responsible for the riot and feud (or rather, if the truth must be told, the war) with the Jews, although your envoys, particularly Dionysius son of Theon, confronting ... put your case with great zeal, nevertheless I was unwilling to make a strict inquiry, though guarding within me a store of immutable indignation against any who renewed the conflict; and I tell you once for all that unless you put a stop to this ruinous and obstinate enmity against each other, I shall be driven to show what a benevolent emperor can be when turned to righteous indignation. Wherefore once again I conjure you that, on the one hand, the Alexandrians show themselves forbearing and kindly toward the Jews, who for many years have dwelt in the same city, and dishonor none of the rights observed by them in the worship of their god but allow them to observe their customs as in the time of the deified Augustus which customs I also, after hearing both sides, have confirmed. And, on the other hand, I explicitly order the Jews not to agitate for more privileges than they formerly possessed, and in the future not to send out a separate embassy as if they lived in a separate city — a thing unprecedented — and not to force their way into gymnasiarchic or cosmetic games, while enjoying their own privileges and sharing a great abundance of advantages in a city not their own, and not to bring in or admit Jews from Syria or those who sailed down from Egypt, a proceeding which will compel me to conceive serious suspicions; otherwise I will by all means proceed against them as fomenters of what is a general plague of the whole world. If, desisting from these courses, you both consent to live with mutual forbearance and kindliness, I on my side will exercise a solicitude of very long standing for the city, as one bound to us by ancestral friendship. I bear witness to my friend Barbillus of the solicitude which he has always shown for you in my presence and of the extreme zeal with which he has now advocated your cause, and likewise to my friend Tiberius Claudius Archibius. Farewell. (translated Lewis and Reinhold, adapted)

This is a section of a letter written in Greek by the emperor Claudius (dated 10 November AD 41) to the citizens of Alexandria. Founded in 331 BC by Alexander the Great, Alexandria was one of the largest cities in the Roman empire, and had always been famous as one of the chief intellectual centres of the Hellenistic world. At this time, however, it was the tension between the various elements of its mixed population – native Egyptians, Greeks and Jews – that brought the city to the attention of the imperial administration.

Claudius wrote this important letter as a result of a visit or embassy he received from a number of its prominent citizens (C), who, it would appear, congratulated him on his accession, and, in connection with this, requested his acceptance of various honours (D); secondly, they asked for certain favours (omitted in the translation); and finally they apologized for recent anti-Jewish riots (E). Apparently he answered their requests by means of this letter; he did not give it to the members of the embassy, but sent it to the city through the prefect Aemilius Rectus.

Each section of the letter merits comment (the divisions in the translation are not ancient ones, but have been inserted to simplify discussion).

The first section (A) consists of a statement added to Claudius' letter by the prefect of Egypt, Lucius Aemilius Rectus, whilst (B) contains Claudius' own titles – he does not appear here as 'father of his country', since that title was not assumed until 6 January 42. The next section (C) lists the members of the embassy; Barbillus and Archibius were perhaps the most important and influential ambassadors, since Claudius refers to them as his 'friends' in the last lines of the letter. Barbillus (the form 'Balbillus' is also found) may well be identical with, or perhaps father of, the Tiberius Claudius Balbillus who became prefect of Egypt in 55. Again, the Alexandrian philosopher Chaeremo who tutored Nero and who was notorious for his anti-Semitic attitude (Josephus, *Against Apion* 1.288 ff.) was perhaps related to the Chaeremo of the embassy, if indeed he was not the same person. Claudius' description of the relationship between Rome and Alexandria contains a degree of diplomatic misrepresentation if we are to judge by the tone of some of the so-called 'Acts of the Pagan Martyrs' (**93**).

The reference to his brother Germanicus is not without interest. In 19, his visit to Alexandria, ostensibly to alleviate a food shortage, had resulted in public demonstrations in his favour, so much so that he judged it advisable to issue an edict urging more moderate behaviour (**78**). It is hardly surprising that Claudius refers diploma-tically to his brother's reception in Alexandria some thirty years before; again, the fact that Claudius and Germanicus were the sons of Mark Antony's daughter Antonia made them even more popular in that city.

Section (D) lists the honours voted to Claudius and is extremely valuable in assessing his attitude to the imperial cult. The early emperors' public position towards this institution was extremely conservative, though they often allowed themselves to be 'persuaded' by the more enthusiastic sections of the empire to abandon their reluctance to be worshipped. Tiberius, for instance, 'vetoed the dedication of temples, flamens and priests in his honour and even the setting up of his statues and busts without his permission' (Suetonius, *Tiberius* 26.1); one might well compare Tiberius' own statement of his attitude in the Gytheum inscription (**24**). Claudius was only a little more accommodating. He refused the offer of temples and the appointment of a high priest, and in so doing stated his position with regard to the whole question: 'I do not wish to be offensive to my contemporaries, and my opinion is that temples and the like have by all ages been granted as special honours to the gods alone'. On the other hand, he did permit them to celebrate his birthday once a month ('as an Augustan day') and also to erect statues to himself; but the latter concession was justified, it should be noted, only because a precedent already existed ('for I see that . . . reverence for my house'). He also allowed them to rename one of the existing tribes after him and to erect statues (presumably of Claudius himself) given by the previous prefect of Egypt, Vitrasius Pollio. So far the honours accepted were in accord with the principle stated above, as was the refusal of Barbillus' suggestion of two golden statues. However, his attitude towards the establishment of sacred groves and the erection of statues in four-horse chariots at the three entrances to Egypt is less easy to understand, especially if, as the letter seems to imply, they are to be dedicated to the emperor himself. Possibly he did not wish to appear too ungracious, and thus was somewhat illogical in this regard; after all it would not be inconsistent with his character as it appears in the literary sources. On the other hand, section (A) of the letter does indicate the extent to which the emperor's representative attempted to extend the scope of the imperial cult ('in order that you may admire the majesty of our god Caesar'); whatever Claudius' intentions were, no matter how well-meaning his official statements, Aemilius Rectus – and no doubt other imperial representatives in other provinces – clearly set out to develop the imperial cult into the worship of the living ruler as a god.

The last section is of special interest, for it throws some light on the problem of anti-Semitism in the ancient world. In Alexandria, the Jews formed an important element in the population from the earliest times (Josephus, *Jewish War* 2.487), occupying a quarter called the 'Delta': by Philo's time (*c.* AD 40), two of the five quarters of the city were predominantly Jewish and many individual Jews lived in other parts of the city. They were exposed to the hostility of their neighbours for a number of reasons. According to H. I. Bell, *Jews and Christians in Egypt* (Oxford 1924), p. 11:

Economic factors were not without influence; for the Jews, besides being dangerous rivals in commerce, were not infrequently tax-farmers or farmers of the royal domains, and many of them were persons of great wealth. Even more powerful, however, were political and religious prejudice. Precluded by their religion from sharing in many of the activites of their fellow-townsmen, to whom the *polis* was above all things a religious community united by the common service of the ancestral gods, and yet enjoying special privileges of their own and favoured, not by the Ptolemies only but by many of the Hellenistic monarchs, as later by the Romans, the Jews were naturally objects of suspicion and dislike. . . . In the Roman period, it (anti-Semitic feeling) was accentuated by political causes and led to open hostilities. . . . The Jews had deserted the national dynasty on the arrival of the Romans, and they received their reward in the confirmation of their privileges and in the special favour of the emperors. But the Alexandrines, who saw their city degraded from a royal capital to a subordinate position under imperial Rome, were constantly hostile to the emperors, and consequently hated their Jewish protégés the more bitterly. Moreover, the Jews, encouraged no doubt by the favours they had received, seem to have been aiming at yet further privileges, in particular at the full Alexandrian citizenship.

There had indeed, just a few years before, been a violent anti-Jewish campaign in Alexandria. It was vividly described by Philo (30 BC–AD 45), the leader of the city's Jewish community (and uncle of the apostate Tiberius Julius Alexander, prefect of Egypt under Nero and almost certainly promoted to prefect of the praetorian guard by Vespasian):

Alexandria has five quarters named after the first letters of the alphabet, two of these are called Jewish because most of the Jews inhabit them, though in the rest also there are not a few Jews scattered about. So then what did they do? From the four letters they ejected the Jews and herded them into a very small part of one. The Jews were so numerous that they poured out over beaches, dung-hills and tombs, robbed of all their belongings. Their enemies overran the houses now left empty and turned to pillaging them, distributing the contents like spoil of war, and as no one prevented them, they broke open the workshops of the Jews which had been closed as a sign of mourning for Drusilla, carried out all the articles they found, which were very numerous, and bore them through the middle of the market-place, dealing with other people's property as freely as if it was their own. A still more grievous evil than the pillaging was the unemployment produced. The tradespeople had lost their stocks, and no one, husbandman, shipman, merchant, artisan, was allowed to practise his usual business. . . . After the pillaging and eviction and violent expulsion from most parts of the city the Jews were like beleaguered men with their enemies all round them. They were pressed by want and dire lack of necessities; they saw their infant children and women perishing before their eyes through a famine artificially created, since elsewhere all else was teeming with plenty and abundance, the fields richly flooded by the overflow of the river and the wheat-bearing parts of the lowlands producing through their fertility the harvest of grain in unstinted profusion. Unable any longer to endure their privation, some of them contrary to their former habits went to the houses of their kinsmen and friends to ask for the mere necessities as a charity, while those whose high-born spirit led them to avoid the beggar's lot as fitter for slaves than for the free went forth into the market solely to buy sustenance for their families and themselves. Poor wretches, they were at once seized by those who wielded the weapon of mob rule, treacherously stabbed, dragged through the whole city, and trampled on, and thus completely made away with till not a part of them was left which could receive the burial which is the right of all. Multitudes of others also were laid low and destroyed with manifold forms of maltreatment, put in practice to serve their bitter cruelty by those whom savagery had maddened and transformed into the nature of wild beasts; for any Jews who showed themselves anywhere, they stoned or knocked about with clubs, aiming their blows at first against the less vital parts for fear that a speedier death might give a speedier release from the consciousness of their anguish. Some, made rampant by the immunity and licence which accompanied these sufferings, discarded the weapons of slower action and took the most effective of all, fire and steel, and slew many with the sword, while not a few they destroyed with fire. Indeed, whole families, husbands with their wives, infant children with their parents, were burnt in the heart of the city by these supremely ruthless men who showed no pity for old age nor youth, nor the innocent years of childhood. (*In Flaccum* 55 ff. *passim*: Loeb translation)

The accuracy of Philo's narrative cannot be checked, but it would appear that the Jews were quickly able to return to their districts and send an embassy to Gaius, led by Philo himself. At the same time, or soon after, they planned revenge, and some sort of incident occurred at the time of Claudius' accession (Josephus, *Jewish Antiq.* 2.487); they also, it seems, sought assistance from their compatriots in Syria and other areas of Egypt (section E). At all events, despite these pogroms and riots, Claudius assumed an attitude of strict impartiality in reply to the representations of both parties. He reprimanded the intolerance of the Alexandrians towards the Jews and confirmed the latter's privileges. These did not include the citizenship which was possessed by individual Jews, but not by the entire community as such. Indeed, Claudius refused to extend their privileges and bluntly warned them to cease causing disturbances. It is clear, though, that neither side had cause to complain at Claudius' attitude: the impartiality and firmness revealed here ought to be taken into account in any assessment of his ability as emperor and compared with the hostile evidence of the biased literary sources.

Apart from its evidence already discussed, the letter is of some interest for the light it throws on the emperor's personality and the character of his government. It can be regarded as certain that Claudius himself was directly responsible for the decisions announced regarding the imperial cult and the Jewish problem, though he doubtless took advice from his senior officials. It does not follow, though, that the actual wording of the letter was his. There is none of the irrelevant pedantry or other idiosyncracies of **25**. On the other hand, there are some very characteristic touches, e.g. the reference to 'my brother Germanicus', his attitude towards the acceptance of honours ('I am not partial to such things'), to the Alexandrians and Jews ('I was unwilling to make a strict inquiry'), and finally the outburst against the latter ('I will by all means proceed against them as fomenters of what is a general plague of the whole world'). It should, incidentally, be noted that some scholars have assumed, probably wrongly, that this is a reference to Christianity (if so, it would be the earliest known to us).

80   (*P. Lond.* 1171 = S 381)

Proclamation of Lucius Aemilius Rectus: No one is to requisition transport from the people in the country areas nor demand provisions without payment or anything else without a permit from me; and each person possessing such a permit may take sufficient supplies on payment of the price for them. But if any of the soldiers or police or anyone at all among the aides in the public services is reported to have acted in violation of my edict or to have used force against anyone of the country people or to have exacted money, I shall inflict the severest penalty upon him. Year 2 of the emperor Tiberius Claudius Caesar Augustus, Germanicus 4th. (translated Lewis and Reinhold)

This proclamation, which is in Greek, was issued in AD 42 by the prefect of Egypt, Lucius Aemilius Rectus. The month Germanicus is the Egyptian month Pachon (26 April–25 May), so renamed in honour of Claudius – or perhaps of his brother Germanicus.

One of the perennial problems facing the administrators of the empire was the corruption and extortion practised by certain provincial governors; the affair of Julius Bassus, governor of Pontus-Bithynia under Trajan, has been considered elsewhere (**15**). A number of emperors attempted to protect the provincials from these abuses. Domitian, for instance, issued the following order to one of his procurators:

From the orders of the emperor Domitian Caesar Augustus, son of Augustus, to the procurator Claudius Athenodorus: From amongst the matters of importance demanding great attention from me, I am aware that the concern of my father, the deified Vespasian, was directed to the welfare of the cities, intent upon which he ordered that the provinces should not be oppressed by either forced rentals of beasts of burden or importunate demands for lodgings. Nevertheless, wittingly or not modification has taken place and that order has not been enforced; there subsists to this day an old and persistent custom which would gradually develop into law if it were not forcibly prevented from prevailing. Therefore I order you also to see to it that no one requisition a beast of burden unless he has a permit from me; for it is most unjust that the influence or rank of any persons should occasion requisitions which no one but me is permitted to authorize. Nothing, then, is to occur which will annul my order and thwart my purpose most useful to the cities, for it is just to come to the aid of exhausted provinces which with difficulty provide for their daily necessities; no one is to oppress them contrary to my wish, nor requisition a guide unless he has a permit from me: for if the farmers are snatched away, the lands will remain uncultivated. And you whether leasing beasts of burden or using your own, will do best ... (M&W 466)

Domitian's letter is particularly clear and definite; he prohibits abuses in the requisitioning of beasts of burden, since he was determined to see the property of the provincials respected and also to guarantee the efficient functioning of the empire's economy.

Beginning with an edict of Germanicus in 19 (**78**), there are a number of similar documents issued by various emperors or their representatives (such as Aemilius Rectus) designed to check the extortion practised by soldiers and local officials; and even in Egypt, which was under the emperor's direct supervision, it seems that this was a difficult problem and remained so. The success of these edicts cannot be assessed, but their persistent reappearance suggests that the malady was a lingering one. In addition, most provinces were governed by senators and erring governors were judged in the senate: consequently it required determined action by the emperor to ensure impartiality or at least a fair trial.

81 (*P. Lond.* 1178 = S 374)

Tiberius Claudius Caesar Augustus Germanicus Sarmaticus, pontifex maximus, of tribunician power for the 6th time, designated to a 4th consulship, saluted as victorious commander 12 times, father of his country, greets the association of touring athletes. I received with pleasure the gold crown which you sent me on the occasion of my victory over the Britons, as a token of your loyalty to me. The envoys (who brought the crown) were Tiberius Claudius Hermas, Tiberius Claudius Cyrus and Dio son of Mykkalos, citizen of Antioch. Farewell.

In this document, a letter written in Greek, Claudius records his thanks for the gift of a gold crown sent by an association of athletes to honour his victory in Britain. The letter can be assigned to the period 25 January–31 December AD 46, for although his sixth tenure of tribunician power ended on 24 January 47, the first twenty-four days of 47 must be excluded as Claudius entered his fourth consulship on 1 January. The document is in fact one of three imperial rescripts appended to a membership certificate in the association that was issued on 23 September AD 194 to Herminus, a boxer from Hermopolis. The three rescripts are intended to indicate the support and privileges granted to the association by earlier emperors. For the complete text, see Lewis and Reinhold, II, pp. 232–3.

Note the title 'Sarmaticus'. In a series of military operations extending from the Caspian to the estuary of the Don, Claudius' troops under Julius Aquila removed the threat to the client kingdom of the Bosporus posed by Mithridates and a number of Sarmatian tribes. Rome's prestige in these distant regions was restored, and the Greek cities of the Black Sea coast were, not unexpectedly, the first to show their appreciation by honouring Claudius with this new title.

His legions had landed in Britain in 43, and by the following year the emperor was able to lead them personally into the capital, Colchester. After his sixteen-day stay on the island he returned to Rome, when the senate, 'on hearing of his achievement voted him the title "Britannicus" and permission to celebrate a triumph. It was further enacted that ... two triumphal arches should be erected, one in Rome and the other in Gaul' (Dio Cassius 60.22). The inscription from the first of these has survived: 'To Tiberius Claudius, son of Drusus, Caesar Augustus Germanicus, pontifex maximus, of tribunician power for the 11th time, consul 5 times, saluted as victorious commander 22 times, censor, father of his country, the senate and Roman people (erected this arch) because he received the surrender of 11 Kings of Britain, conquered without loss, and because he first brought the barbarian tribes beyond the ocean into the dominion of the Roman people' (*ILS* 216 = S 43b). It must have been erected during the period 25 January 51 to 24 January 52, when Claudius held tribunician power for the eleventh time. No reference was made to Julius Caesar's expeditions to the island about a century previously.

This conquest, the chief feature of Claudius' foreign policy, was commemorated in all of the official propaganda. There is, for instance, an *aureus* from the mint in Rome with the legend: 'Tiberius Claudius Caesar Augustus, pontifex maximus, of tribunician power for the 6th time, saluted as victorious commander 10 times' (Obverse): '(In commemoration of the victory) over the Britons' (Reverse: *BMC* I, p. 168, no. 29 = S 43a). But despite Dio's statement that he was voted the title 'Britannicus', Claudius never used it himself but reserved it for his son.

82   (*P. Oxy.* 39)

Copy of a discharge certificate, signed and dated in the 12th year of the emperor Tiberius Claudius Caesar Augustus Germanicus on the 29th day of the month Pharmouthi.
This man was discharged by Gnaeus Vergilius Capito, Prefect of Upper and Lower Egypt:
Tryphon, son of Dionysius, weaver, with weak sight because of a cataract.
From the list of those from the city of Oxyrhynchus.
Examined at Alexandria.
Examined at Alexandria.
Examined at Alexandria.

This document, which is in Greek, was issued on 24 April AD 52, and appears to be a discharge certificate, indicating that Tryphon was rejected from the army on medical grounds. The administrative procedure of the imperial bureaucracy in Egypt is indicated by the triple check at the end of the document: the phrase 'Examined at Alexandria' is written in three different hands. In the early empire, service in the army was normally voluntary, and it would seem that there was no lack of prospective recruits. A careful selection policy was adopted, part of which was a medical examination, and Tryphon apparently failed to satisfy the doctors. The Roman imperial army's selection procedure was quite rigid and we can be certain that not every prospective recruit was admitted. Possibly this explains, in part at least, the success of Rome's army.

83 (S 297b)

Copy of a (?) petition. The legionaries came forward; on the road of the camp near the Temple of Isis. Tuscus the prefect replied to us: 'Do not speak impiously. No one is troubling you. Write on tablets where each of you is stationed and I will write to the magistrates that no one is to bother you.'

On 1 September we gave him the tablets in the Headquarters and he said to us: 'Have you given them to me individually?' and the legionaries said to him: 'We have given them individually'.

On 2 September we greeted him near the Paliurus and he returned our greeting, and on the 3rd we greeted him in the Atrium, he being seated on the tribunal. Tuscus said to us: 'I said to you in the camp and I say the name now. There is one set of duties for the legionaries, another for the auxiliary forces and another for the rowers. Each of you go to his own tasks and do not become idle.'

The document, which is in Greek, describes the activities of a delegation of soldiers who lodged a complaint with the prefect of Egypt and secured a reply. The prefect's rare cognomen enables us to identify him and also to assign an approximate date to the document: he was presumably Gaius Caecina Tuscus who is attested elsewhere as governing Egypt on 5 September 63 and also on 17 July 64, and thus the document can tentatively be assigned to the period 63/4.

It is very unusual both in form and in content. Clearly it is unofficial, for it reports the proceedings from the petitioner's point of view (note the repetition of 'we' and 'us'). Its purpose is far from clear, but perhaps it was prepared by one of the delegation for the information of those whom he represented, with the intention of showing just how little the central bureaucracy cared for the ordinary soldier's problems.

Note that the first meeting was held beside the road near the Temple. We cannot identify the place from the information supplied, but it would appear that the camp was at Nicopolis, near Alexandria, where Egypt's two legions (3 Cyrenaica and 22 Deiotariana) were stationed. Perhaps the meeting was accidental; at all events it was much less formal than the others referred to later in the document. It is difficult, too, to deduce the reason for their complaint. Perhaps the local authorities had disregarded their immunity rights; Tacitus, *Annals* 13.51, refers to Nero's legislation reinforcing these rights and infringements certainly occurred later – see, for instance, *ILS* 9059 translated in Lewis and Reinhold, II, p. 527. But whatever their complaint, the soldiers were clearly upset ('Do not speak impiously'). The prefect instructed them to put their complaints in writing, individually, and he would forward them to the appropriate authority – a not unfamiliar bureaucratic manoeuvre and one no doubt designed to lessen the tension and hostility. Subsequently, more formal meetings were arranged and it seems that their petition was finally granted, but with a stern warning that they must maintain the discipline that was traditional for soldiers of the legions, and not waste any more time.

Now this incident occurred just a few years before the military plot of AD 66, which was suppressed only with the execution of one of Nero's most famous generals, Domitius Corbulo, and it is possible that the unrest that led to it was not confined to any one area of the empire. Again, Nero's failure to visit Egypt would have done little to win the soldiers' support. He did contemplate such a visit, but apparently changed his mind – and set in train events that resulted in the removal from his post of the Tuscus of this document: 'Tuscus, the governor of Egypt (was dismissed) for bathing in the bath that had been specially constructed for the emperor's intended visit to Alexandria' (Dio, 62.18.2: Loeb translation). Suetonius, *Nero* 35 provides a similar explanation for Tuscus' dismissal.

The document, then, provides an insight into the attitude of one small section of the Egyptian legions just a few years before the military revolt against Nero and indicates that at that time there were positive signs of unrest amongst the troops.

84 **(P. Gen. 1 = M&W 405)**

In the consulship (of Lucius Flavius Silva Nonius Bassus and) Lucius Asinius (Pollio Verrucosus)

a				b			
Quintus Julius Proculus, of Damascus				Gaius Valerius Germanus, of Cyrene			

(Received) 1st pay of 3rd year of our Lord:			*Dr* 248	Received 1st pay of 3rd year of our Lord:			*Dr* 248
Deductions:				Deductions:			
(Bedding)	10			Bedding	10		
Food	80			Food	80		
Boots & socks	12			Boots & Socks	12		
?Regt. Dinner	20			?Regt. Dinner	20		
Clothes	60			Clothes	100		
(Total) Expenses	182			(Total) Expenses	222		
Remainder Deposited		66		Remainder Deposited		26	
Previous Balance		136		Previous Balance		20	
Total Credit Balance			202	Total Credit Balance			46
Received 2nd pay in same year			248	Received 2nd pay in same year			248
Deductions:				Deductions:			
Bedding	10			Bedding	10		
Food	80			Food	80		
Boots & Socks	12			Boots & Socks	12		
?Burial Club	4			?Burial Club	4		
(Total) Expenses	106			(Total) Expenses	106		
Remainder Deposited		142		Remainder Deposited		142	
Previous Balance		202		Previous Balance		46	
Total Credit Balance			344	Total Credit Balance			188
Received 3rd pay in same year			248	Received 3rd pay in same year			248
Deductions:				Deductions:			
Bedding	10			Bedding	10		
Food	80			Food	80		
Boots & Socks	12			Boots & Socks	12		
Clothes	146			Clothes	146		
(Total) Expenses	248			(Total) Expenses	248		
Present Balance			344	Present Balance			188

The document, which is in Latin, is a unique piece of evidence; it is the pay sheet of two Roman soldiers, Quintus Julius Proculus

(under heading (a)) and Gaius Valerius Germanus (under heading
(b)), who were presumably members of the legion 3 Cyrenaica or
22 Deiotariana, the legions stationed in Egypt. The reference to the
consulship of Flavius Silva and Asinius Pollio enables it to be
assigned to AD 81. The legionaries received 744 *drachmae* per year
in three equal instalments of 248 *dr.* and deductions were then
made for a variety of items – bedding, food, clothes, regimental
dinner and burial club. The remainder was credited to their
account. It is interesting to note that no deductions seem to have
been made for weapons. This is surprising in view of a famous
passage in Tacitus where a certain Percennius lists the grievances
of the legionary soldier: 'Body and soul are valued at ten *asses* a day;
out of this we have to pay for our clothing, our weapons, and our
tents . . .' (*Annals* 1.17). Presumably, weapons appeared as an item
on the pay sheets only on the relatively few occasions when new
equipment was issued, or else weapons were no longer regarded
as a deduction.

At this period Roman soldiers were paid three times a year only,
but later in the century Domitian added a fourth pay period,
according to Suetonius (*Dom.* 7.3), without reducing the amount
paid on each occasion, and thus managed to increase the pay of
Rome's huge standing army by a third. It would appear that a
savings-bank system existed in the army. Consider the account of
Julius Proculus. At the beginning of 81 he had a credit balance of
136 *dr.*; 248 *dr.* were added in the first pay period and 182 *dr.*
deducted, leaving a credit of 202 *dr.* to be carried over for the
second period. Presumably the balance was made available to him
when he was finally discharged. It would also appear that neither
soldier withdrew any money to spend outside the camp; and even
if most necessities were provided for within the unit, it is hard to
believe that the men did not wish to find entertainment outside
and that they never required money for that purpose. Possibly they
demanded bribes from the local population, but it is extremely
doubtful if this could be relied on to provide a regular source of
income. According to some scholars, the amount of 248 *dr.* is
significant. They assume that it is equivalent to 62 Italian *denarii*
and point out that, at this period, the amount of each instalment
was 75 *denarii*. The remaining 13 *denarii* were, it is thought, given
to the soldiers in cash. For further discussion of this problem, see
the article, 'The Pay of the Auxilia' by M. Speidel in *Journal of Roman
Studies*, 63, 1973, pp. 141–7.

The document provides precise evidence of the method by
which the legionaries in Egypt were paid and also gives some sort
of indication of their standard of living.

85   (*P. Berl.* 8334)

... (by reason of) your (character) and devotion, my dear
Maximus ... and you have always received (rewards) from me
... I have not been satisfied that (appointment as) prefect (of
Egypt) should be the pinnacle of your career; but (when) I
transferred Julius (Ursus), who was long desirous of it, to the
most honourable order, I immediately considered your most
devoted (loyalty and industry) and have made you (col)league
... of (Cornelius) Fuscus ... I do not doubt that you (will be)
most anxious to be by my? side (at Rome).

This important letter, which was written in Latin, is usually
assigned to the first century AD. References to Julius (Ursus) and
(Cornelius) Fuscus, if this is the correct restoration of the names in
the papyrus, suggest that the writer is the emperor under whom
both attained prominence – Domitian. He is addressing a certain
Maximus whose virtues are praised; it seems that Maximus has
already received one reward and further promotion ('colleague of
Fuscus') is indicated. Now this document could well be valuable
evidence for the careers of two important Domitianic administrators. Firstly the Maximus to whom the letter is addressed could
well be Lucius Laberius Maximus who is attested in another
papyrus as prefect of Egypt on 9 June 83; he would then have been
promoted by Domitian to joint commander of the praetorian
guard, according to this document. It so happens that one of the
commanders at that period, Cornelius Fuscus, is known already,
and consequently we can be fairly certain that Fuscus and
Maximus held this important post *c.* 83. In the early years of the
empire the senior equestrian post was the prefecture of Egypt, and
it was normal for promotion to occur to it from the command of
the praetorian guard in Rome. But after Vespasian's accession, the
order of seniority was reversed, and thus, by the reign of Domitian,
movement from Egypt to Rome was to be considered a promotion;
indeed an equestrian could proceed to no higher post – unless, of
course, the emperor was prepared to admit him to senatorial
status.

Julius Ursus was one of Domitian's more important senators. It
is known that, some years earlier, he was prefect of the corn supply
and then prefect of Egypt (*AE* 1939, 60); it would appear that
subsequently he was appointed to the command of the praetorian
guard in Rome, a promotion that the Maximus of this document
was also to receive a year or so later. Now Dio refers on two
occasions to a man called Ursus who was prominent in the early
years of Domitian's reign:

Domitian planned to put his wife, Domitia, to death on the ground of adultery, but having been dissuaded by Ursus, he divorced her, after murdering Paris, the actor, in the middle of the street because of her. (67.3.1: Loeb translation)

And again:

Domitian pretended to take pleasure in the honours voted by the senate; but he came close to putting Ursus to death because he failed to show pleasure at his sovereign's exploits, and then, at the request of Julia, he appointed him consul. (67.4.2: Loeb translation)

Before the discovery of the letter to Maximus, Ursus' precise status at this period was uncertain: it appeared unusual to refer to promotion to the consulship as an honour for a senator, since as many as twelve senators each year could be so promoted. Consequently, some scholars suggested that he may rather have been the commander of the praetorian guard, for whom such an elevation was indeed rare. Domitian's letter to Maximus makes this virtually certain. Promoted from Egypt to the guard in Rome, he had reached the pinnacle of the equestrian career; but due to imperial favour he was 'transferred to the most honourable order', i.e. granted senatorial status. But his rank in that body was not a lowly one; on the contrary, he was almost at once made consul, and is presumably the Ursus referred to by Dio. Furthermore, the consular lists for 84 are known, and in May of that year a certain –RSUS is attested (M&W 56). It is tempting to identify him both with Dio's Ursus and also with the Ursus of Domitian's letter. Such rapid promotion was without precedent, and it is therefore interesting to observe that he found favour with Trajan as well. In 98 he was consul for a second time, and in 100, as an inscription found just a few years ago proves, was awarded the extremely rare honour of a third consulship. If the interpretation suggested is correct, the evidence provided by the letter is most valuable, for it assists in the restoration of the career of this eminent official of the last quarter of the first century. From prefect of the corn supply, he rose to prefect of Egypt and then to commander of the praetorian guard. Granted senatorial status, he proceeded to hold the consulship on three separate occasions, becoming one of the eminent senators of the early years of Trajan's reign. For another example of this type of document, see Jones, II, p. 138.

86   (*CPL* 102)

Titus Flavius Longus, *optio* in the legion 3 Cyrenaica, in the
century of ? Arellius gave as guarantors, on oath, . . . Fronto, in
the century of Pompeius Reg . . . (two more names) and he
swore an oath by . . . that he was freeborn, a Roman citizen and
had the right of serving in a legion. At this point, his guarantors
Fronto and (two more names, as above) swore by Jupiter Best
and Greatest and by the divine spirit of the emperor Caesar
Domitian Augustus Germanicus that the above Titus Flavius
Longus was freeborn, a Roman citizen and had the right of
serving in a legion. Done in the Augustan camp, in the winter
quarters of the 3rd legion on the ? 16th of . . . in the 17th year
of the emperor Caesar Domitian Augustus Germanicus: in the
consulship of Quintus Volusius Saturninus and Lucius Venuleius Montabus Apronianus.

This document, which is in Latin, is a certificate of Roman
citizenship and survives on a papyrus fragment. There are a
number of errors towards its end. The Latin text reads *anno XVII
imperatoris Caesaris Domitiani* . . . , i.e. 'in the seventeenth year of the
emperor Caesar Domitian . . .', which is clearly incorrect, since
Domitian died in 96, the sixteenth year of his reign. The names of
the consuls provide a clue. They held office in 92 and so the Latin
text should be emended to read *anno XII* rather than *anno XVII*.
Again, the consul Venuleius was named 'Montanus' and not
'Montabus'.

It would appear that doubts had been raised as to whether Titus
Flavius Longus, a legionary soldier who had already been promoted to the rank of *optio* (deputy to the centurion) did in fact
possess the qualifications necessary to serve in the army. In the first
place, it must be observed that service in the imperial army was
usually voluntary and that the Romans resorted to conscription
only in times of need – hence Tacitus' comment in *Annals* 4.4 on
the lack of volunteers in AD 23. Again, slaves or ex-slaves were not
allowed to enlist; thus Ulpian, a writer on military/legal matters,
records (49.16.8) that a person whose free birth was in doubt must
not enlist, even if he was freeborn, until the matter had been
settled. This was a serious problem, as Pliny discovered when he
was governor of Pontus-Bithynia *c.* 109. He had to ask the emperor
(Trajan) for advice:

Sempronius Caelianus, who is an excellent young man, has
discovered two slaves among his recruits and has sent them to
me. I have postponed judgement on them until I could ask your

advice on what would be a suitable sentence, knowing that you are the founder and upholder of military discipline. My chief reason for hesitating is the fact that the men had already taken the oath of allegiance but had not yet been enrolled in a legion. I therefore pray you, Sir, to tell me what course to follow, especially as the decision is likely to provide a precedent. (*Ep.* 10.29: Loeb translation)

Trajan's reply was comprehensive:

Sempronius Caelianus was carrying out my instructions in sending you the slaves. Whether they deserve capital punishment will need investigation; it is important to know if they were volunteers or conscripts, or possibly offered as substitutes. If they are conscripts, then the blame falls on the recruiting officer; if substitutes, then those who offered them as such are guilty; but if they volunteered for service, well aware of their status, then they will have to be executed. The fact that they were not yet enrolled in a legion is immaterial, for the truth about their origin should have come out on the actual day they were accepted for the army. (*Ep.* 10.30: Loeb translation)

So it would seem that when there was some doubt about the status of Titus Flavius Longus, a member of the third Cyrenaican legion stationed in Egypt, he had to affirm on oath that he did in fact possess the necessary qualifications and was supported in his statement by three other citizens.

87 (*P. Oxy.* 3022)

The emperor Caesar Nerva Trajan Augustus Germanicus, pontifex maximus, of tribunician power for the 2nd time, consul, to (? the city of) the Alexandrians ... (In view of) your city's outstanding loyalty towards the emperors, and bearing in mind the benefits which my deified father conferred on you ... of his reign, and for my own part also, these claims of yours, having a personal feeling of benevolence towards you, I have commended you first of all to myself, then, as well, to my friend and prefect Pompeius Planta, so that he can take every care to provide for your undisturbed tranquillity, your food-supply, and your communal and individual rights. From which (it will be) clear ...

The document, which is in Greek, is an official communication from the emperor Trajan to the city of Alexandria, and was written at some time between 1 October and 9 December AD 98.

In the first year of Trajan's reign (he came to the throne on 28 January 98), he held tribunician power three times – his first tenure began on the accession, the second on 1 October, and the third from 10 December. The last date was selected since it was the traditional time for the tribunician elections under the Republic, and from this time it was regarded by every emperor in the same way, regardless of the actual date of his accession. The tribunician dating, then, enables the letter to be assigned to this narrow period of time; there remains, however, an error in the emperor's consular year – since he held his first (ordinary) consulship in 91 and his second in 98, the document should refer to his second and not to his first tenure of the office.

It is only rarely that individuals are precisely attested as a 'friend' of an emperor: Pompeius Planta, however, is so described on a second occasion, in a letter from Trajan to Pliny (Pliny, *Ep.* 10.7). Unfortunately, very little is known of this 'prefect and friend'. He could well be the ·us Planta whom Vespasian appointed procurator of Lycia-Pamphylia *c.* 74 (*IGRR* III 466), and, if so, one would have to argue that his advancement was delayed by Domitian for some reason. With such scanty evidence, though, speculation is profitless.

Trajan's fragmentary letter, written just after his accession, appears to be a reply to Alexandria's request for him, as the new emperor, to confirm the city's privileges. His relationship with the Alexandrians deteriorated, to judge by the tone of one of the 'Acts of the Pagan Martyrs' (**93**); but it must be remembered that this letter was part of the requests for privileges and that expressions of loyalty were customary on a new emperor's accession, and did not necessarily reflect the Alexandrians' true attitude to the Roman overlords.

88 (*P. Oxy.* 1022)

Copy of letter. Gaius Minicius Italus to his dear Celsianus, greetings. The 6 recruits approved by me are to be entered on the rolls of the cohort which you command, as from 19 February. I have attached their names and marks of identification to this letter. Farewell, dearest brother.
C. Veturius Gemellus, aged 21, no identification mark;
C. Longinus Priscus, aged 22, scar on left eyebrow;
C. Julius Maximus, aged 25, no identification mark;
(?) Lucius Secundus, aged 20, no identification mark;
C. Julius Saturninus, aged 23, scar on the left hand;
M. Antonius Valens, aged 22, scar on the right forehead.

Received 24 February in the 6th year of our emperor Trajan, delivered by the orderly Priscus.
I, Avidius Arrianus, *cornicularius* of the 3rd Ituraean Cohort, have certified that the original is in the record-office of the cohort.

This letter from the prefect of Egypt, Minicius Italus (see **69**), written in Latin, can be assigned to AD 103, since it was issued during the sixth year of Trajan's reign. The Roman imperial army, as has been seen (**82**), selected its recruits with care. Following a detailed medical examination, the recruit was interviewed, and if all was satisfactory, was granted his *probatio* ('approved by me'). These six recruits received theirs on 19 February and then were posted to their unit (the 3rd Ituraean Cohort) for training. One other point of interest in the prefect's letter lies in the recruits' personal details. Each is described by his name, age in years only and any distinguishing marks; the latter appears frequently in legal documents from Egypt. The fact that they have three names, but no indication of their tribe or origin, suggests that, like most recruits for the auxiliary forces at this period, they were not Roman citizens.

89   (*P. Lond.* 904, Col. II = S. *N–H* 459)

Proclamation of Gaius Vibius Maximus, prefect of Egypt. As the house-to-house census has started, all those who for any reason whatsoever are absent from their nomes must be summoned to return to their own hearths, so as to perform the customary business of registration and apply themselves to the cultivation that concerns them. Knowing, however, that some of the people from the country are needed by our city, I desire all those who think they have a satisfactory reason for remaining here to register their reasons with . . . Festus, prefect of the squadron, whom I have appointed for this purpose, from whom those who have shown their presence to be necessary shall receive signed permits in accordance with this edict up to the 30th of the present month E(peiph) . . . return within . . . days . . .

The edict, which is in Greek, was issued by the prefect of Egypt, Gaius Vibius Maximus, in 104: in Column I of the papyrus (not translated here) reference is made to the seventh year of Trajan's reign. Every fourteen years, the Roman administration conducted a census in Egypt (and at various times in each of the other provinces). The heads of every household were required to provide a list of all living under their roof, vital information for levying the various taxes. All householders had to return to their own nome (one of the thirty-six territorial divisions of Roman Egypt), and this was the point of the prefect's opening sentence. Some people, unable to pay their taxes, had abandoned their lands, and either moved to Alexandria or else adopted a nomadic existence (hence the inclusion of the phrase 'the cultivation that concerns them'). All were required to return to the nome where they were born, apart from those whose services in Alexandria were regarded as essential: they were obliged to apply to Festus. The edict provides useful information on the machinery of the census in Egypt.

90 (*BGU* 140 = S. *N–H* 333)

... I know, my dear Rammius, that those whom their parents during their military service acknowledged as their issue have been debarred from succeeding to their fathers' property, and this measure did not appear to be harsh as their action was contrary to military discipline. But I myself have much pleasure in stating a principle which allows me to interpret more liberally the rather strict rule established by previous emperors. For although those who were acknowledged as such in the period of military service are not legitimate heirs of their fathers, nevertheless I rule that they too are able to claim possession of the property through that clause of the edict which gives this right to kinsmen by birth. It will be your duty to make well known both to my soldiers and to the veterans this generosity of mine, not that I may take credit in their eyes, but that they may make use of this privilege, should they be ignorant of it.

This letter of 4 August 119, written in Greek, was issued by the emperor Hadrian to the prefect of Egypt, Rammius Martialis: the first nine lines, which contain the emperor's and prefect's title, together with the date and the areas where the letter was publicly displayed, have not been included in the translation.

As has been previously noted (**34**), Roman soldiers during their period of service could not contract legally valid marriages; thus any children they had at that time were technically illegitimate and remained so until their father's discharge. One consequence was that they could not inherit property in the normal way and this prohibition was enforced until the father's period of service was concluded and he received his military diploma; but should he die before this time, his technically illegitimate children were severely penalized. It was this problem that Hadrian sought to solve.

He recognized the difficulties that the strict interpretation of the law imposed on his soldiers, and acknowledged that his predecessors had been rather severe in administering it. The wording and tone of his letter suggest that the benefit was intended not only for the legionaries in Egypt (it was posted up in the legionary camp there) but for all soldiers without exception – hence the reference to 'veterans', who, presumably may have been penalized in the past. Instead of waiting for appeals from individual soldiers, Hadrian seems to have taken the initiative and modified a long-standing rule so as to benefit every soldier.

B.　Semi-Official and Private Documents

91　(*P. Oxy.* 2435)

The *exegetes*: 'I have given both decrees to the general'.

The general: 'I who was sent by my father, men of Alexandria...'

The crowd called out: 'Hurrah, Lord! Good luck! You will gain blessings!'

The general: 'You, men of Alexandria, you who have set great store by my addressing you, wait till I have completed my answers to each of your questions before you applaud. I, who was sent by my father, as I said, to regulate the overseas provinces, a difficult assignment, in the first place because of the sea voyage, and then because it has torn me from the embrace of my father, my grandmother, my mother, my brothers, my sisters and my children and intimate friends... the... a new sea in order in the first place to see your city...'

The crowd called out: 'Good luck!'

The general: 'Even before now I thought it to be a dazzling spectacle, in the first place because of the hero who is your founder, to whom a common debt is due from those who have the same aspirations, in the second place because of the good offices rendered to my grandfather Augustus and my father... as is right in your case towards me. And I do not speak...'

The crowd called out: 'Well done! May you live all the longer!'

The general: '(I do not speak) of what everyone knows, but I do remember how I have found your greetings multiplied through being stored in your hearts...'

The document, which is in Greek, appears to be a copy, subsequently edited, of a speech delivered by Germanicus in AD 19 at the moment of his arrival in Alexandria. The unnamed general must be Germanicus – note the reference to 'my grandfather Augustus'. Only two of Augustus' grandsons are known to have visited Alexandria – Gaius Caesar, son of Agrippa, natural grandson and also adopted son of Augustus, and Germanicus, nephew of his stepson Tiberius who adopted him as son in AD 5 on Augustus' orders. Both visited the East with special powers but only Germanicus had children. Gaius Caesar, on the other hand, was not married until the very moment of his departure for the East. Finally, the last sentence of the general's second speech ('because it has torn me from the embrace of . . .') is significant in that he omits a reference to his wife, who obviously had not been left in Rome but was with him on his mission. Germanicus' wife, the elder Agrippina, accompanied him throughout his Eastern trip: her reaction following his death at Antioch on 10 October of this same year is recorded by Tacitus (*Annals* 2.72) and is eloquent testimony to her continued presence on this fatal mission.

The document's author is unknown and its accuracy cannot be guaranteed. But, at face value, it is quite interesting. It provides a lively account of his arrival in Alexandria and of his reception both by the crowd of ordinary citizens and by the leading Greek officials. His speech seems to have been hastily improvised as if he had not been prepared for such an enthusiastic welcome: note the repetition of the phrase 'in the first place'.

More important, though, is his attitude to his own position there. In this connection, Tacitus' version of the visit must be considered: 'In the consulship of Marcus Silanus and Lucius Norbanus, Germanicus set out for Egypt to study its antiquities. His ostensible motive however was solicitude for the province. He reduced the price of corn by opening the granaries and adopted many practices pleasing to the multitude. He would go about without soldiers, with sandalled feet, and apparelled after the Greek fashion. . . . Tiberius having gently expressed disapproval of his dress and manners, pronounced a very sharp censure on his visit to Alexandria without the emperor's leave, contrary to the regulations of Augustus. That prince, among other secrets of imperial policy, had forbidden senators and Roman knights of the higher rank to enter Egypt except by permission . . .' (*Annals* 2.59: translated Church and Brodribb). The regulation was clear and Germanicus had contravened it. His comment in his second speech of the document is vital ('I, who was sent by my father . . . to regulate the overseas provinces'), and indicates that he included Egypt amongst 'the overseas provinces'. His instructions before departing are recorded by Tacitus: 'By decree of the senate, the provinces beyond sea were entrusted to Germanicus, with greater powers wherever he went than were given to those who obtained their provinces by lot or by the emperor's appointment' (*Annals* 2.43: translated Church and Brodribb). But it was always under-stood that Egypt was the preserve of the emperor himself and the senate's decree was not intended to alter its status. Perhaps Germanicus was merely careless and acting with the best motives; Tacitus certainly suggests as much. But the ever suspicious Tiberius regarded the visit far less charitably.

The document also provides an insight (that may well be accurate) into Germanicus' nature. He seems to have abandoned what might be called the traditional Roman reserve, overwhelmed no doubt by the warmth of his welcome, and Tacitus reports that he continued in the same vein. The anonymous author presents him as attractive, headstrong but straightforward, as does Tacitus, in contrast to the dissimulating Tiberius.

92   (*P. Oxy.* 1292)

Greetings from Hermogenes to his brother Ischyras. Please put 200 empty jars on board for me, as I asked you before. You have the 16 *drachmae* of silver through Saras, and I've given Hermas 12 *drachmae* for you. If you specially require two pieces of wood to bring down to me the wheel of the machine, they shall be brought up to you by ... Good-bye. (Addressed) To my dearest Ischyras.

The document, which is in Greek, is a private letter from Hermogenes to his brother Ischyras. It is probably to be assigned to *c.* AD 30, since the papyrus with which it was found seems to belong to that year and to have been addressed to the same person.

It is typical of the numerous personal notes that have survived from Roman Egypt, referring to rather humdrum matters that are interesting none the less, for very few areas of the ancient world provide anything like similar evidence of the lives of ordinary citizens. This letter would appear to be repeating a request for 200 jars, all (or perhaps only some) of which had been paid for already, and also indicates the writer's willingness to supply his brother with wood in order to facilitate the transport of a water-wheel.

93 (*BGU* 511 = S 436)

Tarquitius of senatorial rank ... Aviola of senatorial rank ...
the Alexandrian envoys were summoned and the emperor
postponed their hearing till the following day. The 5th day of
Pachon, in the ?13th year of Claudius Caesar Augustus ... The
2nd day: the 6th day of Pachon. Claudius hears the case of
Isidorus, gymnasiarch of Alexandria versus King Agrippa in
the ... gardens. With him sat 20 senators and, in addition, 16
of consular rank; and the women of the court also attended
Isidorus' trial. Isidorus was the first to speak: 'My Lord Caesar,
I beg you to listen to my account of my native city's sufferings.'
The emperor: 'I shall grant you this day.' All the senators who
were sitting as assessors agreed with this, knowing the kind of
man Isidorus was.
Claudius Caesar: 'Say nothing impious against my friend. You
have already done away with two of my friends, Theon the
exegetes and Naevius the prefect ...' The embassy ... The city ...
Lampon to Isidorus: 'I have already looked upon death ...'
Claudius Caesar: 'You have killed many friends of mine,
Isidorus.'
Isidorus: 'I merely obeyed the orders of the emperor of the day.
Tell me whom *you* wish me to denounce and I will do so.'
Claudius Caesar: 'Are you really the son of an actress, Isidorus?'
Isidorus: 'I am neither slave or actress' son, but gymnasiarch of
the glorious city of Alexandria. You are the cast-off son of the
Jewess Salome! And therefore ...'
Lampon said to Isidorus: 'We might just as well give in to a
crazy emperor.'
Claudius Caesar: 'Those whom I told (to perform) the execution
of Isidorus and Lampon ...'

The document, which is in Greek, describes the trial before
Claudius of two Alexandrian Greeks, Isidorus and Lampon; only
the first part (p. 130 of S 436) is translated here. This remarkable
piece of dialogue is one of the fragments of the so-called 'Acts of
the Pagan Martyrs', a collection of Alexandrian nationalist literature surviving only on papyrus.

The majority of the fragments give, in dramatic form, reports of the
hearing of Alexandrian embassies and of the trial of Alexandrian
nationalist leaders before various Roman emperors. The episodes
related ... are probably basically historical and the accounts appear to
be derived to some extent from official records. But they have been
coloured up ... for propaganda purposes to caricature the emperors, to

stress the fearless outspokenness of the Alexandrians, who are sometimes surprisingly rude to the emperors, and to represent their punishment, usually execution, as martyrdom in the nationalist cause. This
literature is in general bitterly hostile to Rome, reflecting the tensions
between Alexandria and her overlord during the first two centuries of
Roman rule. (*OCD²*, p. 7)

In this fragment, it would appear that the nationalist heroes
Isidorus and Lampon had come to Rome to lodge a complaint
against King Agrippa whose favours to the Jews of Alexandria had
aroused the enmity of the Greek section of the city. Some scholars
argue that the Agrippa of our document is Agrippa I, grandson of
Herod the Great and close associate of Claudius whose accession
he had assisted. However, it is now thought that the trial occurred
in AD 53, nine years after the death of Agrippa I (see A. Garzetti,
From Tiberius to the Antonines, London 1974, p. 141), and therefore
it was his son Agrippa II who appears here. Born *c.* AD 27, he had
lived at Claudius' court until 49 when Claudius had him made King
of Chalcis and he subsequently ruled other kingdoms; his sister
Berenice had married the brother of Tiberius Julius Alexander (**79**)
and subsequently fell in love with Vespasian's son Titus (see
Suetonius, *Titus* 7). Brother and sister are mentioned on an
inscription found near the Grand Mosque in Beirut marking the
restoration of a building: 'Queen Berenice, daughter of his majesty
King Agrippa, and King Agrippa fully restored this (building) built
by King Herod their great-grandfather which had collapsed
through age and adorned it with marble and six columns' (M&W
244). The close and consistent connection between this family and
the Roman emperors was not welcomed by the Greeks of
Alexandria to whom Claudius' comment ('Say nothing impious
against my friend') must have appeared particularly ominous.
Whilst the precise charge that Isidorus and Lampon brought
against Agrippa is not known, the implication of Claudius'
comment is that it was a capital one. At all events, the emperor
took advantage of the situation, decided in favour of his friend
Agrippa, and had his two troublesome Alexandrian critics
executed.

Whilst the dramatic details of the trial may well be suspect, the
incident referred to is no doubt historical. Note how carefully the
author sets the scene in one of the imperial gardens in Rome. With
Claudius as judge there were thirty-six senators, including sixteen
of consular rank, who acted as assessors, and the ladies of the
imperial court were also present. The senators were represented
as strongly favouring Isidorus.

Claudius immediately accused Isidorus of having a number of his supporters executed during Gaius' reign, the most important victim being Naevius (Macro), Sejanus' successor as praetorian prefect. Macro had been influential in securing Gaius' accession, but the emperor became suspicious of his power and forced him to commit suicide, together with his wife, in 38, after designating him prefect of Egypt. The author of this fragment of the *Acta* does not, unfortunately, explain how the Alexandrian Isidorus was involved in his fall. Claudius then, indignant at Isidorus' attack on his impartiality ('Tell me whom *you* wish me to denounce and I will do so'), exchanged insults with him — Isidorus' version of Claudius' origins would appear to be particularly incredible, for Salome, the sister of Herod the Great (presuming that she is the Salome meant), was about 60 when Claudius was born. The final aside ('We might just as well give in to a crazy emperor') presents a version of Claudius not inconsistent with that of Suetonius (though that does not guarantee its accuracy): 'Claudius' mother often called him a "monster: a man whom Mother Nature had begun to work upon but not finished": and, if she accused anyone of stupidity, would exclaim: "He is a bigger fool than my son Claudius!" ' (*Claudius* 3.2: Loeb translation, adapted).

Whilst Isidorus and Lampon are portrayed as heroes by the author of the *Acta*, the Jewish writer Philo saw them somewhat differently. According to him, Lampon 'had been put on trial for impiety to Tiberius Caesar', and, as assistant to a judge, 'he took the minutes of the cases, . . . would then expunge some of the evidence or deliberately pass it over and sometimes insert statements that had not been made . . . Frequently the whole people, truly and appropriately, denounced him as a "pen-murderer" whose writings had done multitudes to death . . .' (*In Flaccum* 128–32: Loeb translation). Philo added further details and then went on: 'Such was . . . Lampon. And with him was Isidorus, nothing behind him in villainy, a mob courter, popularity hunter, practised in producing disturbance and confusion, a foe to peace and tranquillity, adept at creating factions and tumults where they do not exist and organising and fostering them when made, even at pains to keep in contact with him an irregular and unstable horde of promiscuous, ill-assorted people . . .' (*In Flaccum* 135: Loeb translation). Philo's comments on Isidorus should perhaps be read in the context of the pogroms referred to in the discussion of Claudius' letter to the Alexandrians (**79**).

The anonymous author of the *Acta* presents, not unnaturally, a diametrically opposed version, glorifying Isidorus and Lampon as heroes unjustly executed for championing the cause of their city's liberty.

94   (*P. Oxy.* 2725)

... The Lord Caesar entered on the 30th at the second hour, first in the camp ... to the Serapeum, from the Serapeum to the ?Hippodrome ... The proceedings in his ?honour you shall know ... Year 3 of the emperor Caesar Vespasian Augustus, month Germaniceus 4.

This recently published document, which is in Greek, is a private letter from a certain Adrastus to his friend Spartacus and can be assigned to the third year of Vespasian's reign, i.e. AD 71: he dated his reign from July 69, when he was proclaimed in Alexandria, and an inclusive method of counting was used. The fourth of Germaniceus is equivalent to 29 April. Only the last few lines of Adrastus' letter have been translated here; the first section contains various items of private business – trading, legal matters and pig fodder, but is too fragmentary to merit inclusion. It would appear, though, that the writer was in a major city, possibly Alexandria.

The reference to the 'Lord Caesar' who had arrived on the 30th is particularly important. Presumably he means Vespasian's son Titus, who must have reached Alexandria by the 30th of the previous month, i.e. Pharmouthi, and so we can assign Titus' arrival in the city to 25 April AD 71.

Rome had been left in charge of Domitian and Mucianus following the civil war, and neither Vespasian nor Titus hurried to the capital. This new document is of considerable assistance in plotting Titus' route back from the East and we can now be certain that around seven in the morning of 25 April 71, Titus entered Alexandria. We have no direct evidence of the length of his stay there, nor of the date of his entry into Rome. Suetonius, however, reports that 'whilst on his way to Alexandria, Titus wore a diadem at the consecration of the bull Apis in Memphis, an act quite in accord with the usual ceremonial of that ancient religion, but unfavourably interpreted by some. Because of this, he hastened to Italy, ... and went with all speed to Rome ... as if to show that the reports about him were groundless' (*Titus* 5.3: Loeb translation).

95   (*P. Oxy.* 266)

The 16th year of the emperor Caesar Domitianus Augustus, on the (?) of the month Germanicus, at Oxyrhynchus in the

Document 94   A section of a letter from Adrastus to Spartacus.
Reproduced by courtesy of the Egypt Exploration Society of London.

Thebaid. Thaesis daughter of Thonis son of Amithonis, her mother being Sintheus, having with her as guardian her stepfather Onnophris son of Onnophris son of Pammenes, his mother being Taarthonis, acknowledges to her late husband Petosarapis son of Thompekusis son of Sarapion, his mother being Sinthonis, all parties inhabitants of Oxyrhynchus, by agreement executed in the street, that she has received from him the capital sum of 400 silver *drachmae* of the imperial coinage which she brought him as a dowry on herself, his mother Sinthonis daughter of Petosarapis son of ... being guarantor, in accordance with a contract of marriage drawn up through the office of the clerk in Oxyrhynchus on the intercalary days of the 14th year of the emperor Caesar Domitianus Augustus Germanicus, and that she has herewith returned to him the authoritative document crossed and cancelled because the marriage is dissolved, and that she neither makes nor will make any claim nor will proceed against him on account of the aforesaid sum or of her personal effects since she has received them back, or of anything else up to the present date. Petosarapis likewise acknowledges, in the street as said, that he neither makes nor will make any claim nor take proceedings against Thaesis or her assigns about any matter whatsoever up to the present day . . .

The document, which is in Greek, is a deed of divorce, and can be assigned to the sixteenth (and last) year of Domitian's reign, AD 96. The usual type of marriage contract, such as the one referred to in this deed of divorce, lists the bride's dowry and also her personal effects (jewellery, furniture and clothing are the items regularly noted); it was drawn up before a public notary ('in the street') and was known as a *gamos eggraphos* ('recorded marriage'). Many of these survive; for an example, consider the following from AD 66:

Copy of contract. The 13th year of the emperor Nero Claudius Caesar Augustus Germanicus, the 22nd of the month Apellaeus (or the 22nd of Phaophi) at Bacchias in the division of Heraclides in the Arsinoite nome. Chaeremon son of Appollonius, Persian of the Epigone, aged about 34 years, with a scar on the middle of the nose, acknowledges to Sisois son of Peteesis, aged about 71 years, with a scar on the left eyebrow, that he has received from him as a dowry on his daughter Thaisarion, who has previously been living with Chaeremon as his wife, a hundred *drachmae* of coined silver and as personal effects a pair of gold earrings weighing four quarters, a gold crescent of three quarters, two gold rings of two quarters, a pair of silver armlets weighing 44 *drachmae* of uncoined metal, two bracelets weighing 16 *drachmae* of uncoined metal; clothing consisting of two robes, one white and one narcissus, and five mantles; copper vessels and a basin, weighing in all four *minae*; two copper . . . unweighed, and five *minae* of tin; and . . . (various tracts of land, amounting to 10¾ *arurae* are then listed). Wherefore let the parties to the marriage, Thaisarion and Chaeremon, live together blamelessly as they have previously been doing, Chaeremon conducting all the agricultural work of each year on the 10¾ *arurae* of the holding which forms the gift, sowing and harvesting the yearly crops and after-crops grown thereon from the said current year and carrying them to the common home of their wedded life, and paying thereon all the yearly public dues both in corn and in money from the said current year. If on a difference arising between them they separate from each other, whether Chaeremon sends Thaisarion away or she voluntarily leaves him, the above-mentioned holding of 10¾ *arurae* shall belong to Thaisarion's father Sisois or, if he be no longer alive, to Thaisarion herself; and Chaeremon shall moreover return to her the aforesaid dowry and her personal effects in whatever state they may eventually be through wear, in the case of dismissal immediately, and in the case of her voluntary departure within thirty days from the date of the demand. (*P. Ryl.* 154)

There was another legally recognized form of marriage, the *gamos agraphos* or 'unrecorded marriage', in which both parties agreed to live together with the provision that the relationship could be terminated at the will of either party. It might later be converted into a *gamos eggraphos*. The 'unrecorded' type of marriage can be illustrated by the case of Tryphon whose wife Demetrous deserted him and took some of his personal effects. His complaint to the chief magistrate has survived:

To Alexander, chief magistrate, from Tryphon, son of Dionysius, of the city of Oxyrhynchus. I lived in marriage with Demetrous, daughter of Heraclides, and I indeed made provision for her even beyond my means. But she became dissatisfied with our union, and finally left the house and carried off my possessions, of which a detailed list is subjoined. I therefore beg that she be brought before you in order that she may receive what she deserves, and may give me back my possessions. This petition is without prejudice to the other claims I have or may have against her. Of the stolen articles there are: a ... worth 40 *drachmae* ... (*P. Oxy.* 282)

The relationship with Demetrous was *agraphos* and so there was neither dowry nor personal effects for her to return since the bride was not required to furnish these items in such a union. For further examples of marriage and divorce contracts, see Lewis and Reinhold, II, pp. 407–8.

96 (*P. Michigan* 203)

Warmest greetings from Saturnilus to his mother Aphrodous. I pray especially for your health and happiness. I want you to

know that I've sent you three letters this month, and have received in full the monthly allowances which you sent me by Julius and a basket of olives by Julius' lad; that I've another son whose name, the Gods willing, is Agathos Daimon ... and that I've been three months now at Pselkis but haven't yet found an opportunity to come to you. I was afraid to come just a while ago because it was rumoured that the Prefect was on his rounds; he might take the letters from me, send me back to the troops, and then I'd incur the expense in vain. But I want you to know that if another two months pass and I don't come to you before the month of Hathur, then I've eighteen months more of sitting in garrison until I can enter Pselkis again and come to you. Take care of my children's pigs so that if my children come they may find them. The next chance you have, please send whatever allowance you can to Julas, son of Julius, and regard him as my son, just as you love me and I love my children. If Julius' brother isn't busy, have him come to me at once so that I can send my children and their mother to you by him. Give my regards to Sokmenius and his children ... and ... to Sabinus, Thaisas, and her children, to my brothers, my sister Tabenka, her husband, and her relations-in-law. Tell me if she's had a child. Give my regards to my sister Tasokmenis ... (and various other relatives) ... I pray for your health.
The ... year of Trajan, the Best, Caesar, our Lord ...

The letter, which is in Greek, was written by Saturnilus, a soldier on active duty in Pselkis, to his mother Aphrodous. The reference to Trajan enables it to be assigned to the period 98–117.

Whilst on active duty, Saturnilus clearly wrote to his mother at regular intervals, providing ample evidence of the closeness of their family, but very little about his military service. We are not told why he feared the prefect (perhaps he was absent without leave), why the latter should seize Saturnilus' letters or why he had to leave Pselkis for over eighteen months. Apparently, it was the absence, or the nature of the terrain where he was to be sent, that persuaded him to send his family to his mother's home. Again, this is valuable evidence for the social rather than the military historian.

97   (*P. Oxy.* 2190)

Warmest greetings from Neilus to Theon, his lord and father. I am no longer despondent since you've made it clear that you weren't worried about that incident in the theatre ... Now, as

I've already told you, the chariots, in which the direct journey would have been made, were smashed up two days ago ... I've written to Philoxenus ... and he says that Didymus who is apparently a friend of his, had some spare time and would be sailing down. According to Philoxenus, he would be more careful than the others, and he's also persuaded the sons of Apollonius, son of Herodes, to go to Didymus; both of them and also Philoxenus have up to now been looking for a cleverer teacher, as their former one, Philologus, had died. My own view is that, if only I had found someone decent, I'd never want to lay eyes on Didymus, even from a distance; for what disturbs me is that this fellow who used to be merely a teacher in the provinces, sees fit to compete with the rest. However, knowing as I do that apart from paying useless and excessive fees there is no good to be had from a teacher, I am depending on myself. If you've any thoughts on the matter, write to me soon. As Philoxenus also says, I've got Didymus ever ready to spend his time on me and do everything in his power. Moreover, with any luck, I shall do well for myself by hearing the lecturers, one of whom is Posidonius.

What worries me about this, and it's making me neglect my health, is that those who have not yet succeeded ought not to concern themselves with these matters, especially when there are none who are bringing in any money. For in the past the useful Heraclas, curse him! used to contribute some *obols* each day, but now, after being deservedly punished by Isidorus, he's escaped and gone back, I think, to you. You can be sure that he'd never hesitate to intrigue against you, for, of all things, he felt no shame at gleefully spreading reports in the city about the incident in the theatre nor at telling the sort of lies that not even a prosecuting lawyer would utter; but so far from getting his just deserts, he's been released and behaves in every respect as though he were a free man. Just the same, if you don't send him back, you could still hand him over to a carpenter (I'm told that a young worker makes two *drachmae* a day) or else have him do some other work at which he'd earn more money. You could then collect his wages, and in due course send them to us — you know that Diogas is also studying.

While you are sending the little one, we will look about for more spacious rooms in a private house; for in order to be near to Dionysius, we've been living in rooms much too small ...

Farewell.

The letter, which is in Greek, was written by Neilus, a student living

possibly in Alexandria, to his father Theon, and can be assigned to
the first century AD.

It is an unusually interesting document, providing the historian
with valuable evidence on various aspects of human activity and
on the attitudes of certain groups towards such institutions as
education and slavery. It would appear that Neilus and his young
brother Diogas were students in Alexandria at a time when there
was a shortage of professors and teachers in Egypt. Apparently
Neilus had been involved in some trouble or other connected with
the theatre, for he refers to this obliquely on two occasions, and is
quite annoyed at his slave's persistence in 'gleefully spreading'
around the details of this escapade. Again, one wonders about
those 'smashed chariots'. Another problem the boys had to face
was a lack of money – they must have supported themselves partly
by the earnings of their slave Heraclas. They were also seeking a
teacher, or more precisely, someone to tutor them at home.
Clearly Didymus was the best of a bad bunch, according to Neilus,
but with nothing to recommend him. The most intriguing section
is his attitude to his slave Heraclas and the latter's relatively
extensive freedom of movement. Letters such as this assist
historians to evaluate more precisely the ancient attitude to slaves
and slavery.

98   (*P. Oxy.* 1154)

Greetings from Theon to his sister Sarapous. Above everything
else do take care of yourself, as I urged you to do when I was
with you, so that I may find you well. Do not worry about me
being away from home, for I know these places personally and
am no stranger here. If I am a soldier . . .

The letter, which is in Greek, was written by Theon to his sister (?
and wife) Sarapous and can be assigned to the latter part of the first
century AD.

Many letters of this type have survived from ancient Egypt,
indicating quite clearly how little change has occurred throughout
the ages in the kind of letter written by a soldier to his wife or
friends at home; for some examples, see Jones, II, pp. 151–2.

99   (*P. Fouad* 76)

Sarapous invites you to dinner for the sacrifice in honour of our
Lady Isis, at her home tomorrow, i.e. the 29th from the 9th hour.

The document, which is in Greek, is a dinner invitation written in the first century of the empire.

It resembles its modern counterpart quite closely in that it was written on a rectangular piece of cardboard, 1½ by 2 inches; its edges have survived intact and it had been folded once.

100 (*P. Tebtunis* 278)

Baker, dyer, fuller, spear-maker, oilman, painter, cobbler, breastplate-maker, doctor, locksmith, mason, millstone-maker, shipwright, scraper-maker, armourer, tablet-maker, ... engraver, glassworker, ... goldsmith ...

My (?garment) is lost; violent was he (?who took it), well-born was he who took it. It was bought for ten coins; if it had been a cloak, I should not have minded. I seek but do not find it. It was taken without cause. He will meet with anger. Just so he took it, my lovely garment. A lion he was who took it, a fool who lost it. It was taken at night. He was a stranger who took it, it was nothing to one like him. I will choke myself, for I am cold ...

This unusual document, which is in Greek, consists of a pair of acrostics written in two separate columns; it can be assigned, from the style of writing, to the first half of the first century AD. The first is a list of various traders, each beginning with a different letter of the alphabet from A to Z. The second column is somewhat more ambitious; it gives in sentences the story of the loss of a garment, and, once again, each sentence begins with a different letter of the alphabet in order. Apparently it is an ancient equivalent of an alphabetical nursery rhyme, intended to reinforce learning of the alphabet.

101 (*P. Oxy.* 32)

Greetings to Julius Domitius, legionary tribune, from Aurelius Archelaus, his *beneficiarius*. I have already recommended my friend Theon to you, and once again I beg you, Sir, to consider him in your eyes as myself. For he's just the sort of person you like. He's left his family, his property and his business and followed me, and in every way he's kept me free from worry. And so I beg you to let him see you, and he can tell you everything about our business. . . . Hold this letter before your eyes, Sir, and imagine that I'm talking with you. Goodbye.

The letter, which is in Latin, was a testimonial for a soldier named Theon, and is usually assigned to the early part of the second century AD. It was sent by a senior non-commissioned officer, Aurelius Archelaus, to his superior, Julius Domitius. In the Roman imperial army, a prospective recruit, or indeed a soldier seeking promotion or a transfer, would, if he were wise, first obtain a letter of recommendation; normally, it would be provided by a member of the family circle or a close friend with military connections. Without it, his chances of success were limited, and no doubt this is one of the reasons why, over the centuries, service in the army tended to become more and more the privilege of a particular section of society. In this document it would appear that Theon had already been recommended by Aurelius and was undeterred by his previous failure. Large numbers of similar documents have survived in the papyri and in literature. Probably the most famous is the letter Pliny wrote in an effort to secure the post of military tribune in Britain for his friend, the historian Suetonius:

You give proof of your high regard for me by the delicacy with which you frame your request that I should transfer to your relative Caesennius Silvanus the military tribunate which I obtained for you from the distinguished senator Neratius Marcellus. For myself, I should have been delighted to see you as a tribune, but I shall be equally pleased if Silvanus owes his office to you. If one has thought a man worthy of promotion it is, I think, illogical to begrudge him the right to show his family feeling, seeing that this does him more honour than any official title. I see too that as the performance of services is as laudable as the deserving of them, you will win praise on both accounts if you give up to someone else what you merited yourself, and I realize that some credit will be reflected on me, too, if as a result of your action it is known that my friends are free either to hold the office of tribune themselves or to give it away. Your wish is thus excellent in every way and shall be granted. Your name is not yet entered on the lists, so it is easy for me to substitute that of Silvanus; and I hope that your service will please him as much as mine pleases you. (*Ep.* 3.8: Loeb translation)

Apparently Pliny had managed to persuade the governor of Britain, Neratius Marcellus, to appoint Suetonius to his staff, but then Suetonius changed his mind about serving in Britain and asked Pliny to transfer the post to someone else, his relative Caesennius Silvanus; no doubt Suetonius' second letter required the 'delicacy' to which Pliny refers. But it is important to note that the eminently proper and respectable Pliny regarded this entire practice as quite normal. It was, then, a standard procedure both for recruits to the army and also for soldiers seeking to better themselves, and could be regarded as equivalent to our system of referees' reports and testimonials. For further examples of this type of document, see Jones, II, pp. 136–7, 142–3.

102 (*P. Giessen* 3 = S. *N–H* 519)

Phoebus: Having just mounted aloft with Trajan in my chariot of white horses, I come to you, O people, I, Phoebus, a by no means unknown god, to proclaim the new ruler Hadrian, whom all things serve on account of his virtue and the Genius of his divine father.
Demos: Let us make merry, let us kindle our hearths in sacrifice, let us surrender our souls to laughter, to the wine of the fountains and the unguents of the stadium; for all of which we are indebted to the reverence of our *strategos* for our Lord and his zeal on (?our) behalf.

The document, which is in Greek, is a fragment of a dramatic performance in honour of Hadrian's succession. The phrase, 'Let us make merry', which in S. *N–H*, p. 192, is attributed to Phoebus, has been assigned to the Demos in the translation.

The accession of a new emperor inevitably prompted congratulatory messages and expressions of loyalty from throughout the empire; at Heptakomia in Egypt it was celebrated with some sort of pageant, of which this tiny fragment alone has survived. In it, Phoebus is portrayed as having returned to earth 'to proclaim the new ruler Hadrian' after accompanying his 'divine father' to heaven. This, presumably, refers to the deification of Trajan and suggests that the document is to be assigned to 117 or not long afterwards. No doubt it was officially inspired, and the stress on the legitimacy of the new emperor's position is significant, for there were rumours that Trajan had not nominated a successor and that Hadrian's accession was facilitated by the praetorian prefect and Trajan's wife (see **19**) acting illegally.

103 (*P. Oxy.* 1242 = S. *N–H* 516)

... Dionysius, who held several procuratorial posts, and Salvius, Julius Salvius, Timagenes, Pastor the gymnasiarch, Julius Phanias, Philoxenus the gymnasiarch-elect, Sotion the gymnasiarch, Theon, Athenodorus, and Paulus of Tyre, voluntary advocate for the Alexandrians. When the Jews learned this, they too elected envoys from their own group, and thus were chosen Simon, Glaucon, Theudes, Onias, Colon, Jacob, with Sopatros of Antioch as their advocate. They set sail, then, from the city, each party taking its own gods along, the Alexandrians ... He conversed with their companions; and at the end of the winter, they landed at Rome. When the emperor learned that the envoys of the Jews and Alexandrians had arrived, he appointed the day on which he would hear both parties; and Plotina approached the senators in order that they might oppose the Alexandrians and support the Jews. Now the Jews entered first, and greeted the emperor Trajan who returned their greeting most cordially, having already been won over by Plotina. After them the Alexandrian envoys entered and greeted the emperor. He, however, did not go to meet them, but said: 'You say "hail" to me as though you deserved a greeting — after all that you have dared to do to the Jews! Be off with you and ... You must be eager to die, having such contempt for death as to answer even me with insolence.'

Hermaiscus said: 'Why, we are grieved to see your Council filled with impious Jews.'

Caesar said: 'This is the second time I tell you, Hermaiscus: you are answering me insolently, taking advantage of your birth.'

Hermaiscus said: 'What do you mean, I am answering you insolently, greatest emperor? Explain this to me.'

Caesar said: 'Pretending that my Council is filled with Jews.'

Hermaiscus: 'So, then, the word "Jew" is offensive to you? In that case you ought rather to help your own people and not play the advocate for the impious Jews.' (lines 4–50)

The document, which is in Greek, is a particularly interesting account of the members of a Jewish and of an Alexandrian embassy to the emperor Trajan, and of a supposed conversation between the emperor and one of the Alexandrians. It is another fragment of the so-called 'Acts of the Pagan Martyrs', discussed in **93**. The section translated lists the members from each side, and some interesting points emerge. Dionysius, for instance, the first of the Alexandrians, is known to us from other sources and was probably a grandson of the Gaius Julius Dionysius of Claudius' famous letter to the Alexandrians (**79**, sec. C); from the text it would appear that he was regarded as the leader of the group. Hermaiscus, who is particularly prominent in the section trans-lated, is not even listed, either through error, or else because he was already in Rome and was co-opted by the others on their arrival in the capital. Now whilst most of the *Acta* are violently anti-Roman, the general tone of this fragment is anti-Semitic. As we have observed elsewhere (**79**), racial tension certainly existed in Alexandria and in other cities, and it is reflected in the reported remarks of Hermaiscus who, like his Alexandrian colleagues, regarded the Romans as pro-Jewish – an opinion not shared by the Jewish writers of this time, needless to say. There is no other evidence or even suggestion of the alleged Jewish sympathies of Trajan's wife, Plotina. Perhaps the support supposedly given them by Poppaea, Nero's wife (Josephus, *Jewish Antiq.* 20.195), was applied by extension to Plotina as well. At all events the accusation is quite unlikely. Another claim of the Greek propaganda was that the emperor's 'Privy Council' was 'filled with impious Jews'. During the Julio-Claudian period at least, the Herods were always on good terms with the imperial household, whilst Nero's and Vespasian's promotion to high rank of the apostate Jew Tiberius Julius Alexander has already been noted (**79**); under Trajan we hear of another Tiberius Julius Alexander, procurator of Crete, and also of a Tiberius Julius Alexander Julianus, a senator, both of whom may well have been related to Vespasian's prefect. It is just possible that Julianus was a member of Trajan's Council. Obviously, then, there is very little supporting evidence of the *Acta*'s claim and it would seem not unreasonable to regard the accusation as baseless, or, at best, highly exaggerated. The fragment is a valuable document none the less. Whatever the historical accuracy of the facts reported, the attitude of the Alexandrians no doubt reflected faithfully the feelings of the Greek community there, and provides us with some indication of how Rome's subjects regarded her.

104 (*P. Tebtunis* 381)

18 December in the 8th year of the emperor Caesar Trajan Hadrian Augustus, at Tebtunis in the division of Polemon of the Arsinoite nome. Thaesis daughter of Orsenouphis son of Onnophris, her mother being Thenobastis, of the aforesaid village of Tebtunis, aged about 78 years, having a scar on her right forearm, acting with her guardian, her relative Cronion son of Ameis, aged about 27, having a scar between his eyebrows, acknowledges that she, the acknowledging party, Thaesis, has consented that after her death there shall belong to Thenpetesuchus, her daughter by her late husband Pomsais, and also to Sansneus, son of Tephersos, the son of her other daughter Taorseus, now dead, to the two of them, property as follows: to Thenpetesuchus, the house, yard and all effects

belonging to Thaesis in the said village of Tebtunis by right of
purchase from Thenpetesuchus daughter of Petesuchus, and
the furniture, utensils, household stock and apparel left by
Thaesis, and the sums due to her and other property of any
kind whatsoever, while to Sansneus she has bequeathed 8
drachmae of silver, which Sansneus shall receive from Thenpetesuchus after the death of Thaesis; on condition that the
daughter Thenpetesuchus shall properly perform the obse-
quies and laying out of her mother, and shall discharge such
private debts as Thaesis shall prove to owe, but as long as her
mother Thaesis lives she shall have power to . . .

The document, which is in Greek, is the will of a certain Thaesis
from Tebtunis and can be assigned to 18 December AD 124. It
throws light on legal procedures and practices in Roman Egypt.
According to its terms, she bequeathed to her daughter Thenpetesuchus all of her property apart from 8 *drachmae* of silver, which
were to go to her grandson Sansneus. The daughter was also
charged with providing for her burial. Note how carefully the
family tree is explained. It might be summarized as follows:

Onnophris
|
Orsenouphis m. Thenobastis
|
Thaesis m. Pomsais
|
Thenpetesuchus   Taorseus m. Tephersos
|
Sansneus

It is clear that the Thenpetesuchus daughter of Petesuchus from
whom Thaesis purchased various property must be distinguished
from Thaesis' daughter of the same name. Like other legal and
semi-legal documents from Egypt, this will illustrates the care
taken to identify the principal persons involved – both Thaesis and
her guardian Cronion bore scars that were precisely recorded in
the document; for further examples, see Lewis and Reinhold, II,
pp. 277–82.

105   (*P. Fayum* 19 = S. *N–H* 123)

Greetings from the emperor Caesar Hadrian Augustus to his
most esteemed Antoninus. Above all, I want you to know that I
am being released from my life neither before my time, nor
unreasonably, nor piteously, nor unexpectedly, nor with facul-
ties impaired, even though I shall almost seem, as I have found,
to do injury to you who are by my side whenever I am in need

of attendance, consoling and encouraging me to rest. From such considerations I am impelled to write to you as follows, not by Zeus, as one who subtly devises a tedious account contrary to the truth, but rather making a simple and most accurate record of the facts themselves, . . . and he who was my father by birth fell ill and passed away as a private citizen at the age of forty, so that I have lived half as long again as my father, and have reached nearly the same age as that of my mother . . .

The document, which is in Greek, purports to be a letter written by the emperor Hadrian in AD 138 to his adopted son, the 52-year-old Titus Aurelius Fulvus Boionius Arrius Antoninus who subsequently became the emperor Antoninus Pius (i.e. the emperor Caesar Titus Aelius Hadrian Antoninus Augustus Pius). He was adopted following the death of Lucius Aelius Caesar (**21**) on 1 January 138; seven months later, on 10 July, Hadrian himself died.

Some scholars have doubted whether the document is genuine. After giving the Greek text, S. *N–H*, p. 58, notes that 'the first five lines (of the letter) are . . . repeated, with some mistakes, in another hand'. It could well be argued, then, that the document was produced by a teacher of rhetoric and then copied out, with a few errors, by one of his pupils as some sort of exercise. In favour of such a view of the letter is the rather strained comparison between the length of the emperor's life and that of his parents which occurs towards the end of the section translated. Other references, though, suggest that it might be genuine.

Whilst insisting that death would be a relief to him, Hadrian was concerned at the reaction of Antoninus, for he had once before objected ('as I have found') to Hadrian's stated intention to commit suicide, and, in the rest of the letter, the emperor apparently prepared a reasoned and detailed argument to support his plan to be 'released from life'. According to Dio Cassius he did indeed consider suicide: 'He . . . began to be sick; for he had been subject even before this to a flow of blood from the nostrils and at this time it became distinctly more copious. He therefore despaired of his life. . . . And indeed Hadrian did linger on a long time in his illness, and often prayed that he might expire, and often desired to kill himself. There is, indeed, a letter of his in existence which gives proof of precisely this – how dreadful it is to long for death and yet be unable to die' (69.17.3: Loeb translation). The anonymous author of the *Life of Hadrian* also claims that a suicide attempt was prevented by Antoninus who 'begged him to endure with fortitude the hard necessity of illness, declaring furthermore that he himself would be no better than a parricide, were he, an adopted son, to permit Hadrian to be killed' (24.9: Loeb translation). This could well explain the statement 'as I have found' in the letter. It is, then, not impossible that the document is in fact genuine: possibly it is a later version of the letter referred to by Dio. If so, it should be added to the few other surviving pieces of genuine Hadrianic composition, throwing some light on the emperor's attitude to death and suicide.

Examples of Historical Reconstruction

A. A Vespasianic War of Conquest in Germany

The following passage is from E. T. Salmon's *A History of the Roman World: 30 B.C. to A.D. 138* (London 1968), p. 241:

Between the Upper Rhine and the Upper Danube there is a triangle of land which is mostly occupied by the Black Forest. This area, so Tacitus implies, was called the Agri Decumates, a title, possibly obsolete and native, that has never been satisfactorily explained. In 73 Vespasian instructed Cn. Cornelius Clemens, legate of Upper Germany, to annex the region. Frontier rectification was presumably his main motive: the boundary would thus become shorter and straighter, and intercommunication between Rhine and Danube camps would be facilitated. In the process Vespasian would safeguard the growing civil life on the left bank of the Rhine and would also obtain land on which to settle his veterans. He may even have hoped to derive a large revenue from the area, a consideration to which the thrifty Flavian would certainly not be indifferent. To find a pretext was not difficult. The area was sparsely populated and of uncertain ownership: if Rome did not claim it, somebody else probably would. The annexation was achieved without undue difficulty, although it did not proceed very rapidly. With each step forward fortresses were established to consolidate gains; some of these ultimately grew into towns and cities. By 79 Roman arms had at least reached a line that stretched from Argentorate (*Strasbourg*) by way of

Arae Flaviae (*Rottweil*), where a centre of Caesar-worship was instituted, to Lake Constance; and they may even have got as far north as the line that runs from Baden to Günzburg on the Upper Danube. This would seem to be the area of the Agri Decumates proper.

The passage describes military operations of considerable extent, based on a well-thought-out policy in the area of the upper reaches of the rivers Rhine and Danube, and several motives for these activities are suggested. It may come as a surprise, therefore, to learn that there is no mention of this war, its causes and consequences in any of our surviving literary works. The passage is based on the interpretation and piecing together of a number of inscriptions, the excavations of archaeologists and the conjectural connection with these pieces of information of a passage from the *Germania* of Tacitus, which gives no indication of the date to which the passage refers and only a vague indication of the geographical area which is the subject of the passage. Here is the passage, given in the Penguin translation of the *Germania* of H. Mattingly, revised by S. A. Handford. The *Germania*, it should be noted, may have been composed in or about AD 98, but even this is a matter of dispute.

I am not inclined to reckon among the peoples of Germany the cultivators of the *agri decumates*, although they have established themselves between the Rhine and the Danube. All the most disreputable characters in Gaul, all the penniless adventurers, seized on a territory that was a kind of no man's land. It was only later, when the frontier line of defence was drawn and the garrisons moved forward, that they came to be regarded as an outlying corner of the empire and a part of a province.

Some comments may immediately be made on the passage. (i) We do not know what the word *decumates* means in the phrase *agri decumates*; and this is acknowledged by Salmon. The phrase may mean 'fields on which a tithe (of the produce) is paid'; it may alternatively mean 'land divided up into groups of ten districts or communes'. (ii) These *agri decumates may* have been situated between the rivers Rhine and Danube; and this area *may* have been 'a triangle of land which is mostly occupied by the Black Forest', though this is not a necessary conclusion. All that can be said with certainty is that 'between the Rhine and the Danube' implies an area east of the Rhine and north of the Danube. The Latin text also admits of another interpretation: the people who settled between the Rhine and the Danube, whom Tacitus does not regard as Germans but as Gauls, came thither from a part of Gaul that had the name *agri decumates*. (iii) The final sentence of the passage suggests that these settlers were eventually enclosed within the defensive frontier line known as the *limes*, when they thus became 'a part of a province' or 'a part of *the* province', though in neither instance is the province specified. If the *Germania* was written in AD 98, we are looking at an area 'between the Rhine and the Danube' which extended from Mainz on the Rhine, through Heidelberg and Stuttgart, to Ulm on the Danube. The 'province', because of its enclosure within the *limes* system, can only have been either Raetia or Upper Germany; and the two Germanies (Upper and Lower) did not gain true provincial status until about AD 90. The passage, then, is full of uncertainties; and the best that can be said of it is that it *may*, on the basis of the evidence to be cited next, apply to the Black Forest and *may* refer to the reign of Vespasian.

Next, we may look at the evidence which enables Salmon to write that 'In 73 Vespasian instructed Cn. Cornelius Clemens, legate of Upper Germany, to annex the region'. There is considerable epigraphical evidence attesting the presence of Cn. Pinarius, son of Lucius, Cornelius Clemens as legate with the rank of propraetor of the army in Upper Germany (and note that (i) though the year of Clemens' consulate is not known, it must have been before this command, which was invariably consular; and (ii) his correct title of legate 'of the army in Upper Germany', not 'of the province' of Upper Germany, shows that he held this command before the Germanies attained provincial status). In the following inscriptions the major conjectural restorations will be indicated by their inclusion in square brackets.

(a) **M&W 50 (= *ILS* 997), from Hispellum in Umbria:**
Cn. Pinarius, son of Lucius, of the Papian tribe, Cor[nelius Clemens ...], legate with the rank of propraetor of the army which [is in Upper Germany, commissioner] of sacred [buildings] and of public places ... with triumphal adornments [... on account of activities successfully carried out] in Germany.

We may note, firstly, that this inscription gives us no indication of or help in the dating of any part of it; but that Cn. Pinarius, son of Lucius, received the very prestigious award of triumphal adornments for successful activities in Germany is a pretty certain restoration. The unrestored inscription, however, does not tell us whether the Germany is Upper or Lower.

(b) **M&W 399 (= *ILS* 1992), a military diploma from Sikator in Upper Pannonia (only the relevant sections will be translated here):**

The emperor Caesar Vespasian Augustus, pontifex maximus, of tribunician power for the 5th time, saluted as victorious commander 13 times, father of his country, consul for the 5th time, designated for the 6th time, censor, to the cavalrymen and infantrymen, who are serving in the 6 cavalry squadrons and 12 infantry cohorts, which are called ... [then follow the names of the units] ... and are in Germany under Cn. Pinarius Cornelius Clemens ...

On the day before the 12th day of the Calends of June, in the second consulship of Q. Petillius Cerialis Caesius Rufus and the second consulship of T. Clodius Eprius Marcellus.

The diploma gives us several pieces of important information, as well as recording the full name of Cornelius Clemens and his command in Germany (though note that the text does not tell us whether it is Upper or Lower Germany). It gives us a precise date – day, month and year – of issue: 21 May AD 74; the year can be corroborated both by the consuls in office, whose place in the consular lists is definitely known, and by the tribunician power of Vespasian, whose fifth year of power extended from 1 July AD 73 to 30 June AD 74. Clemens, then, was in command of the army of (Upper) Germany in the first half of AD 74. It may be significant that the veteran soldiers of the units mentioned in the document, whilst given citizenship and the other customary related privileges, are not given their discharge. The implication is that war was either still in progress or had so recently finished or was expected to break out so soon that it was felt that these soldiers had to be retained by their units, despite the completion of their period of service.

(c) M&W 446 (= *ILS* 5957), a boundary stone marking the result of a boundary determination, found in the Graian Alps at the Col de la Forclaz between Chamonix and St Gervais-les-Bains: On the authority of the emperor Caesar Vespasian Augustus, pontifex maximus, of tribunician power for the 5th time, consul for the 5th time, designated for the 6th time, father of his country, Cn. Pinarius Cornelius Clemens, his legate with the rank of propraetor of the army of Upper Germany, determined [the boundary] between the people of Vienna and the Ceutronae.

Again on the basis of Vespasian's tribunician power and consulship, the inscription gives us a fairly precise date: between 1 January AD 74, when Vespasian entered his fifth consulship, and 30 June AD 74, when his fifth year of tribunician power came to an end. It also provides us with a further piece of specific information: Cornelius Clemens was legate of the army of *Upper* Germany.

(d) M&W 416 (= *ILS* 5832), a milestone from Offenburg:
... when Caesar, [son of Augustus, Domiti]an was consul [for the third time] (and) Cn. Cor[nelius Cleme]ns was legate [of the emperor with the rank of propraetor], the road was d[riven from Arge]ntorate to R[aetia?] ... F[rom Argentorate ? miles ...].

The text is very fragmentary; however, some restorations are fairly certain, e.g. the name of Domitian, whose name is joined with those of his father and brother Titus on other milestones; uncertain, however, is the consular number. The restoration of the full name of Cornelius Clemens and his rank are also reasonably certain, as is that of the first two syllables of the city Argentorate (modern Strasburg). The terminal point of the road has been conjecturally restored from the surviving letter R as Raetia; but some editors would restore it, in Latin, to in r[ipam Danuvii], i.e. 'to the bank of the Danube'. It is not possible to give a precise date to the inscription, because of the loss of Domitian's consular number. He was consul for the second time in AD 73 and for the third time in either 74 or 75; at the time of Titus' death in AD 81 he was consul for the eighth time. As it is highly unlikely that Clemens was in Upper Germany in AD 71, the year of Domitian's first consulship, it would seem reasonable to restore the consulship to the third, of AD 74 or 75, the former of which is the only attested year of Cornelius Clemens' legateship. The milestone recorded the distance from Argentorate, through Offenburg, as far as Arae Flaviae (modern Rottweil); where it went from Rottweil is guess-work. If the restoration 'to Raetia' is accepted, Lake Constance seems to be a reasonable terminal-point, as in the Salmon passage ('to Lake Constance'); if the restoration 'to the bank of Danube' is preferred, Tuttlingen or Laiz would seem reasonable terminal-points.

These pieces of evidence enable us to say definitely that Cn. Pinarius Cornelius Clemens was commander of the army of Upper Germany in AD 74 and possibly AD 75 and that at or near this time he obtained a success, either military or diplomatic or both, which enabled Vespasian to award him the triumphal adornments. We can also say that during his period as legate, he was responsible for the construction of a road that cut across the eastern boundary of the Black Forest area; and it is well known that Roman roads invariably had a military purpose, in order to facilitate the swift movement of troops from one strategic – and usually frontier – area to another. This evidence can be taken with the evidence of archaeological excavations, which reveal the construction of forts during the reign of Vespasian along the line of the road across the Black Forest, at Offenburg, Waldmössingen and Rottweil. It is also possible, though the archaeological evidence is vaguer and less precise even than for the forts on the roads across the Black Forest, that several of the auxiliary forts of Raetia were transferred by Vespasian to the northern bank of the Danube. If this is so, then it indicates that Vespasian intended to link the Roman frontier on the Rhine with that on the Danube, thereby shortening the frontier and enclosing behind it the Black Forest area. The military activities of Cornelius Clemens and his road-building work, revealed by the inscriptions, will have been the means of occupying this area and pacifying it. The military operations, which may have had Argentorate as their starting-point, will have been either accompanied or succeeded by the road-building and construction of the forts. The organization and conduct of this enterprise must have been on a grand scale; and Cornelius Clemens, who never again appears in history, must have thoroughly deserved his triumphal adornments. He might also have expected to receive the further honour of a second consulship, but if he did, no trace of it has so far been revealed from epigraphical material. It should be stressed that there is no direct evidence linking the building of the Vespasianic forts across the Black Forest with the activities of Cornelius Clemens, but the assumption of such a link can be regarded as not only plausible but inevitable; and a further piece of indirect evidence, to be discussed shortly (see Addendum), throws further light on the large scale of the operation. It should also be repeated that the passage in Tacitus' *Germania* (chapter 29), which refers to the *agri decumates*, *may* be referring to this operation, but that we cannot be more positive than this. It can thus be seen how the evidence of inscriptions is here the sole evidence preserved to us of a large-scale war in southern Germany that occurred under the rule of Vespasian and formed an important part of his plans for the northern frontier of the empire.

Addendum: the following inscription (M&W 340 = *ILS* 2729) may well throw further light on the scale of Clemens' operation across the Rhine. It is a monument, from Rome, erected by a mother to her son.

To Titus Staberius, son of Titus, of the Quirinian tribe, Secundus, prefect of a cohort of Chalcidians in Africa, military

tribune of the legion 7 Gemina Felix in Germany, prefect of cavalry of the Moesian squadron Felix Torquata, Staberia, his mother, [erected this] at her own expense.

The military postings of T. Staberius Secundus are in ascending order, i.e. the cavalry prefecture being the one most recently held. From another inscription it is known that Staberius was holding the cavalry prefecture in April AD 78. His military tribunate must, therefore, have been held before this date. The legion 7 Gemina had not been one of the Rhine legions before the accession of Vespasian. Originally from Spain, it formed part of the Pannonian garrison at the time of Vespasian's bid for power and under its legate, Antonius Primus, had spearheaded the invasion of Italy and the capture of Rome; nor at that time did it have the honorific title Felix, 'the Fortunate' (i.e. successful in battle). Tacitus tells us, *Histories* 4.39, that Mucianus, probably in January AD 70, as a means of breaking the excessive and disruptive influence of Antonius Primus, sent off the seventh legion (i.e. Gemina) into winter quarters away from its commander. Unfortunately, Tacitus does not tell us where these winter quarters were, although a return to Pannonia, whose garrison had been reduced by the transfer of legion 13 Gemina to Lower Germany, seems possible. The evidence of the Staberius inscription shows that at some time before April AD 78, 7 Gemina was in Germany and that by this date it had acquired the title Felix. Other epigraphical evidence has revealed that the legion's stay was in Upper Germany and it is known from yet another inscription that it had been transferred back to its native Spain by AD 79. A reasonable conclusion to draw from all of this evidence is that 7 Gemina was temporarily attached to the army of Upper Germany during Vespasian's reign and that during this time it gained for itself the honorific title Felix. Whether it was brought back to Germany from Pannonia or elsewhere or whether it was sent directly by Mucianus to winter quarters in Germany cannot be said. Be that as it may, the garrison of Upper Germany appears to have been temporarily increased to five legions and the date and purpose of this increase seems most probably to have been the operations of Cornelius Clemens in the Black Forest area. We may note that an army of five legions, together with the large number of auxiliary units, represented the most powerful army in the whole Roman empire and, situated as it was in Upper Germany, the one nearest to Italy and Rome. This in itself is yet another indication of the confidence that Vespasian must have had, not only in the military abilities of Cornelius Clemens, but in his absolute loyalty.

Two further inscriptions may be briefly mentioned here. These are M&W 299 and 300 (= *ILS* 990 and 991), both from Fulginiae in Umbria and both from monuments erected in honour of two brothers, Cn. Domitius Afer Titius Marcellus Curvius Lucanus and Cn. Domitius . . . Curvius Tullus (the name of the second brother is lost from the inscription and restored from literary evidence). Each of the two brothers is referred to in his own inscription as having been 'prefect of all the auxiliary troops against the Germans' and as having been presented by 'the emperor Vespasian Augustus and Titus Caesar, son of Augustus' with various military decorations. It has been assumed by many scholars that these prefectures took place during service with Cornelius Clemens during his Black Forest campaign (cf. R. Syme, *Cambridge Ancient History*, Cambridge 1969, p. 161: 'two senators who held in succession the command over the auxiliary forces were also decorated'). It should be noted, however, that neither inscription tells us whether the Germans were those of Upper or Lower Germany. Moreover, the assigning of these two prefectures to Clemens' operations in the mid-70s depends on the conjectural dating of the rest of the careers of the brothers; and it can be argued, with equal plausibility, that their offices should be dated several years earlier than has traditionally been done and that therefore their German commands should be assigned to operations in Vespasian's reign earlier than those of Clemens, perhaps the operations against Civilis and the Batavians in Lower Germany in AD 70. The inscriptions are therefore mentioned here, but not made part of the reconstruction.

B.   The Revolt of Saturninus

The following passage, describing a revolt against Domitian by L. Antonius Saturninus, is from Salmon, *A History of the Roman World*, pp. 232–3:

In one province, serious internal trouble did develop, in Upper Germany. In 88 L. Antonius Saturninus, commander of Legions XIV Gemina and XXI Rapax stationed at the 'double' camp of Moguntiacum, raised the standard of revolt. . . .

Domitian, however, had followed his father's example in carefully cultivating the provincial armies, and his popularity with them now stood him in good stead. Although the Danubian legions were unavailable, he was able to muster overwhelming forces against the insolent pretender: the other two legions of Upper Germany, the four legions of Lower Germany under L. Appius Maximus Norbanus, and the Spanish legion which the future Emperor Trajan rapidly trasferred. Domitian himself hurried north with some of his Praetorians in January 89. But before he arrived Saturninus had already been defeated and killed by Norbanus somewhere north of Moguntiacum on the left bank of the Rhine. An unseasonable thaw prevented the Chatti from participating in the battle: the ice broke up, so that they could not cross the river.

Saturninus' was not the first conspiracy against Domitian, but it was the most dangerous. Domitian's fears may even have magnified it, for he could not discover its ramifications. Any papers that might have implicated others were destroyed by Norbanus in the rebels' camp.

The passage describes a revolt led by Lucius Antonius Saturninus who held one of the most strategically significant posts available to a senator, the governorship of the imperial province of Upper Germany. As 'legate of the emperor with the rank of propraetor', he had overall control of the province's four legions together with their auxiliary forces; his loyalty and efficiency were vital for the empire's security as well as for the emperor's survival. Yet even though a revolt by an officer of this rank was an event of critical importance, both contemporary and later literary sources are singularly unhelpful in the information they provide about Saturninus himself, the causes of his revolt, the general who suppressed it and even about when it began.

It is worthwhile examining such literary evidence as we have so as to discover the basis for Salmon's account. Four contemporary or near contemporary writers refer to aspects of the revolt. According to Suetonius, 'A civil war which was set on foot by Lucius Antonius, governor of Upper Germany, was put down in the emperor's absence by a remarkable stroke of good fortune; for at the very hour of the battle the Rhine suddenly thawed and prevented his barbarian allies from crossing over to Antonius. Domitian learned of this victory through omens before he actually had news of it' (Suetonius, *Dom.* 6.2). Plutarch's account is even vaguer: '. . . Antonius was in revolt from Domitian and a great war was expected from Germany; . . . (Domitian) was already on the march when messages and letters announcing the victory came to meet him' (*Life of Aemilius Paullus* 25). Martial attacked an Antonius (presumably the same man) in the fourth book of his *Epigrams* (the first poem of which was written for Domitian's thirty-seventh birthday, 24 October AD 88): 'While, swollen with pride, you rejoiced overmuch in an empty name and were ashamed, wretched man, to be Saturninus, you awoke such impious war. . . . Did the Rhine promise you what the Nile did not give him?' (*Epigr.* 4.11: Martial is comparing Saturninus with Mark Antony).

In his *Panegyricus* to the emperor Trajan, delivered on the occasion of his consulship in 100, Pliny refers to Trajan's role in helping to suppress Saturninus' revolt: '(Domitian) had called you from Spain to be his surest support during these very German wars, unwilling as he was to bestir himself and jealous of another's virtues even when he was in dire need of them' (*Pan.* 14.5). Two points should be borne in mind. In an attempt to gloss over Trajan's support of Domitian, whose memory had been officially condemned (**59**), Pliny denigrates the emperor's role in the revolt – compare the account of Plutarch previously cited. Secondly, he has adopted the 'official' designation of the war: it was not to be referred to as a 'civil war' (as Suetonius does in his *Life of Domitian* 6.2) but rather as a 'German war'.

Dio Cassius, writing a century later, adds some significant details: 'A certain Antonius, who was governor of Germany at this period, revolted against Domitian; but Lucius Maximus overcame him and destroyed him. Now so far as this victory was concerned Maximus does not deserve any particular praise . . . but for his action in burning all the papers that were found in the chest of Antonius, thus esteeming his own safety as of slight importance in comparison with the preventing of their use for the purpose of blackmailing anyone, I do not see how I can praise him enough' (67.11.1–2). His account seems to be at variance with that of epitomator of Aurelius Victor, *De Caesaribus* (fourth century AD), who states that the revolt was suppressed by Norbanus Appius (or Norbanus Lappius – the manuscripts vary in their spelling of the name: *Epit. de Caes.* 11.10). Two further literary references should be noted. In one of his letters to the emperor Trajan (*Ep.* 10.58.6), Pliny quotes a letter that Domitian had written to L. Appius

Maximus who was almost certainly a proconsul of Pontus-Bithynia, whilst Martial addressed an epigram to a certain Norbanus, praising his 'loyalty to your master Caesar' (*Epigr.* 9.84). Some scholars have attempted to solve the problem by assigning the name Lucius Appius Maximus Norbanus to Dio's 'Lucius Maximus': note, for example, Th. Mommsen, *The Provinces of the Roman Empire from Caesar to Diocletian* (tr. W. P. Dickson, Ares Reprint, Chicago 1974), p. 151, B. W. Henderson, *Five Roman Emperors* (Cambridge 1927), p. 114, and also Salmon in the passage cited above.

The literary evidence, then, suggests that a governor of Upper Germany, Lucius Antonius Saturninus, revolted against Domitian probably not long after the emperor's thirty-seventh birthday, that he had hoped for assistance from Rome's traditional enemies, the transrhenine Germans, that someone possibly named Lucius Appius Maximus Norbanus suppressed the revolt (burning any incriminating evidence), that Trajan came from Spain to assist the emperor, and that, before Domitian himself could reach Germany, the revolt was over. This, essentially, is the information provided by Salmon. It can, however, be amplified and, in one aspect, corrected by epigraphical evidence.

On four occasions, the minutes of the Arval Brothers for January 89 refer to prayers offered for the emperor's victory and safe return: they do not, unfortunately, provide any reason for his absence from Rome. One of these four inscriptions is translated below with any conjectural restorations indicated by their inclusion in square brackets. '. . . During the consulship of the same men (i.e. AD 89), on 12 January, on the Capitol, the [Arval Brothers] pronounced [vows] for the safety and vict[ory and return] of the emperor Domitian Caesar Augustus Ger[manicus] in accordance with a decree of the Senate' (M&W 15, lines 14–16). A possible interpretation of this and the three other similar inscriptions is that Domitian was at the time on his way to Germany, attempting to suppress the revolt by his consular legate, Saturninus.

An inscription from Rome adds further information: 'to . . . elia, (wife of) [L]appius Maximus, twice consul, who brought the German war to a conclusion' (*ILS* 1006 = M&W 60). We note that, as in Pliny's *Panegyricus*, the official designation of the revolt, the 'German war', has been used, and that the senator who 'brought the German war to a conclusion' had received two consulships, a singular honour indeed and one that is not mentioned by the literary sources. The magnitude of the honour can be seen from an examination of the known consuls of Domitian's reign: thanks to the work of epigraphists during the last forty years or so, over 115 consuls of his reign are now definitely attested. Lappius – and it will be shown later that this *is* his name – held his first consulship from 1 September to 31 December 86 (M&W, p. 8) and the second from 1 May to 31 August 95 (M&W, p. 10). It is also clear that he was the only senator to whom Domitian granted two consulships. He was therefore one of that emperor's favourites, held in high esteem for, presumably, his loyalty and efficiency.

The discovery, in Upper Germany, of some legionary tiles of the legion 8 Augusta bearing the name Lappius (see the discussion in **51**) should have led scholars to review the name assigned to the man who suppressed the revolt. Mommsen, however, assessed the value of the tiles as follows: 'The tiles of this same Appius [sic], which have been found in the province of Upper Germany, . . . must be referred to the epoch after the defeat of Antonius' (p. 151 n. 1). Other scholars went further: they argued that, since 'Appius' must have been governor of Lower Germany at the time of the revolt whereas the titles were found in the Upper province, he must have been given control of all of Germany together with Gaul for a period after the revolt, until, presumably, the area was pacified. Such is the view of S. Gsell, *Essai sur le Règne de l'Empereur Domitien* (Paris 1894), p. 257. Were it true, this would be an unparalleled grant of power to an individual senator. The argument has to be rejected, for it involves misreading the clear evidence of the tiles. As was previously noted (**51**), the tiles refer to Lappius: it is a very rare name but it does exist elsewhere. Again, they were found in Upper Germany, the province where the legion 8 Augusta had been stationed for some years. Since tiles bear the name, not of the provincial governor, but merely of the legionary legate, they presumably indicate that Lappius commanded the 8 Augusta; he would have done so at least ten years before his first consulship, at some time during the reign of Domitian's father, Vespasian. That the medieval copyists found difficulty with the name Lappius is perhaps understandable. It is comparatively rare and hence was read as 'L. Appius', i.e. 'Lucius Appius': the manuscripts of both Pliny and Dio therefore refer to 'Lucius Maximus'. On the other hand, one would not have expected so many scholars to have rejected the clear evidence of his name on the legionary tiles.

The name Norbanus has also caused confusion. Domitian had a praetorian prefect of that name in 96, and in 89 an officer named Norbanus had come to Germany to assist the emperor in suppressing the revolt. Presumably, this was the same·Norbanus. His loyalty in 89 was subsequently rewarded. The epitomator of

Aurelius Victor, writing three centuries after the revolt, is the first to equate the senatorial Maximus and the equestrian Norbanus. The reasons for the conflation remain obscure; but there can be no doubt that Lappius and Norbanus were two different persons – the discovery of Lappius' complete name (**35**), Aulus Bucius Lappius Maximus, is evidence of this.

We can summarize the epigraphic evidence of Lappius' career as follows: probably towards the end of Vespasian's reign, when he was in his mid-thirties, he was legate of the legion 8 Augusta stationed in Upper Germany (this post was, at this time, held a few years after the praetorship, which one usually attained at or around the age of thirty); a few years later, possibly *c.* 82, he was appointed proconsul of Pontus-Bithynia (Pliny, *Ep.* 10.58.6, previously cited); then, in September 86, he gained the consulship; his role in the revolt of Saturninus can most logically be explained by assigning to him the governorship of Lower Germany in the years immediately after his consulship (note, however, that we have no epigraphic evidence for his tenure of this post); finally, after being appointed governor of another consular province, Syria (**35**), he returned to Rome to receive the prestigious award of a second consulship.

All this information was known well before 1960, so it is surprising to read in the second edition of the *Oxford Classical Dictionary* (1970), under the rubric 'Norbanus', that 'Aulus Lappius Maximus Norbanus won great credit for destroying the conspirators' papers before Domitian arrived. . . . He does not seem to have been employed again by Domitian' (p. 738). Yet, almost ten years before, in 1961, a military diploma (**35**) had been found, indicating that (a) Lappius' full name was Aulus Bucius Lappius Maximus (there is no mention whatsoever of 'Norbanus') and (b) he was governing the province of Syria on 12 May 91. Lappius had obviously been 'employed again by Domitian'. His conspicuous loyalty in 89 had earned him the strategically important command of Syria – and it is only rarely that a senator was appointed to a second imperial consular province (compare, however, Lucius Funisulanus Vettonianus, **59**). Then, on his return from Syria, he also received another rare honour, a second consulship.

According to Dio, Lappius had burned 'all the papers that were found in the chest of Antonius, thus esteeming his own safety as of slight importance' (67.11.1–2). The fact that Dio relates a similar story elsewhere (72.29.1 – of Marcus Aurelius, and 72.29.2 – of Verus) leads one to suspect its accuracy. In addition, if Lappius had really destroyed any dangerous evidence, Domitian would almost certainly have learned of it from his 'examination' of Saturninus' soldiers. Under torture (Suet., *Dom.* 10.5), they would have revealed the extent of any support that their leader expected or received from his counterpart in Lower Germany, and the slightest suspicion of treachery would have been enough for Domitian. Lappius' subsequent promotions indicate that not only did the emperor 'employ him again' but also that he trusted him implicitly.

Epigraphy then has widened our knowledge of Saturninus' revolt, so inadequately treated by the literary sources. It probably occurred early in January 89 and was rapidly suppressed by the consular legate of Lower Germany, whose name and career are now known to us: Lappius emerges as one of Domitian's most loyal and decorated supporters. There is, as well, a clear indication of the danger of misreading epigraphic evidence – or rather, of attempting to make it fit in with one's preconceived notions. For many years, scholars simply refused to believe that the clearly inscribed Lappius on the legionary tile (**51**) was accurate: it should, they thought, have been 'L. Appius'. The error was then compounded. Since the tile was found in Upper Germany (whereas Lappius was consular legate of the lower province), they assumed that Domitian must have amalgamated the eight legions of Germany, Lower and Upper, creating one huge (and unprecedented) unit, and then appointed Lappius as its governor, even though legionary tiles bear the name of the commander of a single legion.

Salmon's account of Saturninus' revolt must therefore be slightly modified. For 'Norbanus' and 'L. Appius Maximus Norbanus', we should read 'A. Bucius Lappius Maximus', and we need to be told that Domitian rewarded Lappius by appointing him, probably almost immediately, to the prestigious command of Syria, an appointment that casts doubt on Dio's account of Lappius' destruction of any incriminating evidence found in the rebels' camp.

Appendices

As stated in the Introduction (p. xv), the purpose of these appendices is to suggest some of the more significant aspects and issues of the early empire and to show how our selection of documents can be used to illustrate these. The issues chosen are, for the most part, broad ones and often overlap each other; similarly individual documents frequently illustrate or are relevant to more than one topic. We have deliberately not included an appendix of 'historical events', but have concentrated on broad issues which extend over the whole period covered by our documents.

Appendix 1 Constitutional Matters

Under this heading we have included documents which illustrate the constitutional powers, offices and position of the emperors and the gradual development of a regular and formal imperial titulature, together with new powers and titles added to the basic framework by different emperors. We have also included under this heading documents which illustrate the attempts of the various emperors to found or consolidate a family dynasty and the means that they employed to do this. The use of propaganda and religion for this purpose forms the subject of two separate appendices.

Documents: 1 2 3 4 5 6 7 8 9 10 12 13 14 16 17 18 19 20 21 22 23 27 28 30 32 33b 33d 33e 34 35 38 39 43 44 45 48 73 76 77 78.

Appendix 2   Imperial Propaganda

Under this heading we have included documents issued either by the emperor or by others on his behalf or referring to him in a laudatory manner. The subject matter of the documents mainly reflects achievements, real or pretended, of the emperor and attitudes and beliefs that he held or wanted people to believe he held or were held about him by others. Any official document issued by 'the government' can be said to have a propagandist purpose to a certain extent, since any government will try to present itself in the best light; we have selected documents which have specific messages (e.g. benefits conferred on the people; criticisms of previous emperors; vows for the ruler's safety, intended to show his popularity). Coins, the ancient instrument of mass propaganda, naturally form a large part of this topic.

Documents: 2 5 7 8 10 11 12 14 17 20 30 33a 33c 33d 48 58 73 102.

Appendix 3   Religious Aspects of the Emperor's Position

Under this heading we have included documents which illustrate such matters as: the emperor's position in the religious practices of the Roman state; the attitude of towns and individuals outside of Rome, in Italy and the provinces, to the emperor as a beneficent deity; and the attitude of certain emperors to the frequent attempts to worship them publicly as gods.

Documents: 18 23 24 26 33a 33b 33c 33d 33e 73 74 75 78 79 102.

Appendix 4   Municipal and Provincial Administration

Under this heading we have included a wide range of documents which illustrate many aspects of the relationship between the emperor and his government and the towns, cities and provinces of the empire: the formation of new provinces; changes in provincial status; municipal charters; the patronal representation of cities in Rome; deputations to the emperor from provincial cities; benefits conferred on provinces, cities and individual provincials by different emperors. Documents illustrating the religious relationship of the provinces to the emperor can be found in Appendix 3.

Documents: 1 4 15 23 24 25 26 29 30 31a 31b 32 40 41 42
43 44 45 46 47 48 49 50 52 53 54 58 59 60 61 62 63 64
65 66 67 74 75 76 78 79 80 87 89 91 93 95 103.

Appendix 5 The Army

Under this heading we have included a selection of documents
which illustrate various aspects of service in the Roman imperial
army: privileges granted to retired soldiers; rates of pay and
methods of payment; non-military activities of the army; military
decorations won by soldiers for valour; letters of recommendation
to a position in the army; and even a letter from an ordinary
soldier to his mother.

Documents: 34 35 36 37 38 40 44 45 51 53 55 65 66 67 68
69 80 82 83 84 86 88 90 96 101.

Appendix 6 The Frontiers

Under this heading we have included a number of documents
which illustrate several aspects of Rome's activities on the frontiers
of her empire, those parts where pacification was still incomplete
and which adjoined nations which were a potential danger to the
empire. Such activities include: troop movements in frontier areas;
the building of roads behind the frontier; expeditions undertaken
across the frontiers; the 'provincialization' of what had previously
been frontier 'military districts'; the provision to friendly 'client'
states across the frontiers of military aid and installations.

Documents: 2 28 34 35 36 37 38 40 44 45 49 50 51 52 53
55 58 59 66 81.

Appendix 7 The Imperial Civil Service

Under this heading we have included a number of documents
which illustrate the development during the first 150 years of the
imperial system of a well-organized administrative machinery, or
civil service, in the service of the emperor and involving the three
main educated classes of the empire: senators; *equites* or knights;
and the mainly Greek *liberti* or freedmen of the emperor. The
creation of this highly efficient administrative and bureaucratic
organization, with well-defined career and promotional patterns,
is one of the greatest benefits conferred by the emperors on the
Roman empire.

Documents: **54 56 57 58 59 60 61 62 63 64 65 66 67 68 69 70 71 72 85.**

Appendix 8   Roman Egypt

Egypt, one of the richest and most important provinces of the empire and virtually the private possession of the emperor, has left us a mass of documentary evidence, mainly in the form of papyrus documents, illustrating a wide range of aspects of life under Roman rule: administrative arrangements and appointments; racial and 'ethnic' problems; economic matters; military service; private and public legal procedures; the ordinary daily life of the people, to mention but a few. Egypt well deserves study as an example of Roman provincial administration; and our selection provides a broad sampling of papyrus documents in part III (**78–105**) which will be of considerable use in such a study. Document **63**, the famous inscription of Cornelius Gallus, is a significant document of the first year of direct Roman rule in Egypt; and document **71** is an illustration of one part of Rome's security measures for the province.

Glossary of Military, Administrative and Official Terms

(*Note*: where we, or a translation that we have used, have retained the original Latin or Greek word, we have set this out in the glossary in such a way that it is obvious that the word used is in the original language and have added a brief explanation of its meaning. We have also indicated where the original word is a Greek term.)

adlected among the ex-tribunes, ex-praetors = *adlectus inter tribunicios, praetorios*

aedile = *aedilis*, i.e. at Rome, the magistrates who ranked below the praetors; in the municipalities, the magistrates who ranked below the duovirs

aides in the public service = *hyperetai en tais demosiais* (Greek)

arbitrator = *iudex*

augur = *augur* (i.e. a member of one of the priestly colleges at Rome)

Augustus, son of = *Augusti filius*

benefactor = *euergetes* (Greek)

beneficiarius = *beneficiarius*, i.e. a soldier with special privileges

cavalryman = *eques* (pl. *equites*)

censor, perpetual = *censor perpetuus*

censorial power, with = *censoria potestate*

centurion, senior = *primus pilus* or *primipilaris*

clerk = *agoranomos* (Greek)

cognomen = *cognomen*, i.e. a distinguishing name added to the gentile, or clan, name, and usually the third of the three names possessed by a Roman citizen, e.g. Marcus Tullius *Cicero*

cohort (of auxiliary infantry) = *cohors*

college of three, for the casting and striking of bronze, silver and gold coinage, member of = *IIIvir* (i.e. *tresvir*) *aere argento auro flando feriundo*

college of three, responsible for the execution of justice, member of = *IIIvir capitalis*

college of four (or two), for the administration of justice, member of = *IIIIvir* (i.e. *quattuorvir*) or *IIvir* (i.e. *duovir*) *iure dicundo*

college of four, appointed every five years, member of = *IIIIvir quinquennalis*

college of seven, concerned with sacred banquets, member of = *VIIvir* (i.e. *septemvir*) *epulonum*

college of fifteen, for the performing of sacrifices, member of = *XVvir* (i.e. *quindecimvir*) *sacris faciundis*

colleges, member of all the priestly = *collegiorum omnium sacerdos*

colony = *colonia*

commissioner, for the Aemilian Way = *curator viae Aemiliae*

commissioner, for the Flaminian Way = *curator viae Flaminiae*

commissioner, for the Gallic census = *curator census Gallici*

commissioner, for public works and sacred buildings = *curator operum publicorum et aedium sacrarum*

commissioner, for public records = *curator tabularum publicarum*

commissioner, for the shrine of Hercules the Victor = *curator fani Herculis Victoris*

commissioner, for the Trajan Way = *curator viae Traianae*

commonwealth, parent of = *parens reipublicae* (periphrastic for *pater patriae*)

community = *civitas*

conscript = *(miles) lectus*

conscripti = *conscripti*, i.e. members of a municipal council

consul = *consul*, i.e. the most senior of the 'Republican' magistrates

cornicularius = *cornicularius*, i.e. a military rank similar to that of adjutant

country, father of his = *pater patriae*

curiae = *curiae*, i.e. voting units in provincial and Italian municipalities (sing. *curia*)

decorations, praetorian, consular, triumphal = *ornamenta praetoria, consularia, triumphalia*

decorations: crowns (mural, rampart, naval, golden) = *coronae (murales, vallares, classicae, aureae)*; spears, untipped = *hastae purae*; pennants = *vexilla*; neckchains, medallions, armlets = *torques, falerae* (or *phalerae*), *armilla* decree of the senate = *senatus consultum*; by decree of the senate = *senatus consulto*; in accordance with a decree of the senate = *ex senatus consulto*

decuriones = *decuriones* (see 'town councillors')

deified, the = *divus*

deified, son of the = *divi filius*

deified, grandson of the = *divi nepos*

deputy-master (of the Arval Brothers) = *vice magistri (fratrum Arvalium)*

designated (consul) = *designatus (consul)*

diocese, Carthaginian, of the province of Africa = *dioecesis Carthaginiensis provinciae Africae*

divine power and providence (of the emperor) = *numen ac providentia (Caesaris)*

divine spirit (of the emperor) = *genius (Caesaris)*

duovir = *duovir* (pl. *duoviri*), one of the two senior magistrates in provincial and Italian municipalities

emperor, the = *imperator* (i.e. the *praenomen imperatoris*); see discussion of document **22**

ephebarch = *ephebarchos*, i.e. the magistrate who supervised the young men in a Greek city

ephors = *ephoroi* (Greek), i.e. the senior municipal magistrates of Gytheum in Laconia

exegetes = *exegetes* (Greek), i.e. one of the senior magistrates at Alexandria

fetial = *fetialis*, i.e. a member of one of the Roman priestly colleges

financial secretary of the emperor = *a rationibus Augusti**

fiscus see 'imperial treasuries'

freedman / freedwoman = *libertus/liberta*

friend of Caesar and of the Romans = *Philokaisar kai Philorhomaios* (Greek; in Latin *amicus Caesaris et Romanorum*)

gymnasiarch = *gymnasiarchos* (Greek), i.e. the magistrate who supervised the gymnasium in a Greek city

imperial treasuries = *fisci*; sing. *fiscus*, i.e. the imperial treasury, the emperor's privy purse

in charge of correspondence = *ab epistulis**

in charge of (the department of) the inheritances = *ab hereditatibus**

in charge of (the department of) the petitions = *a libellis**

in charge of the patrimony = *a patrimonio**

infantryman = *pedes* (pl. *pedites*)

judicial powers, with full = *ius gladii* (sc. *habens*); literally: 'having the right of the sword'

keeper of weapons = *custos armorum*

*often prefixed by the title *procurator* (q.v.)

Leaders of the Youth = *principes iuventutis*
legate of the ____th legion = *legatus legionis* (+ numeral)
legate (of the emperor) with the rank of propraetor of the province
    of ____ = *legatus (Augusti) propraetore provinciae* ____
nomes = *nomoi* (Greek), i.e. administrative districts in Egypt
optio = *optio*, i.e. assistant or deputy centurion
patron = *patronus*
plebiscites = *plebiscita* (literally: 'resolutions of the plebs')
police = *machairophoros* (Greek) (literally: 'sword-bearer')
pomerium = *pomerium*, i.e. the sacred boundary of the city of Rome
pontifex maximus = *pontifex maximus*, i.e. the head of the Roman
    state religion; in Greek inscriptions translated as *archiereus*
    megistos
praetor = *praetor*, i.e. the second most senior magistrate of the
    'Republican' magistracies
prefect of the alimentary system = *praefectus alimentorum*
prefect of the cavalry of the ____ squadron = *praefectus equitum alae*
    ____
prefect of the 1st cavalry squadron of individual Roman citizens =
    praefectus equitum alae I singulorum civium Romanorum
prefect(ure) of the city = *praefectus (praefectura) urbi* (or *urbis*)
prefect of a cohort = *praefectus cohortis*
prefect of the 1st cohort of Breucian cavalry of Roman citizens =
    praefectus cohortis I Breucorum equitum civium Romanorum
prefect of ____th urban cohort = *praefectus cohortis urbanae* ____
prefect of the communities of ____ = *praefectus civitatium* ____
prefect of the detachments = *praefectus vexillariorum*
prefect of Egypt = *praefectus Aegypti*
prefect of the grain supply = *praefectus annonae*
prefect of the legion II Trajana Fortis = *praefectus legionis II Traianae*
    Fortis
prefect of the military treasury = *praefectus aerarii militaris*
prefect of the Praetorian Guard = *praefectus praetorio*
prefect of the province of Sardinia = *praefectus provinciae Sardiniae*
prefect of the treasury of Saturn = *praefectus aerarii Saturni*
prefect of the Watch = *praefectus vigilum*
priest = *pontifex* (but note that the *pontifex* is only one of many
    different kinds of priest in the Roman religion)
priest of Ceres = *flamen Cerealis*
priest of the deified Claudius = *flamen divi Claudi*
priest, chief, of the Augusti for life = *archiereus ton Augouston dia biou*
    (Greek)
prince = *princeps*
proconsul = *pro consule*

procurator = *procurator*, i.e. the equestrian official in charge of a minor imperial province; the equestrian or freedman official in charge of an imperial bureau or the collection of a particular tax

procurator for the poll-tax of the Jews = *procurator ad capitularia Judaeorum*

procuratorial district = *eparcheia* (Greek)

quaestor = *quaestor*, i.e. the junior magistrates both at Rome and in the municipalities

quaestor, as candidate of the deified Hadrian = *quaestor candidatus divi Hadriani*

recruit = *tiro*

Roman Knight = *eques Romanus*

saviour and benefactor = *soter kai euergetes* (Greek)

sesquiplicarius = *sesquiplicarius*, i.e. a soldier who received 50 per cent more than the basic rate of pay

soldier (ordinary) = *gregalis*

squadron (i.e. of cavalry) = *ala*

staff officer of Claudius Caesar in Britain = *comes Claudi Caesaris in Britannia*

standard-bearer = *aquilifer*

strategos = *strategos*, i.e. chief magistrate of an Egyptian city

subprefect of the fleet of Alexandria = *subpraefectus classis Alexandrinae*

substitute (soldier) = *vicarius*

town councillors = *decuriones*

townspeople = *municipes*

tribe, of the ____ = *tribu* ____, i.e. one of the geographical districts in which all Roman citizens were enrolled

tribune, military = *tribunus militum*

tribune of the plebs = *tribunus plebis*

tribune of the ____ Praetorian cohort = *tribunus* ____ *cohortis praetoriae*

tribune, as candidate of the deified Hadrian = *tribunus candidatus divi Hadriani*

tribunician power, of, for the ____ time = *tribunicia potestate* ____

veteran soldier = *veteranus*

victorious commander, saluted as for the ____ time = *imperator* ____ (see discussion on **22** for the difference between this and the *praenomen imperatoris*)

viginivirate = *viginiviratus*, i.e. a junior magistracy, held before entry to the senate and consisting of a board of twenty, divided into four separate colleges, two of which are the two 'colleges of three' cited above

volunteer = *voluntarius*

watch = *vigiles*

Select Bibliography

Ashby, T., *The Aqueducts of Ancient Rome*, Oxford 1935.

Basore, J. W. (tr.), *Seneca: Moral Essays*, Loeb edn, Cambridge, Mass. and London 1928.

Bell, H. I., *Jews and Christians in Egypt*, Oxford 1924.

Bennett, C. E. (tr.), *Frontinus*, Loeb edn, Cambridge, Mass. and London 1925.

Brunt, P. A., 'The Lex de Imperio Vespasiani', *Journal of Roman Studies*, 67, 1977, pp. 95–116.

Cary, E. (tr.), *Dio Cassius*, Loeb edn, Cambridge, Mass. and London 1917.

Champlin, E., 'Pegasus', *Zeitschrift für Papyrologie und Epigraphik*, 32, 1978, pp. 269–78.

Church, A. J. and Brodribb, W. J. (tr.), *The Complete Works of Tacitus*, ed. M. Hadas, New York 1942.

Colson, F. H. (tr.), *Philo*, Loeb edn, Cambridge, Mass. and London 1941.

Conole, P. and Milns, R. D., 'Neronian Frontier Policy in the Balkans: The Career of Ti.Plautius Silvanus', *Historia*, 32, 1983, pp. 183–200.

Garzetti, A., *From Tiberius to the Antonines: A History of the Roman Empire A.D. 14–192*, tr. J. R. Foster, London 1974.

Grant, M., *Roman History from Coins: Some Uses of the Imperial Coinage to the Historian*, Cambridge 1968.

Gsell, S., *Essai sur le Règne de L'Empereur Domitien*, Paris 1894.

Hammond, M., *The Augustan Principate*, Cambridge, Mass. 1933.

Henderson, B. W., *Five Roman Emperors*, Cambridge 1927.

Magie, D. (tr.), *The Scriptores Historiae Augustae*, Loeb edn, Cambridge, Mass. and London 1921.

Marrou, H. I., *A History of Education in Antiquity*, tr. G. R. Lamb, London 1956.

Mitford, T. B., 'Some Inscriptions from the Cappadocian *Limes*', *Journal of Roman Studies*, 64, 1974, pp. 160–75.

Mommsen, Th., *The Provinces of the Roman Empire from Caesar to Diocletian*, tr. W. P. Dickson, Ares Reprint, Chicago 1974.

Nicols, J., *Vespasian and the Partes Flavianae* (*Historia Einzelschrift* 28), Wiesbaden 1978.

Perrin, B. (tr.), *Plutarch's Lives*, Loeb edn, Cambridge, Mass. and London 1926.

Radice, B. (tr.), *Pliny: Letters and Panegyricus*, Loeb edn, Cambridge, Mass. and London 1969.

Rolfe, J. C. (tr.), *Suetonius*, Loeb edn, Cambridge, Mass. and London 1914.

Rossi, L., *Trajan's Column and the Dacian Wars*, London 1971.

Rostovtzeff, M., *The Social and Economic History of the Roman Empire*, Oxford 1957.

Salmon, E. T., *A History of the Roman World: 30 B.C. to A.D. 138*, London 1968.

Seager, R., *Tiberius*, London 1972.

Speidel, M., 'The Pay of the Auxilia', *Journal of Roman Studies*, 63, 1973, pp. 141–7.

Syme, R., 'Flavian Wars and Frontiers', *Cambridge Ancient History*, Vol. XI, Cambridge, repr. with corrections 1969, pp. 131–87.

Comparative Tables

I. Coins

BMC I

p.	no.	doc.
73	427	2
106	650	1
133	95	3
151	33	5
168	29	81
200	1	6
251	261	7
369	10	8

BMC II

p.	no.	doc.
81	397	30
131	604	11
180	748b	10
311	62	12
323	111	13
324	115	13
326	129	13

BMC III

1	4	14
94	454	17
98	484	46
100	498	18
108	531	16
237	5	19
401	1120	20
544	1919	21

II. Inscriptions

S	doc.	M&W	doc.	S. *N–H*	doc.
9	33a	1	27	1	33e
13	33b	2	33d	6	20
16	33c	35	9	22	16
43a	81	44	11	50	77
43b	81	45	30	59	47
57	7	53	30	60	47
64	26	79	9	62	20
106	6	82	8	64	77
172	70	83	10	72	32
182	71	86	44	91a	14
228	58	97	57	101	76
233	56	105	45	108	16
234	56	114	12	110a	19
258	64	203	72	110b	19
276	5	237	28	111	19
297b	83	244	93	119b	21
308b	48	274	58	123	105
309	48	283	53	133	18
317	49	298	43	141b	19
340	40	307	59	208	15
343	41	314	60	225	62
368	25	315	61	231	38
370	79	336	67	317	55
374	81	337	42	321b	55
381	80	338	65	321i	55
436	93	347	68	333	90
		369	28	343	36
		372	66	344	37
		399	34	347	38
		405	84	357	37
		408a	48	378a	17
		408b	48	378b	17
		419	43	399	47
		439	50	408a	46
		453	31	408c	46
		454	31	424	47
		461	29	459	89
		466	80	479	19
				516	103
				519	102

ILS	doc.
91	1
100	39
113	22
158	75
168	3
170	3
206	25
216	81
218	48
244	27
263	45
264	30
297	76
309	77
966	56
967	56
984	57
985	58
986	58
1005	59
1035	38
1061	62
1339	69
1349	64
1374	67
1447	65
1448	68
1519	72
1546	70
1992	34
2816	71
5866	46
6044	4
6089	31
6090	31
6092	29
8682a	54
8704a	53
8710	50
8781	23
8784	73
8904	44
8995	63
8996	4
9200	66
9485	61

IG	doc.
VII 2713	26

OGIS	doc.
583	74

RG	doc.
25	23
27.1	1
29.2	2
34	57
35.1	39

AE	doc.
1937, 112	34
1950, 32	16
1957, 336	38
1961, 319	35
1967, 355	52

SEG	doc.
IX 252	47
XI 923	24

TAM	doc.
II 563	60

IGRR	doc.
III 133	28
III 551	60

RIB	doc.
1340	55
1499	55
1762	55

SIG³	doc.
838	32

CIL		doc.
III	1443	19
III	1445	19
VII	1201	49
VIII	10119	43
X	8024	42
XIII	9145	40
XIII	12168(7)	51
XVI	46	36
XVI	69	38
XVI	160	37
XVI	163	37

E&J	doc.
14	1
15	1
21	63
27	2
50a	4
52	75
53	4
77	73
82	22
91	3
92a	3
102b	24
134	74
220	4
315	23
320b	78

III. Papyri

CPL	doc.
102	86

P. Mich.	doc.
203	96

BGU	doc.
140	90
511	93

P. Fouad	doc.
76	99

P. Teb.	doc.
278	100
381	104

P. Oxy.	doc.
32	101
39	82
266	95
282	95
1022	88
1154	98
1242	103
1292	92
2190	97
2435	91
2725	94
3022	87

P. Lond.	doc.
904, Col. II	89
1171	80
1178	81
1912	79

P. Giessen	doc.
3	102

P. Fayum	doc.
19	105

P. Ryl.	doc.
154	95

SP	doc.
211	78

P. Gen.	doc.
1	84

P. Berl.	doc.
8334	85

Indexes

1. Chronological Index

Date	Document	Page
Reign of Augustus		
15 April		
28 BC	63	98
28 BC	1	2
19 BC–2 BC	73	112
18/17 BC	2	2
3 BC	23	23
3–2 BC	39	66
Reign of Tiberius		
15 or 16	24	26
19	78	119
c. 19	91	142
21	22	21
22–3	3	3
16 Nov. 29	74	113
c. 30	92	114
31	4	4
19 Oct.		
31–37	75	114
Reign of Gaius		
37–8	5	5
27 Oct. 39	33a	49

Date	Document	Page
Reign of Claudius		
10 Nov. 41	79	119
41 or 53	93	145
26 April–		
25 May 42	80	127
6–12 Jan. 43	33b	49
44–5	40	67
15 March 46	25	27
46	81	129
46–7	41	67
49–50	49	77
24 April 52	82	130
52–3	48	74
41–54	56	82
41–54	64	99
41–54 or		
later	70	109
1st half i AD	100	155
Reign of Nero		
54	6	6
11 Dec. 55	33c	50
c. 63–4	83	131
64–6	7	7
28 Nov. 67	26	29
54–68 or		
later	71	110

Date	Document	Page
Reign of Vitellius		
14 March 69	33d	51
69	8	8
69	9	8
Reign of Vespasian		
c. Jan. 70	27	32
70	10	9
71	94	148
71	11	10
21 May 74	34	53
74	42	68
74	50	77
74–9	58	87
75	28	37
76	43	68
76	44	69
77	29	38
c. 77–9	51	78
79	53	79
69–79	52	78
69–79	57	84
69–79 or later	65	100
69–79 or later	72	111
Reign of Titus		
80	45	71
80–1	30	40
81	84	132
Reign of Domitian		
81–4	12	10
81–4	31	41
81–4	61	95
84–9	60	93
84–96	54	80
87–8	13	12
87–92	59	92
89–96	66	102
12 May 91	35	58
92	86	137
96	14	12
96	95	148

Date	Document	Page
81–96	85	135
i AD	97	152
i AD	98	154
i AD	99	154
Reign of Trajan		
98	87	138
98–102	15	13
8 May 100	36	60
25 March 101	33e	52
103	88	139
104	89	140
105	67	105
11 Aug. 106	37	61
108–9	46	72
112	16	13
112–13	17	14
112–14	18	15
113–14	76	115
117	19	16
98–117	68	107
98–117	96	151
98–117	103	157
Reign of Hadrian		
118	77	116
118	20	17
4 Aug. 119	90	141
119	47	73
17 July 122	38	63
18 Dec. 124	104	159
128–9	32	47
137	21	18
138	105	160
117–38	102	157
122–38	55	81
early ii AD	101	155
c. middle ii AD	62	96
c. middle ii AD	69	108

2. Index of Names

Note that this index is not intended to be exhaustive. Entries are limited to persons who are important for the understanding of the relevant documents and our discussion of them.

Acilius, P. Attianus, 17, 157
Acilius, M' Aviola, 81, 145
Acraephians, 32
Adrastus, 113–14
Adrastus, 148
Aelius Gallus, 5
Aelius, L. Caesar, 18, 19, 161
Aelius, L. Lamia, 90
Aemilius, L. Rectus, 119, 123, 124, 127, 128
Aemilius, M. Bassus, 62
Agricola, Cn. Julius, 79, 80, 83, 96
Agrippa, M. (Vipsanius), 76, 112, 143
Agrippina (the Elder), 4, 143
Agrippina (the Younger), 6, 50
Alexander, Ti. Julius, 125, 146, 159
Alexandrians, 119–27, 138, 139, 142, 145, 146, 147, 158, 159
Alfius, M. Olympiacus, 102, 105
Anauni, 28
Antiochus (King of Commagene), 102, 103
Antonia (mother of Claudius), 123, 147
Antonius Pius (emperor), 98, 109, 160, 161, 162
Antonius, L. Saturninus, 59, 171–6
Antonius, (M.) Primus, 169
Antony, M. (triumvir), 3, 123, 172
Aphrodous, 151, 152
Apronianus (Cassius?), 17
Aristobulus (King of Lesser Armenia), 70

Artabanus (King of Parthia), 8
Arval Brethren, 18, 20, 35, 48–52, 173
Attius, Sex. Suburanus, 52
Augustus (emperor), xv, 1, 2, 3, 4, 7, 9, 16, 20, 21–3, 24–6, 27, 28, 32, 34, 36, 38, 39, 42, 47, 48, 49, 50, 54, 55, 66, 74, 83, 87, 93, 98 (= Caesar, son of the deified), 99, 112, 113, 119, 142, 143
Aurelius Archelaus, 155, 156
Aurelius, L. Patroclus, 67, 68
Aurelius, M. (emperor), 75
Aurelius, Q. Pactumeius Fronto, 69

Baebius, C. Atticus, 99–100
Baebius, P. Italicus, 93–4
Bassaeus, M. Rufus, 100
Bastarnae, 87
Berenice, 146
Britannicus (son of Claudius), 50, 130
Britons, 61, 62, 129, 130

Caecina, C. Tuscus, 131, 132
Caesar (son of Domitian), 10, 11
Caesennius, A. Gallus, 71
Caesennius, L. Paetus, 71
Caesius, Sex. Propertianus, 100–2
Caristanius, C. Fronto, 95–6
Chaeremo, 120, 123
Chaeremon, 150, 151
Chatti, 94, 103, 171, 172
Cilnius, C. Proculus (cos. suff. 87), 60

Cilnius, C. Proculus (*cos. suff.* 100), 60

Civica Cerealis, 106

Civilis, (Julius), 170

Claudius Athenodorus, 128

Claudius (emperor), 6, 7, 8, 22, 25, 27–9, 32, 34, 36, 42, 47, 49, 50, 54, 55, 57, 67, 74, 75, 76, 77, 80, 82–4, 87, 88, 90, 99, 100, 105, 107, 110, 119–27, 128, 129, 130, 145, 146, 147

Claudius, Ti. Archibius, 120, 122, 123

Claudius, Ti. Atticus, 53, 58

Claudius, Ti. Barbillus, 120, 122, 123, 124

Claudius, Ti. Saturninus, 109–10

Coeidius, L. Candidus, 84

Corbulo, Cn. Domitius, 91, 132

Cornelius, C. Gallus, 98–9

(Cornelius), Cn. Lentulus Gaetulicus, 49

Cornelius Fuscus, 135

Crassus, M. Licinius (triumvir), 3

Dacians, 52, 87, 92, 93, 102

Deceangli, 78

Decebalus (Dacian King), 102, 104

Decidius, L. Saxa, 3

Demetrous, 151

Domitia Longina (wife of Domitian), 10, 11

Domitian (emperor), 8, 9, 10, 11, 12, 13, 14, 37, 38, 41, 42, 45, 56, 58, 65, 68, 69, 70, 71, 72, 78, 80, 85, 87, 88, 90, 92, 93, 94, 95, 96, 102, 103, 104, 105, 106, 107, 108, 111, 128, 134, 135, 136, 137, 139, 148, 150, 163, 167, 171–6

Domitilla (daughter of Vespasian), 58

Domitius, Cn. Afer. . . Lucanus, 170

Domitius, Cn. . . . Curvius Tullus, 170

Domitius, (Cn. Ahenobarbus) (father of Nero), 50

Domitius, L. Ahenobarbus (= emperor Nero), 50

Domitius, T. (?) Decidius, 82–4

Ducennius, Geminus, 85

Drusilla (sister of Caligula), 125

Drusus (the Elder), 67, 74, 76, 130

Drusus (the Younger), 3, 4, 5

Egnatius, Q. Catus, 69

Epaminondas, 30, 32

Eprius, T. Clodius Marcellus, 53, 54, 58, 166

Erastus, L., 47, 48

Festus, 140, 141

Flavia Aphrodisia, 111

Flavius, Sabinus (brother of Vespasian), 85–7

Flavius, T. Euschemon, 111

Flavius, T. Longus, 137, 138

Funisulanus, L. Vettonianus, 92–3, 175

Gaius Caesar (son of M. Agrippa), 4, 143

Gaius Caligula (emperor), 4, 5, 6, 8, 22, 25, 27, 36, 49, 54, 74, 75, 76, 77, 92, 126, 147

Galba (emperor), 25, 85, 86, 101

Germanicus (brother of Claudius), 4, 5, 6, 74, 119, 120, 123, 127, 128, 142, 143, 144

Germanicus Caesar (son of Drusus the Younger), 3, 4

Germanicus (title), 14, 23, 45, 94, 95

Greeks (Hellenes) and Nero, 30–2, 112

Hadrian (emperor), xv, 13, 16, 17, 18, 36, 47–8, 63, 64, 65, 73, 74, 81, 96, 97, 98, 109, 115, 116–17, 141, 142, 157, 159, 160, 161, 162

Hellenes (= Greeks), 30

Helvius, L. Agrippa, 68
Hermaiscus, 158, 159
Hermogenes, 144

Iberians, 37
Ischyras, 144
Isidorus, 145, 146, 147

Jews, 10, 40–1, 74, 102, 103, 111, 122–7, 158, 159
Julia (daughter of Titus), 136
Julia (the Elder), 112
Julia (the Younger), 112
Julius Aquila, 129
Julius, C. Bassus, 13, 128
Julius Caesar (dictator), 2, 4, 66, 130
Julius, C. Dionysius, 157, 158
Julius Domitius, 155, 156
Julius, L. Ursus, 18, 135, 136
Julius, L. Ursus Servianus, 18
Julius, Q. Proculus, 133, 134
Julius, Sex. Frontinus, 75, 76, 80
Julius, Ti. Xanthus, 110–11

Laberius, L. Maximus, 135, 136
Lampon, 145, 146, 147
Lappius, A. Bucius Maximus, 59, 78, 171–6
Lepidus, (M. Aemilius), 49
Livia (Drusilla), (wife of Augustus), 26, 27, 49–50, 112, 119
Livia Julia (wife of Drusus the Younger), 3, 4, 5
Longinus, C. Priscus, 139
Lucretius, M. Clemens, 57

Macro, Naevius Sutorius, 145, 147
Marcomanni, 102, 104
Marciana (sister of Trajan), 13, 14
Matidia (niece of Trajan), 13, 14
Matidia (the Younger), 13, 14
Memmius, C., 73
Messalina (wife of Nero), 30–2, 112
Minicius, C. Italus, 105–7, 139, 140

Minicius, L. Natalis Quadronius Verus, 96–8
Mithridates (Iberian King), 37
Mommsen, 174
Mucianus, (C. Licinius), 10, 148, 169
Murena = Pompeius, Q. . . Falco, 63

Neilus, 152, 153, 154
Nero (emperor), 6, 7, 8, 21, 28, 29–32, 36, 38, 47, 50–1, 68, 74, 85, 86, 88, 90, 91, 92, 101, 110, 112, 123, 125, 132, 150, 159
Nerva (emperor), 11, 12, 13, 14, 15, 16, 60, 61, 63, 65, 72, 73, 74, 107
Norbanus, 171, 173, 174, 175, 176

Octavius, Cn. Titinius Capito, 107–8
Otho (emperor), 35, 51, 85, 86

'Pagan Martyrs', 139, 145, 146, 147
Paphlagonians, 24, 26
Parthians, 1, 2–3, 37–8, 102, 103, 115
Pedanius, C. Fuscus Salinator, 18
Pedanius, Secundus, 86
Petillius, C. Firmus, 78, 79
Petillius, Q. Cerialis Caesius Rufus, 53, 54, 57, 58, 79
Petosarapis, 149
Pinarius, Cn. Cornelius Clemens, 53, 56, 58, 163–70
Platorius, A. Nepos, 63, 64, 81
Plautius, Ti. Silvanus Aelianus, 87–91
Pliny (the Younger), 108, 137
Plotina (wife of Trajan), 13, 14, 17, 157, 159
Plotius, D.(?L.) Grypus, 79
[Plo]tius Pegasus, 78, 79
Pompeius, Cn. Collega, 70
Pompeius, Q. . . Falco, 63, 64, 65, 69
Pompeius Planta, 138, 139

Poppaea (wife of Nero), 159

Quadi, 102, 104

Rammius Martialis, 141
Rhoxolani, 87
Rostovtzeff, M., xiii

Sarapous, 154
Sarmatians, 37, 87, 102, 104, 129
Saturnilus, 151, 152
Scythians, 87
Seius, L. Strabo, 4, 5, 25
Sejanus, L. Aelius, 4, 5, 114, 115, 147
Seneca, L. Annaeus, 7
Sinduni, 28
Spartacus, 148
Staberius, T. Secundus, 168–9
Statius, Ti. Claudius . . . Macedo, 108–9
Subrius, Sex. Dexter, 68

Tampius, L. Flavianus, 91
Terentius, D. Scaurianus, 16, 61, 62
Thaesis (daughter of Thonis), 149
Thaesis (daughter of Orsenouphis), 159
Thaisarion, 150, 151
Theon (brother/husband of Sarapous), 154
Theon (father of Neilus), 152, 154
Tiberius (emperor), 3, 4, 5, 6, 21, 22, 23, 25, 26–7, 28, 32, 34, 36, 49, 67, 74, 87, 88, 90, 110, 113–15, 119, 124, 143, 144, 147
Tiberius Caesar (son of Drusus the Younger), 3, 4, 6
Titus (emperor), 9, 10, 11, 22, 23,

37, 40–1, 42, 55, 68, 69, 70, 71, 72, 76, 77, 79, 80, 95, 96, 102, 111, 119, 146, 148, 167, 170
Trajan (emperor), 1, 2, 3, 13, 14, 15, 16, 17, 18, 47, 52, 60, 61, 63, 64, 65, 72, 73, 97, 98, 106, 107, 115, 116, 117, 128, 136, 137, 138, 139, 140, 152, 157, 158, 159, 172
Transdanubians, 87, 91, 104
Tridentini, 28
Tryphon (son of Dionysius), 130, 131
Tryphon (husband of Demetrous), 151
Tulliassies, 28

Ulpius, M. Novantico, 61, 62, 63
Ulpius, M. Traianus (father of Trajan), 15, 71

Velius, C. Rufus, 102–5
Venuleius, L. Montabus Apronianus, 137
Vergilius, Cn. Capito, 130
Vespasian (emperor), 9, 10, 11, 13, 15, 21, 23, 32–6, 37, 38, 39, 40, 41, 42, 45, 51, 53, 54, 55, 56, 58, 68, 69, 70, 71, 72, 75, 76, 77, 78, 79, 80, 85, 86, 87, 88, 90, 91, 95, 96, 101, 102, 103, 105, 106, 111, 118, 119, 125, 128, 135, 146, 148, 159, 163–70
Vibia Sabina (wife of Hadrian), 13
Vibius, C. Maximus, 140
Viriasius, P. Naso, 114–15
Vitellius (emperor), 8, 9, 10, 14, 35, 51, 85, 101, 102, 108, 111, 117
Vitellius, L. (father of emperor Vitellius), 8
Vitrasius Pollio, 120, 124

3. Index of Places

Note that this index is not intended to be exhaustive. Entries are limited to places that are important for the understanding of the relevant documents and our discussion of them.

Achaea, 30, 68
Acraephia, 31, 112
Actium, 25
Agri Decumates, 163–70
Albania, 38
Alexandria, 9, 119, 122–7, 132, 142–4, 148, 154, 158, 159
Anatolia, 70
Antioch, Pisidian, 95, 96
Apollonia, 73, 74
Arae Flaviae, 167, 168
Argentorate, 167, 168
Armenia, 37–8, 91
Armenia, Lesser, 70
Asia Minor, 70–2
Athens, 48
Aventine, 5

Baetica (Hispania), 38, 39, 45
Black Forest, 163–70
Britain, 63, 64, 65, 77, 79, 80, 81, 84, 96, 129–30

Campus Martius, 5
Cappadocia-Galatia, 38, 70, 71
Capri, 5
Caucasus mountains, 37, 38
Cilicia, 17, 65
Colchester, 129
Cologne, 67
Commagene, 103
Corinth, 29
Cyprus, 74, 113–14

Cyrene, 73, 74

Dacia, 14, 52, 61, 104
Dacica, 17
Dalmatia, 78–9, 104
Delta, 124–5

Egypt, 2, 118, 132, 141
Eleusis, 47, 48
Ephesus, 47, 48

Galatia, 24, 95
Gallic Provinces (Census of), 84, 86
Germany, 56, 59, 163–70
Germany, Lower, 56, 165, 166, 169, 170, 171, 174, 176
Germany, Upper, 56, 78, 165, 166, 167, 169, 170, 171, 173, 174, 175, 176
Gytheum, 26

Hadrian's Wall, 64, 81
Hellas (= Greece), 29, 30

Iberia, 37, 38

Jerusalem, 40, 111
Judaea, 10, 41, 64, 69

Lycia–Pamphylia, 93, 94

Macedonia, 68
Malaca, 43, 45–7

Masada, 10
Melik Scherif, 70
Melitene, 70
Memphis, 148
Moesia, 84, 85, 86, 87, 88, 90, 91, 93
Moguntiacum, 67, 171

Nicopolis, 132
North Africa, 69, 73
Numidia, 59, 69

Pannonia, 18, 19, 91, 104
Paphlagonia, 24
Parthia, 3, 15, 37, 102, 103, 115
Peloponnese, 30, 31

Raetia, 102, 104, 165, 167, 168
Rhodes, 47, 48
Rome, 5, 10, 18, 53, 66, 74, 75, 76, 77, 80, 129, 135, 158

Sabora, 38–9
Salpensa, 41–2, 45–6
Sardinia, 67, 68, 71
Satala, 70
Spain, 45, 88, 90, 97
Syria, 12, 17, 59, 126–7, 175

Thebes, 9
Tridentinum, 28–9

Via Traiana, 72

4. Index of Major Topics

Aqueducts, 74–7, 80–1

Calendars, 24, 25, 114
Careers (Equestrian), 82, 98–109, 135–6, 156, 168–9
Careers (Freedmen), 80, 82, 109–11
Careers (Senatorial), 13, 58, 59, 60, 64–5, 69, 71, 78, 79, 82–4, 87–98, 135–6, 165, 175, 176
Citizenship, Roman, 28–9, 31, 41–2, 46, 56–7
Constitutional Matters, 2–19, 23, 24–6, 32–6, 37, 54–5, 59, 66, 67, 68, 69, 71–2, 74, 119

Damnatio Memoriae, 31, 36, 51, 72, 92, 94, 96, 101, 105, 107, 115
Dynastic Succession, 9–10, 25, 37, 41

Egypt (Roman), 98–9, 109, 110, 118–62

Financial Administration, 38–9, 83–4, 109, 110, 111, 116–17, 140–1
Frontier Defence, 3, 10, 12, 15, 16, 37–8, 55–6, 59, 63, 67, 70–2, 73–4, 81, 87–91, 103–5, 129, 130, 132, 143–4, 163–76

Government of Empire (excluding official careers), 13, 28–9, 29–32, 38–40, 41–7, 47–8, 82–4, 93, 95–6, 106, 108, 110, 111, 113–14, 116–17, 119–29, 132, 138–9, 140–1

Imperial Family, 3–4, 5, 6, 9–10, 11, 13–14, 16–17, 18, 50, 58, 67, 71, 72, 74, 76, 79, 84–7, 112, 119, 123, 130, 136, 143–4, 146, 147, 148, 157, 159, 161–2
Imperial Propaganda, 1, 2–3, 7–8, 9–11, 12, 14–15, 17–18, 19, 29–32, 40–1, 74–7, 130, 157
Imperial Titulature, 2, 8, 9, 12, 15, 16, 17, 21–3, 37, 39–40, 47, 50–1, 54–5, 66, 69, 71–2, 76, 77–8, 115–16, 119, 129, 138–9, 148

'Latin Rights', 39, 45, 46
Legislation, 32–6, 41–7, 56–7, 137–8, 141–2

Municipal Administration, 27–9, 38–9, 41–7

Religion and the Emperor, 15, 22, 24, 25, 26–7, 30–2, 42, 48–52, 112, 113–14, 120, 124
Rome and Roman Empire, xi–xvi and *passim*

Slavery, 109–11, 137–8, 154–5